# *F*RANKLIN D. *R*OOSEVELT
## *and the Search for Victory*

# AMERICA IN THE MODERN WORLD
## STUDIES IN INTERNATIONAL HISTORY

**Warren F. Kimball**
**Series Editor**
**Professor of History, Rutgers University**

**Volumes Published**

Lawrence Spinelli, *Dry Diplomacy: The United States, Great Britain, and Prohibition* (1989). ISBN 0-8420-2298-8

Richard V. Salisbury, *Anti-Imperialism and International Competition in Central America, 1920–1929* (1989). ISBN 0-8420-2304-6

Gerald K. Haines, *The Americanization of Brazil: A Study of U.S. Cold War Diplomacy in the Third World, 1945–1954* (1989). ISBN 0-8420-2339-9

Harry Harding and Yuan Ming, eds., *Sino-American Relations, 1945–1955: A Joint Reassessment of a Critical Decade* (1989). ISBN 0-8420-2333-X

Lawrence S. Kaplan, Denise Artaud, and Mark R. Rubin, eds., *Dien Bien Phu and the Crisis of Franco-American Relations, 1954–1955* (1990). ISBN 0-8420-2341-0

Michael L. Krenn, *U.S. Policy toward Economic Nationalism in Latin America, 1917–1929* (1990). ISBN 0-8420-2346-1

Akira Iriye and Warren Cohen, eds., *American, Chinese, and Japanese Perspectives on Wartime Asia, 1931–1949* (1990). ISBN 0-8420-2347-X

Edward M. Bennett, *Franklin D. Roosevelt and the Search for Victory: American-Soviet Relations, 1939–1945* (1990). Cloth ISBN 0-8420-2364-X Paper 0-8420-2365-8

James L. Gormly, *From Potsdam to the Cold War: Big Three Diplomacy, 1945–1947* (1990). Cloth ISBN 0-8420-2334-8 Paper 0-8420-2335-6

# *F*RANKLIN D. *R*OOSEVELT
## *and the Search for Victory*

## American-Soviet Relations, 1939–1945

## Edward M. Bennett

A Scholarly Resources Inc. Imprint
Wilmington, Delaware

The paper used in this publication meets the minimum requirements of the American National Standard for permanence of paper for printed library materials, Z39.48, 1984.

Scholarly Resources Inc.
104 Greenhill Avenue
Wilmington, DE 19805-1897

**Library of Congress Cataloging-in-Publication Data**

Bennett, Edward M., 1927–
    Franklin D. Roosevelt and the search for victory : American-Soviet relations, 1939–1945 / Edward M. Bennett.
        p. cm. — (America in the modern world)
    Includes bibliographical references (p.
    Includes index.
    ISBN 0-8420-2364-X. — ISBN 0-8420-2365-8 (pbk.)
    1. World War, 1939–1945—Diplomatic history. 2. United States—Foreign relations—Soviet Union. 3. Soviet Union—Foreign relations—United States. I. Title. II Series.
D753.B45 1990
940.53'2273—dc20                                                            90-8562
                                                                                              CIP

## About the Author

Edward M. Bennett is currently a professor of history at Washington State University. A specialist in twentieth-century U.S. diplomatic history, Professor Bennett has written many books and articles in the field, including *Franklin D. Roosevelt and the Search for Security: American-Soviet Relations, 1933–1939* (1985).

# Contents

CHAPTER VIII

CHAPTER IX

CHAPTER X

# Acknowledgments

MANY PEOPLE should be thanked for the assistance they have given me in the preparation of this second volume of my study of Franklin D. Roosevelt and American-Soviet relations. The first volume, *Franklin D. Roosevelt and the Search for Security: American-Soviet Relations, 1933-1939,* dealt with FDR's efforts to preserve the peace. All of the people at Scholarly Resources who have worked with me on both studies deserve special recognition for their patience and excellent editorial assistance. When I was invited to participate in the colloquium on American-Soviet relations during the period between 1939 and 1942 held in Moscow in October 1986 and again to participate in the meeting covering 1942–43 held at the Roosevelt Library in Hyde Park, New York, in October 1987, the Scholarly Resources staff accepted the delay in submission of the manuscript and encouraged me to take advantage of these opportunities. Naturally, there are many other people who have made this work possible. I have acknowledged my master's and doctoral students and various library staff in the first volume. Here I must mention particularly the people at the Franklin D. Roosevelt Library, especially its director, William Emerson. Milton Gustafson, Mrs. Pat Dowling, and my former student Connie Potter of the Department of State Records at the National Archives also deserve special mention. I am again indebted to the Houghton Library at the Harvard College Library for its assistance and its permission to quote from the papers of Joseph C. Grew.

In addition to the presentations the author prepared for the two American-Soviet colloquia, part of the material in the chapters dealing with 1939 to 1942 was incorporated in a paper delivered at the 1986 Citadel Conference on War and Diplomacy, "Franklin Delano Roosevelt and American-Soviet Relations: The Move to War, 1939–1942," and the author is grateful to the staff at the Citadel, especially Professor David H. White, Jr., for that opportunity.

No scholar can claim not to be influenced by numerous people whose works have touched on his or her research topic or field of specialization. I owe a special debt to Norman A. Graebner, my mentor and friend of many years, for direction and assistance in seeing American foreign relations in a realistic context. If there are errors in judgment in this volume, however, they are my own.

Those who are familiar with the Russian language will note some discrepancies in spelling. I prefer the Library of Congress style of transliteration, recommended in the 1950s, because it is a more accurate rendering of the language; thus, Konstantin Umanskii is used here rather than the archaic Constantine Oumansky. However, sometimes the name or place is so familiar that it would be confusing to change the spelling, and in these cases the commonly accepted Americanization has been used; for example, Joseph Stalin instead of Josef.

It is not an easy task to evaluate the foreign policy perspective of Franklin D. Roosevelt. He was certainly one of the most complex personalities to serve as president of the United States. There have been hundreds of books written about FDR as a political leader and as director of American foreign policy. I have benefited from the wisdom, and sometimes from the errors, of other authors who have looked at the Roosevelt persona and at the effect that this powerful man had on his time in history. It is possible only to cite those works used in the context of this study, but to those others who contributed in some way to my understanding of the most important president of the twentieth century I owe a word of thanks and empathy for the amount of work they have done in attempting to place FDR in his role as a maker of history. The writings of Frank Friedel, Arthur M. Schlesinger, Jr., Joseph P. Lash, James MacGregor Burns, Warren Kimball, and Robert Dallek have helped me to understand the personality of Franklin Roosevelt, and they therefore deserve special mention, as do Mark Stoler and Theodore Wilson.

To my wife, Margery Harder Bennett, who has once again served as research assistant, editor, and typist and whose training as a historian has been immeasurably helpful during the thirty years we have worked together on various topics in American foreign relations, I owe my deepest gratitude and respect as a fellow scholar. To Margery and to my son, Michael, and my daughter-in-law, Phyllis, both of whom are just beginning their scholarly careers, I dedicate this volume.

# Abbreviations

| | |
|---|---|
| *DSF* | Department of State Files, Record Group 59, National Archives, Washington, DC |
| *FDRL* | Franklin D. Roosevelt Library, Hyde Park, New York |
| *FRUS* | *Foreign Relations of the United States* |
| *OF* | Official Files, FDRL |
| *PPF* | President's Personal File, FDRL |
| *PSF* | President's Secretary's File, FDRL |

# *Chronology*

1939    —August: The U.S. Department of State attempts to analyze Soviet policy toward the major European powers as the USSR prepares to sign the Nazi-Soviet nonaggression pact of August 24.

—September 1: Hitler invades Poland.

—September 4: Secretary of State Cordell Hull meets with Lord Lothian, British ambassador to the United States, to ensure lack of conflict over neutral rights.

—September 5: President Franklin D. Roosevelt announces American neutrality in the war, as required by U.S. law.

—September 17: The USSR invades Poland as arranged in a secret protocol in the pact of August 24.

—October 11: Roosevelt appeals to President Mikhail Kalinin of the USSR to settle differences with Finland amicably.

—November 29: The Soviet Union invades Finland.

1940    —January 1: FDR assigns Sumner Welles the task of feeling out the prospects for peace. Welles's mission to Europe ends unsuccessfully with his return on March 28.

—January 3: Roosevelt sends his $1.8-billion defense budget to Congress along with a warning that the nation faces a worldwide conspiracy of aggressor nations to destroy civilization.

1940  —January 26: The United States announces the expiration of its 1911 commerce treaty with Japan.

—March 13: The Soviets and Finns end the Winter War with Finnish territorial concessions to the USSR.

—May 10: Winston Churchill replaces Neville Chamberlain as British prime minister.

—May 16: FDR asks Congress for $1.18 billion more for defense.

—June 14: The president uses his press conference to warn of the Nazi threat to American security.

—June 17: France surrenders.

—July 15: The USSR holds "plebiscites" in Estonia, Latvia, and Lithuania. Their annexation to the Soviet Union is announced on July 21.

—July 25–26: Roosevelt restricts exports of oil and scrap metal to Japan.

—September 3: The destroyers-for-bases deal between the United States and Great Britain is announced.

—September 19: Secretary of the Treasury Henry Morgenthau pursues a deal with the Soviet Union to provide aid to China, while the Department of State negotiates a new trade agreement with the USSR. Thus FDR tries to win the Russians away from a possible commitment to the Axis powers.

—September 26: Roosevelt places a total embargo on shipments of scrap steel and iron outside the Western Hemisphere except to Great Britain.

—September 27: Japan, Germany, and Italy sign the Tripartite Pact forming the Axis alliance.

—October 8: Germany alarms the USSR by occupying Romania and beginning the Balkan campaign.

—November 12: Chief of Naval Operations Admiral Harold Stark recommends a "Germany first" grand strategy.

—November 29: Roosevelt gives his "arsenal of democracy" address in a fireside chat, emphasizing to the national radio audience the seriousness of the threat to America from the Axis powers.

1941    —January 6: In his State of the Union message, FDR announces the proposed Lend-Lease program and enunciates his Four Freedoms concept.

—March 1: Bulgaria joins the Tripartite Pact, and German forces move into the country in large numbers the next day, instigating a formal protest from Soviet Commissar of Foreign Affairs V. M. Molotov on March 6.

—March 11: Congress approves Lend-Lease.

—March 13: Adolf Hitler authorizes Operation Barbarossa, the planned invasion of the USSR.

—April 9: Denmark agrees to the creation of American bases to defend Greenland.

—April 11: Roosevelt extends the Atlantic patrol area for U.S. Navy units to the Azores.

—April 13: Japan and Russia sign a nonaggression pact.

—May 27: FDR announces an unlimited national emergency.

—June 22: Hitler invades the USSR.

—June 23: Roosevelt announces aid to Russia, but not yet Lend-Lease.

—July 26: FDR freezes Japanese assets in the United States and stops licensing oil shipments to Japan.

—August 12: Churchill and Roosevelt meet at Argentia Bay off Newfoundland and announce the Atlantic Charter.

—August 25: British and Soviet forces occupy Iran.

—September 6: President Roosevelt orders the U.S. Navy to "shoot on sight" German submarines in the neutral zone.

1941 —October 17: A German submarine attacks the USS *Kearny.*

—October 30: The USS *Reuben James* is sunk by a German submarine.

—November 5: The Japanese Imperial Conference makes the decision to attack Pearl Harbor if the Americans do not accede to Japanese demands.

—November 17: FDR signs legislation repealing the neutrality laws.

—December 1: The Japanese emperor and his Privy Council decide to wage war against the United States.

—December 7: Japan attacks the United States at Pearl Harbor.

—December 11: Germany and Italy declare war on the United States.

1942 —January 1: Twenty-six nations sign a United Nations declaration as opponents of the Axis powers.

—January 14: At the Arcadia Conference, the United States and Britain conclude plans for Anglo-American military collaboration.

—February 4: FDR and Secretary Hull reject Soviet demands for recognition of new Soviet borders in eastern Europe.

—May 26: Great Britain and the USSR sign a twenty-year alliance that excludes an agreement on Soviet borders and includes assurance of a second front in Europe to be opened by Anglo-American forces in 1942.

—July 1: The First Protocol is signed, guaranteeing U.S. Lend-Lease aid to the USSR.

—August 12–14: The first Moscow Conference takes place, and Churchill tells Soviet leader Joseph Stalin that the next front to open will be in North Africa instead of Europe. This invasion commences on November 8.

—November 19: The Red Army launches its counteroffensive at Stalingrad.

1943   —January 24: Churchill and Roosevelt meet at Casablanca and agree to attack Sicily and Italy and once again to delay the cross-Channel attack. They attempt to pacify Stalin by announcing the unconditional surrender doctrine.

—April 27: As a result of the Polish reaction to the Katyn Forest massacre, the USSR suspends relations with the Polish government-in-exile at London.

—May 22: Moscow announces dissolution of the Comintern.

—May 25: The Trident Conference concludes in Washington after detailing plans for the buildup of forces for the invasion of France.

—July 10: Operation Husky begins in Sicily.

—July 25: Benito Mussolini resigns as premier of Italy.

—August 11–14: The Quadrant Conference is held at Quebec, where Roosevelt and Stalin meet to confirm plans for Operation Overlord and to establish a China-Burma-India theater of operations. Also in attendance are Canadian Prime Minister Mackenzie King and Chinese Foreign Minister T.V. Soong.

—October 19–30: The Moscow Conference of foreign ministers takes place, at which Stalin is assured that a second front will be opened in France in 1944, and the USSR agrees to the Four Nations Declaration in favor of establishing the United Nations. Stalin tells Secretary of State Hull that he will enter the Far Eastern war as soon as Germany is defeated.

—November 7: The Red Army recaptures Kiev.

—November 26: The first Cairo Conference brings FDR, Churchill, and Chiang Kai-shek together. Chiang agrees to Soviet claims regarding the Kurile Islands and Sakhalin Island, although the Soviet Union is not represented.

1943 —November 28–December 1: Roosevelt, Churchill, and Stalin meet at Tehran to lay final plans for the invasion of France, to gain assurance of a Soviet offensive to coincide with the Normandy invasion, and again to get assurance of Soviet entry into the Pacific war. The United Nations idea is again discussed, along with preliminary plans for the postwar world. FDR tries to soften Soviet demands for expanded borders and influence in eastern Europe by emphasizing the collective security principle to be embodied in the United Nations.

1944 —March 26: Churchill and Stalin try to get American approval of spheres of influence with British preeminence in Greece and Soviet domination of Romania. FDR hedges and gives conditional approval for three months.

—June 6: D-Day. The second front is launched against the coast of Normandy.

—August 1: The Warsaw uprising occurs; the Soviets sit it out on the east side of the Vistula River. As the Polish underground is slaughtered by the Germans, the British and Americans demand that they be allowed to land in the USSR after overflights and supply drops to the Poles. Their requests are denied by the Russians.

—August 21–October 7: The Dumbarton Oaks Conference lays plans for the United Nations Organization. The Soviet Union is not willing to accept Anglo-American proposals on the veto question in the Security Council, on membership, or on several other matters.

—September 10: The U.S. ambassador to the USSR, W. Averell Harriman, reports growing Soviet surliness and arrogance.

—October 9–18: With the reluctant support of FDR, Churchill meets with Stalin in Moscow to arrange spheres of influence. Ambassador Harriman tells FDR what is taking place, and again the U.S. government requests that territorial questions be delayed until the end of the war.

—November 30: Edward R. Stettinius, Jr., replaces Cordell Hull as secretary of state.

1945    —January 21: The Americans regain the territory lost in the Battle of the Bulge.

        —January 23: Soviet occupation of Poland is completed.

        —February 4–11: Churchill, Roosevelt, and Stalin meet at Yalta to discuss the last phases of the war and plans for the peace. Territorial divisions are taken up seriously, and the Americans again oppose Soviet plans for eastern Europe. The Declaration on Liberated Europe is signed; it will be interpreted by the Anglo-American group differently from the way the Soviet Union sees it. Plans to dismember Germany are set in place. Soviet demands for quid pro quos for entry into the Pacific war are partially satisfied.

        —March 1: President Roosevelt addresses a joint session of Congress on the Yalta Conference.

        —March 4: The Bern incident, concerning secret talks in Switzerland with German representatives for surrender, deepens Soviet-American antagonisms. Several communications between Roosevelt and Stalin between March 4 and April 13 concern this matter. The last one reaches its destination after Roosevelt's death.

        —April 11: FDR prepares a speech for April 13, which he never delivers.

        —April 12: Roosevelt dies of a cerebral hemorrhage at Warm Springs, Georgia.

# Introduction

FRANKLIN DELANO ROOSEVELT attempted to establish a foreign policy that was liberal and conservative, isolationist and interventionist, realistic and idealistic, recognizable and hidden. Incredibly, he managed to accomplish all of these things, although not always to his own or his nation's advantage. His determination to remain in control of foreign policy occasioned some of the dualism in his conduct of diplomacy. He was confident of his ability to maneuver to meet changing circumstances, but often he was not sure of the people in the government who assisted him in making and carrying out his policies.

Roosevelt the pragmatist exhibited all of the advantages and disadvantages of this philosophy. On the plus side, he was liberal and open to experimentation, but he rejected dogmatism and looked askance at those who responded to crises ideologically. On the negative side, he seemed incapable of planning for alternatives if the best policy did not prevail. This led him to rely on crisis-to-crisis diplomacy. Postponing decisions about the future was not the best way to foster an amicable relationship with the Russians. Very early in his presidency, an admirer asked him to give the public a long-range plan for American foreign policy that might be used as a guide. He admitted that he did not know how to do this and that he probably would not follow such a program even if he could, because he had learned from Woodrow Wilson that the public could not be attuned to the highest note in the scale without being discomforted.[1] Unfortunately, this meant that too often the scale of notes in Roosevelt's foreign policy led to cacophony.

FDR's pragmatism allowed him to avoid being caught in the rigid web of dogmatism, but it also engendered continuous shifting of short- and long-range U.S. goals. This shifting fueled the mutual suspicions in the American-Soviet relationship and intensified the deep-seated Russian paranoia concerning foreigners. Thus FDR's pragmatism was far less

---

[1]Letter of January 30, 1934, PPF 359, Foreign Affairs Folder, FDRL.

effective when it was applied to foreign affairs than when it was used in domestic crises.

## *II*

When FDR entered office in 1933 he recognized the Soviet Union, mainly because he wished to block the aggressive course Japan had launched in Asia and to offer a warning to Adolf Hitler, whom the president already viewed as a discordant element in Europe threatening to upset the balance of forces there. He believed that Hitler intended to supplant democracy with totalitarianism, thereby endangering America and the rest of the world. Eleanor Roosevelt recalled her husband's reaction after hearing Hitler's first speech as chancellor: "The man is a menace."[2] He never altered his opinion.

FDR's objectives throughout the 1930s remained constant: defend American national interest by promoting arms limitation; establish a cooperative relationship with the Soviet Union, with the intent of using the combined size and power of the United States and the USSR to block threats to the peace; and promote economic stability as a further guarantee of the peace. Roosevelt saw a threat to American security in the disintegration of the world peace structure. When arms limitations failed, he began to build America's military might in order to counteract rising levels of armaments among the Axis powers. His support for arms production was excessively cautious, however, so as to make sure that neither congressional nor public opposition would force him to retreat from his preparedness program. When his efforts to focus public opinion pressure on the dissident powers proved unsuccessful, he encouraged the stiffening of British and French policy to resist the Axis powers. The president attempted to keep the United States out of direct involvement, but he also kept foreign policy troubleshooters working to bring the quarreling European and Asian nations to some accommodation. Russia remained a constant element in FDR's plans to avoid war or, in the event of war, to ensure victory for the side he favored.

Roosevelt's nemesis was Joseph Stalin, for on the hinge of Soviet policy swung the success or failure of FDR's waiting game with the Axis powers. Stalin was an enigma to Roosevelt. He knew that the Soviet dictator was ruthless, shrewd, and to some degree dangerously ideological. The question was: To what degree? At times, when the president assessed the information coming to him from his ambassadors in Moscow and from other sources, he optimistically judged Stalin as merely another pragmatic politician with whom he could deal on matters of obvious mutual interest; there were other occasions when he viewed Stalin as sinister, unfathomable, and devious. Between Roosevelt's first evaluation of the Soviet leader in

---

[2]Interview with Eleanor Roosevelt, summer 1959, Hyde Park, New York.

1933 and the coming of war in 1939, FDR several times changed his perception of Stalin as a person and a political leader, most dramatically during the negotiations Stalin directed with the British, French, and Germans in 1939. Roosevelt waited on tenterhooks to see which way the Russian leader would move and wondered whether his own waiting game would bring success or disaster when the world crisis came. All of his sources told the president that Germany could not win a two-front war, or at least it would not risk one. A neutral Russia threatened both Germany and Japan, because a long and enervating war in which the USSR remained uninvolved only enhanced Soviet prospects to take advantage of Nazi and Japanese weakness.

FDR attempted to mold a foreign policy that isolated potential aggressors and thwarted their moves. The events of 1939 made him fear that his maneuvers might be for naught, that the whole situation might dissolve into an uncontrollable mess. His concern over the state of affairs in Europe seemed warranted at the beginning of the year when Chargé d'Affaires Alexander Kirk, in Moscow, cautioned that Maxim Litvinov might have lost his struggle to direct the USSR toward collective security and that probably his replacement as commissar of foreign affairs was the result of his animosity toward the Nazis.[3] A report from John F. Montgomery at the American embassy in Budapest suggested that Hitler and Benito Mussolini had gone too far to turn back and that most of Europe's leaders thought them beyond recall on the road to war.[4]

In a lengthy dispatch in May 1939, Kirk discounted rumors that firing Litvinov was part of a ploy on Stalin's part to put pressure on the British and French to come to acceptable terms with Russia in the negotiations then in progress. Instead, something really significant was happening that warned of a shift in Soviet policy, and it was not toward a rapprochement with Great Britain and France.[5] Loy W. Henderson, who previously had served in Moscow and who at the time was assigned to duty in Washington, corroborated Kirk's assessment. He thought that possibly a radical shift was coming in Soviet policy that would not be beneficial to the democratic coalition.[6]

All of these warnings and more convinced the president that the Axis powers could not easily be dissuaded or diverted from conquest by fear of the threatened powers coalescing against them. Roosevelt's concern intensified when the Soviets attacked Finland in November 1939, and storm clouds forecasting a general war gathered more ominously over Europe as the

---

[3]Alexander Kirk to Secretary of State Cordell Hull, February 22, 1939, DSF 861.021/38.

[4]John F. Montgomery to Franklin D. Roosevelt, April 21, 1939, PSF II, Departmental Files, State Department, 1939, FDRL.

[5]Kirk to secretary of state, May 4, 1939, DSF 861.01/2160.

[6]Memorandum by Loy W. Henderson for the Division of European Affairs to secretary of state, May 4, 1939, DSF 861.01/2176.

prospect of the Russians siding with the forces of civilization seemed even less likely. Roosevelt reacted angrily in his private correspondence to this betrayal of little Finland and tried to use American influence on behalf of the Finns, but he did not break relations or antagonize the Soviets too forcefully because he knew the West would be in desperate straits if the Russians joined Germany in full alliance. When the Nazi-Soviet nonaggression pact was announced, President Roosevelt already knew that this was a distinct possibility, if not a probability. When Germany and the USSR seemed to be allied in the attack on Poland, FDR remained calm, although he lumped the Russians with the other dictator nations as violators of the peace against which America needed to be on its guard.[7]

## III

While the president worried about the role the Soviets would play in Europe and Asia, the new ambassador to the USSR, Laurence A. Steinhardt, and others evaluated the world crisis and attempted to fathom a course for the United States. Steinhardt received some startling information on July 10, 1939, from his friend Colvin W. Brown, who had heard that Nazi Foreign Minister Joachim von Ribbentrop advocated a campaign against Poland and had told Hitler that he had nothing to fear from the Western democracies opposing such an attack. Concerning Nazi-Soviet relations, Brown had learned that the failure to reach an Anglo-Russian agreement was a great disappointment to conservative elements in Germany that were outwardly Nazi but inwardly hoping for Hitler's downfall. Brown's informant in Germany had told him that Berlin's ambassador to Moscow had offered terms to Stalin including a nonaggression pact, a reciprocal trade agreement with the balance in favor of Russia, suppression of White Russian propaganda and other activities in Germany, denunciation of any right to the German minority in the Ukraine, and cession of India to Russia when the British Empire disintegrated.[8]

Steinhardt passed on the information he thought significant to Undersecretary of State Sumner Welles on August 16, 1939. To get Germany's attention the Russians had leaked the news that Steinhardt had carried a secret letter from FDR to Stalin about Anglo-French-Russian negotiations. He did have such a letter, an appeal for Anglo-French-Russian cooperation in the interests of peace, to which Vyashislav Molotov responded orally that he appreciated President Roosevelt's concern but that the English and French would have to start discussing real guarantees of

---

[7]Press Conferences of Franklin D. Roosevelt, 14, no. 576, September 5, 1939, p. 140, FDRL.

[8]Colvin W. Brown to Laurence A. Steinhardt, July 10, 1939, Box 27, General Correspondence, Laurence A. Steinhardt Papers, Library of Congress, Washington, DC (hereafter cited as Steinhardt Papers).

"mutual" assistance if they wished to impress Russia. Steinhardt concluded that the Soviets intended to continue negotiations with both sides in order to stall until October. This would enable them to avoid war until spring, because no one would attack them during a Russian winter. They also thought that they would find Japan weaker in the spring.[9]

On the same day, Steinhardt intimated to Secretary of State Cordell Hull that U.S.-Soviet relations should concentrate on the Far East, where the two nations' interests coincided. In a talk with President Mikhail Kalinin, Steinhardt bluntly suggested that eventually the United States would take the lead in checking Japan, followed by cooperation from England, France, and the USSR. Kalinin emphasized the peaceful intentions of Russia toward Japan, but he said that they were not reciprocated. However, as the Soviets were ready for Japanese aggression they were not worried, and they felt reasonably secure in Europe. Steinhardt surmised that the Russians were playing a shrewd game in international politics and that, from the point of view of their interests, they were playing it intelligently and successfully. They would fulfill a steadily increasing role in world politics, both in Europe and the Far East, because of their potential and carefully concealed military strength.[10] Steinhardt wrote to a friend in New York, foretelling the outbreak of a general European war in the near future. In fact, he predicted that only a miracle would prevent war within three weeks and that it probably would come before the letter (dated August 25) reached its addressee.[11]

Charles E. Stuart forwarded a letter for the president's attention from Edward A. Loring, a British engineer. Stuart had been considered for the Moscow post when Steinhardt was selected, and he was a partner in an international engineering firm that had conducted business in the USSR during the period of nonrecognition. Stuart had extensive contacts in both the Soviet Union and Great Britain. Loring wrote that war was imminent, that Britain was prepared to fight, "not to save Danzig for the Poles, nor even to save Poland; we all believe that it will be a war to endeavor to save civilization." Even so, he conjectured that in the end "we shall never again see the world as it is to-day, at any rate in our time, unless the war can be successfully ended quickly for the Democracies, otherwise I think it will lead to quite a new order of things."[12]

The sentiment concerning the salvation of civilization coincided exactly with Roosevelt's own assessment of the stakes of a general war. FDR feared that, if the European democracies lost the war, the United States

---

[9]Steinhardt to Sumner Welles, August 16, 1939, Letterbooks, Box 78, Steinhardt Papers.

[10]Steinhardt to Hull, August 16, 1939, DSF 123, STEINHARDT, LAURENCE A./249.

[11]Steinhardt to Hageman E. Hilty, August 25, 1939, Letterbooks, Official Letterbook, p. 50, Steinhardt Papers.

[12]E. A. Loring to Charles E. Stuart, August 25, 1939, OF 198E, FDRL.

would be left alone to hold the torch of civilization. He expressed his fears on this score as early as 1937, when he wrote author James Hilton to congratulate him on his book *Lost Horizon* and to tell him some of the ideas in the book had been used in the "quarantine" speech on Japanese aggression.[13] Later, in a letter to the U.S. ambassador to Italy, William Phillips, FDR suggested that the United States might have to play the role of Shangri-la when the war came by standing aside and waiting "to pick up the pieces of European civilization and help them save what remains of the wreck."[14]

# IV

Perhaps President Roosevelt should have been aware of yet another prospect for Soviet foreign policy, one that was noted in a perceptive analysis by journalist Louis Fischer at the very end of 1939. Fischer had long been a sympathetic observer of the progress of the Soviet experiment. He had encouraged recognition, criticized American reluctance to deal with the Russians on security matters when the Soviet Union did not pay its debt to America, and believed that the strain in relations was at least as much the fault of the Americans as of the Soviet leaders. However, the Nazi-Soviet nonaggression pact convinced Fischer that the Kremlin's policy had become Machiavellian, pure and simple, after the restraining hand of Litvinov was removed and the hard-line Bolshevik Vyashislav Molotov replaced him.

Fischer's essay for the *Nation* suggested what had really caused Russia's decision to sign an agreement with the Nazis. In essence, he turned most analysts' perceptions of Stalin's decision upside down: He proposed that those who credited the Soviet action to a policy of self-defense, intended to keep the Germans at arm's length, did not understand either Hitler or Stalin. Hitler signed the pact not because he believed Britain and France would not fight, as some observers suggested, but because he thought they would. In such a case he would not want a neutral Russia on his flank; otherwise, he would not have shared Poland with Stalin, thereby making his anti-Bolshevik crusade appear so ludicrous. The Russians knew that their bargaining position would give them part of Poland, and this, rather than fear of a German invasion, determined Stalin's course. Bargaining with the British and French made it clear that they were not going to offer the Soviets control of eastern Poland and the Baltic States, but Germany would; it was that simple. Had Franklin Roosevelt read and believed Fischer's article, he would have had less hope for real cooperation with the Soviets

---

[13]FDR to James Hilton, December 20, 1937, PPF, FDRL.

[14]FDR to William Phillips, September 15, 1938, in Elliott Roosevelt, ed., *The Roosevelt Letters: Being the Personal Correspondence of Franklin Delano Roosevelt*, 3 vols. (London: George G. Harrap, 1949–1952), 3:241. Volume 3 covers the years from 1928 to 1945.

but possibly more confidence that the Soviet leadership was not irrevocably committed to a long-term agreement with Hitler.[15]

Fischer subtitled his article "Has Stalin Blundered?" and answered with a resounding "no." Stalin had acted shrewdly, as always, and those who expected altruism in national policy would be badly disappointed. "What looks like idealism in foreign policy," Fischer surmised, "is often merely a long view of selfish ends."[16] This was the part of the article that FDR might have read with the most benefit, for it described to perfection Stalinist foreign policy. The Bolshevik turned tsar never shrank from realpolitik, and this was an early illustration of that reality.

Winston S. Churchill said that Russia is a riddle wrapped in a mystery inside an enigma, but he also thought that perhaps there was a key. In Stalin's case the key was a combination of self-interest, both for himself and for the Soviet Union. Roosevelt never fully believed what was apparent about Stalin, that he had the soul of a Georgian merchant and was trustworthy only inside the framework of what served his own ends. This was the man whom FDR would attempt to charm and manipulate into an acceptable arrangement to win the war and secure the peace. The president's realism told him that he had no choice: If he failed, Hitler would win or the Soviet Union would replace Germany as America's enemy, and Roosevelt's dream of a secure and peaceful world would remain unfulfilled.

---

[15] Louis Fischer, "Soviet Russia Today," *Nation* 149 (December 30, 1939): 728–32.
[16] Ibid., p. 728.

# I

## Roosevelt and the Disintegrating World Order: Where Will Russia Be?

FRANCES PERKINS MARVELED at Franklin Roosevelt's resiliency: "It seemed to me during all the years that I knew him that at the most severe and gloomy stages of our national emergencies that this was the time the president set his jaw and decided that he had to set an example and nearly always did so."[1] Certainly he must have decided it was time to set his jaw during the waning days of 1939. Little imagination is needed to conjure the grim realities of those days for the president as the European crisis deepened and very little news from Asia gave hope of any better prospects there. The Nazi-Soviet agreement made the Russians appear to be contributors to the declining fortunes of the Western nations.

After the pact was signed, on August 24, 1939,[2] the American embassy in Moscow was given the task of discovering the extent of the intended cooperation between Hitler and Stalin. Charles E. Bohlen, second secretary of the embassy, was the person responsible for answering these questions: "Would [the two dictators] be genuine allies, aiding each other economically and militarily and pledging to come to each other's defense? Would they divide Poland and then go their separate ways? Would they, as the British confidently predicted, soon fall into a quarrel, as thieves do? How long would they keep the pledge of nonaggression against each other?"[3] Bohlen thought that he knew the answer to one question immediately: Stalin would stick by the agreement as long as Germany's military strength was undiminished. He was not so sure about Hitler. Some observers were surprised by the Russian attack on Poland, but Bohlen had predicted it because it made sense to keep German military activities as far from Russia as possible. The Soviets did not hesitate to fulfill long-held Russian

---

[1]Interview with Frances Perkins, spring 1958, University of Illinois, Urbana.
[2]Most sources give the date as August 23, but the pact was actually signed at 1:00 A.M. on August 24.
[3]Charles E. Bohlen, *Witness to History, 1929–1969* (New York: W. W. Norton, 1973), p. 88.

ambitions to incorporate areas of Poland with Belorussian and Ukrainian areas of the USSR, and the chance to seize Latvia, Estonia, and Lithuania was too good to pass up.[4]

Incredibly, the British did not see the prospect for the pact as clearly as the Americans, nor did they feel the need to hurry their negotiations. A memorandum from the British secretary of state for foreign affairs warned that it might be necessary to deal with the Russians immediately lest there be an arrangement with the Germans. But the British government stalled and behaved as though it had all the time in the world; also, it flatly rejected Soviet demands for a mutual defense alliance. The Russians were clearly upset by this, as the British already had such a treaty with France and Poland.[5] Sir William Strang, who headed the British mission that negotiated with the Soviets, observed prophetically that perhaps they would have been "wiser to pay the Soviet price for the agreement . . . earlier, since we are not in a good position to bargain and since, as the international situation deteriorates, the Soviet price is likely to rise."[6] In fact, the price was one that the British were unprepared to pay, and, as the Americans and some of the British predicted, Stalin turned to Berlin.

Reports from Moscow to Washington illuminated the extent of collaboration between the Soviets and the Nazis. Ambassador Laurence Steinhardt, Chargé Alexander Kirk, and others pointed out the complaints from the Baltic diplomats concerning their treatment and concerning Soviet demands for facilities to expedite shipment of Russian goods through their territories to Germany. Also, during the internment of the American merchantman *City of Flint* and its crew at Murmansk, the Russians showed favoritism toward the German prize crew, ignoring the ordinary rules of neutrality and civility to the American crew while granting privileges to Germans from other ships who should have been under strict retention, privileges that were denied to the Americans.[7]

Roosevelt watched the Soviet-Finnish War carefully, aware of U.S. sympathy for the small republic under attack by the Communist colossus and of the American desire to pull for the underdog Finns who had gained so much respect by being the only country to pay off the debt they had incurred in the United States during the Great War. At the same time, Roosevelt feared that taking too aggressive a course in support of Finland might push Russia toward a firmer alliance with the Nazis. Economic pressure on

---

[4]Ibid., p. 90.

[5]Memorandum by the secretary of state for foreign affairs, May 1939, British Cabinet Minutes, CAB 24/CP 124 (39), Public Record Office, London, England.

[6]Memorandum, "Anglo-Franco-Soviet Negotiations," circulating a letter from Sir William Strang in Moscow of July 20, 1939, CAB 24/CP 172 (39).

[7]See *FRUS: Diplomatic Papers, The Soviet Union, 1933–1939* (Washington, DC: Government Printing Office, 1952), pp. 934–1013, for complete details of these reports. A prize crew consisted of the capturing navy's manning of a seized ship.

Russia was the best answer the president could come up with, and he wrote to Assistant Secretary of State Adolf A. Berle, Jr., suggesting that it was time to consider curtailing gasoline shipments to Russia and possibly cutting out scrap iron sales as well. "This particular time may be a turning point where one or two comparatively minor matters may tip the scale toward unofficial considerations in the direction of peace."[8]

Although the U.S.-Soviet relationship was strained by the Russian assault on Finland and Stalin's deal with Hitler, the Kremlin continued to imply that mutual interests could still bring the two nations together in joint opposition to Japan. At a luncheon in Moscow, Commissar of Foreign Affairs V. M. Molotov tested Ambassador Steinhardt with a prediction about future Soviet-American cooperation against the Japanese. Molotov suggested that, despite trade and boundary negotiations between the USSR and Japan then in progress, his government still considered Japan to be an enemy. He would not be surprised, he told Steinhardt, to see the Red Army and the American fleet some day collaborating to suppress this common foe. Steinhardt did not respond to this bait.[9] His failure to comment must have seemed strange to Molotov, who no doubt expected a corroboration of the mutual American-Soviet interests in the Far East implied by the ambassador's comments to President Mikhail Kalinin on August 16, 1939, when Steinhardt had predicted that eventually the United States would take the lead in checking the Japanese, followed by the British, French, and Russians.[10]

Loy W. Henderson, in the Division of European Affairs, analyzed the Soviet commissar's intent in speaking to the ambassador about a future conflict with Japan. Henderson contended that, if Steinhardt had in any way indicated agreement that Russia and America shared an enmity against Japan, Molotov would have used this to intimate to the Japanese that the Americans had approached the Russians to build a Soviet-American anti-Japanese front. Henderson thought that the Russians realized that they needed good relations with the United States, because the Americans were the only source of supply for great quantities of badly needed strategic materials. He concluded that "this species of allure has not been used to any extent since it was put away shortly after the establishment of diplomatic relations in 1933."[11] Henderson was dead wrong, as both the Soviet Union and the United States had used the Japanese bogeyman on numerous

---

[8]Roosevelt to Adolf A. Berle, Jr., January 27, 1940, and response of February 1, 1940, PSF II, Departmental Files, State Department, A. A. Berle, Jr., 1938–1940, FDRL.
[9]Steinhardt to Hull, February 28, 1940, DSF 760D.61/1184.
[10]Steinhardt to Hull, August 16, 1939, DSF 123, STEINHARDT, LAURENCE A./249.
[11]Memorandum, Henderson to Hull, March 2, 1940, DSF 760D.61/1184.

occasions since recognition to try to force one another to be more cooperative about foreign policy objectives.[12]

Roosevelt's first real evidence that the Soviet Union might join Germany in its war on Poland came on September 8, 1939, when Steinhardt wrote from Moscow to the State Department that within the preceding twenty-four hours the Soviet government had called up numerous reserves, commandeered nonmilitary automobiles, and called Red Cross nurses to duty. The heaviest concentration was on the USSR's western borders.[13] On September 9, Steinhardt narrowed the possible purposes of the mobilization to two: Either the Russians intended to occupy eastern Poland and possibly the Baltic States, or they planned to take a defensive position against deep German penetration into areas adjacent to the Soviet, Polish, and Baltic frontiers.[14]

Roosevelt must have watched with frustration and apprehension as the European drama unfolded. His concerns about the Soviet position increased on September 18, when Berle sent a dire prediction about Soviet actions to the president. Berle warned of the probable fate of Poland and of Soviet efforts to swing the Turks into their orbit. If this were successful, the entire Danube Valley down to the Black Sea would be German, and German-Russian domination would extend from the Rhine to the Pacific. This new map of Europe and Asia would be particularly forbidding if a Russo-Japanese nonaggression pact were to be signed, which Berle thought very likely. In these circumstances China would be split between Russia and Japan. Such an extension of Axis power, which was all too likely to occur, required immediate U.S. efforts to create a unified Western hemispheric defense policy.[15]

In October 1939, Roosevelt's hopes were raised that Russia might not be fully committed to Germany. When Soviet Ambassador Konstantin Umanskii left for the USSR in late 1939, Presidential Press Secretary Steve Early spoke to journalist Huston Thompson about a telephone interview he had had with the Russian before his departure. Anglo-Soviet rapprochement might not be a lost cause, but cooperation could only stem from a change in the British government, which put Winston Churchill in charge of negotiations with the Soviets.[16]

---

[12]Edward M. Bennett, *Franklin D. Roosevelt and the Search for Security: American-Soviet Relations, 1933–1939* (Wilmington, DE: Scholarly Resources, 1985), pp. 5–7, 14–16, 20, 23–24, 26–30, 117–22.

[13]Steinhardt to Hull, September 8, 1939, DSF 861.20/480.

[14]Steinhardt to Hull, September 9, 1939, DSF 861.20/481.

[15]Memorandum, Berle to FDR, September 18, 1939, PSF, Department of State File, Berle, FDRL.

[16]Memorandum, FDR to Hull, October 26, 1939, PSF II, Departmental Correspondence, State Department, Hull, Box 33, FDRL.

## *II*

Roosevelt decided that there was only one way to determine the seriousness of the threat to the democracies. On January 1, 1940, the president called Sumner Welles to the White House and asked him to undertake a mission to Europe. FDR told him that he had considered for some time "whether there still remained any step which he, as President of the United States, could take to avert the dangers that would so clearly confront the people of this country, as well as the civilized world, if the European war continued."[17] Roosevelt did not believe that there was one chance "in a thousand" that anything could change the course already in progress, but in good conscience he felt that he had to try by sending a personal representative to Germany, France, England, and Italy. Italy was included because it was a part of the Axis alliance, although it was still formally neutral. The Soviet Union was specifically excluded because, due to the Nazi-Soviet pact, the president "did not feel that a visit to Moscow would serve any useful purpose, at least for the time being." He also told Welles that he was not seeking a truce or peace on German terms, for he "had no interest in any temporary or tentative armed truce."[18]

The mission accomplished only one thing. It became absolutely clear there was no chance for a peace based on anything resembling the status quo before the attack on Poland. Welles learned in Italy that Benito Mussolini would do nothing on his own and probably had insufficient influence to do anything to divert Hitler even if he so desired. In Germany, Hitler orchestrated all of the discussions that Welles carried on with Joachim von Ribbentrop, Hermann Goering, Rudolf Hess, and lesser lights in the Nazi firmament. The same arrogant message emerged from all sources: Germany controlled the fate of Europe and would accept no peace agreement except on its own harsh terms. Welles concluded that the only way to stop Hitler was to convince him that if he attacked the democracies the United States would come to their aid with full force.[19]

Certainly earlier pronouncements to both the press and friends indicated that Roosevelt saw no hope for an acceptable peace with Hitler. His radio address of March 16 emphasized that he was not searching for peace at any price. The prerequisites for an acceptable peace agreement were clearly delineated: "Today we seek a moral basis for peace. . . . It cannot be a lasting peace if the fruit of it is oppression, or starvation, or cruelty, or human life dominated by armed camps. It cannot be a sound peace if small nations must live in fear of powerful neighbors. It cannot be a moral peace

---

[17]Sumner Welles, *The Time for Decision* (New York: Harper & Brothers, 1944), p. 73.
[18]Ibid., pp. 73–74.
[19]Ibid., pp. 89–120.

if freedom from invasion is sold for tribute."[20] There was no doubt in Great Britain about what this speech meant. When Neville Chamberlain endorsed it in the House of Commons on March 19, his announcement was followed by cheers from the members.[21] Those in Washington who feared that Welles's mission might bring further appeasement were also heartened by Roosevelt's message.[22]

## *III*

One of FDR's problems was how to approach the American people so that they might see the dangers in the rising Axis menace without becoming alarmed and retreating to a panicky isolationism. In his annual address to Congress on January 3, 1940, he averred that the United States was not going to go to war for others' security. But he did not want people to think that, because America had no intention of fighting its safety was ensured or that it could afford to be uninterested in the developing world war. Circumstances dictated that Americans must take a longer view of external events: "We must look ahead and see the effect on our future generations if world trade is controlled by any nation which sets up that control through military force. . . . It is not good for the ultimate health of ostriches to bury their heads in the sand." This warning was intended to arouse Americans to the dangers Roosevelt recognized: "What we face is a set of world-wide forces of disintegration—vicious, ruthless, destructive of all the moral, religious and political standards which mankind, after centuries of struggle, has come to cherish most."[23]

In his press conference of January 30, FDR attempted to disarm the critics of his defense budget. He announced an expenditure of $1.8 billion and stated that he did not believe that the majority of Americans wanted any cuts. He told the press that unnamed experts on defense thought his appropriation was less than adequate, although he thought it was sufficient. He emphasized the need for it in the face of the world situation and assured the press that the amount would be reduced "when the current emergency has passed."[24]

In his annual meeting with the members of the Society of Newspaper Editors, President Roosevelt continued his campaign to win over the press

---

[20]Franklin D. Roosevelt, *Roosevelt's Foreign Policy: Franklin D. Roosevelt's Unedited Speeches and Messages* (New York: Harper, 1942), p. 225.

[21]Ibid.

[22]W. T. Stone, "Washington News Letter," *Foreign Policy Bulletin* 19 (March 22, 1940).

[23]Franklin D. Roosevelt, *Roosevelt's Foreign Policy: Franklin D. Roosevelt's Unedited Speeches and Messages* (New York: Wilfred Funk, 1941), p. 213.

[24]Press Conferences, 15, no. 612, January 30, 1940, pp. 10–14, FDRL. W. T. Stone analyzed the budget and came up with a figure of $2,247,126,509 for defense. See W. T. Stone, "Washington News Letter," *Foreign Policy Bulletin* 19 (January 17, 1940).

to his concern about the deteriorating U.S. security position. He told them that his armaments program was not caused by a militarist attitude on his part, but, as commander in chief, he was obligated to overcome pressures intended to limit arms at any cost. The "silly, fool, old question of the pacifists: Who are you trying to protect us against? . . . Who is going to attack? What nation? Name it. Where?" had been answered by events in Europe. He asked: If Britain lost the war, how would the United States like to have Nazi Germany as a neighbor in Canada? He stressed the threat of a Nazi presence in Latin America and reminded them how serious it was to have the continent of Europe in the hands of powers antagonistic toward the United States.[25]

On June 14 the president used another press conference to warn about the threat to American security. Hitler had granted an interview to a Hearst correspondent, wherein the Nazi dictator had scoffed at the idea that he would ever consider invading the Western Hemisphere. A reporter asked Roosevelt to comment, but the president demurred except to remark that "it brings up recollections." This comment was followed by laughter. He stated that, although no elaboration was necessary, his remark could be explained by going back a number of years and counting the nations that Hitler had solemnly assured he would not attack and then recalling what had happened to them.[26]

Occasionally, President Roosevelt gave the press a modified Wilsonian lecture on the values and responsibilities that had to be defended and promoted by the United States in the face of attacks by the antidemocratic forces loose in the world. On July 4 he read the Declaration of Independence in his address to the nation, adding that this was a reminder of what America stood for. Its basic ideals encompassed four freedoms that some nations had copied but that men on horseback had overturned in the name of "more efficient" forms of government. Those who listened to such leaders forgot that the American system preserved certain freedoms.

The first of these, freedom of information (which FDR thought was a better description than freedom of the press), was important because "you will never have a completely stable world without freedom of knowledge, freedom of information." Freedom of religious belief was the second; it had been fairly well maintained in democratic countries "and is not maintained in those nations which have adopted other systems of government." Freedom of expression was third, and it should be limited only by prohibiting advocacy of the overthrow of the government. His fourth one was freedom from fear, "so that people won't be afraid of being bombed from the air or attacked, one way or another, by some other nation." Protection and promotion of these freedoms had to be the fundamental objectives of

---

[25]Press Conference, 15, no. 636-A, April 18, 1940, pp. 273 ff., FDRL.
[26]Ibid., no. 653, June 14, 1940, p. 565, FDRL.

American foreign policy. Richard Harkness would have added freedom from want, which he thought meant free trade or the opening of trade to all nations. FDR agreed that Harkness was correct, and he had had that in mind as well but had failed to include it.[27] The president genuinely believed that these were the essential foundations of an acceptable way of life, and the threat of their disappearance from the world gave the American people a mission worthy of the vigilance required to promote their protection. If he could defend these vital freedoms without war, that was best; if it took a fight, then so be it.

## *IV*

Critics of Roosevelt's Russian policy attacked him for dealing with a dictatorship as ruthless, they argued, as Hitler's Nazis. In their view, FDR operated with a double standard and therefore was pro-Soviet, naive, or taken in by Stalin. The president, in fact, was faced with a series of alternatives that left him little choice. He was on record calling Stalin a dictator and the Soviet Union a totalitarian state. He wooed Stalin, however, because Russia was the only strong European power that might aid the democracies. Given the restricted alternatives, Roosevelt's pragmatism led him to make a choice similar to the one he made about Dominican dictator Rafael Leonidas Trujillo Molina. FDR said he knew that Trujillo was a bastard, but he was "our" bastard. If a dictator could be used to support American security, especially when there was nothing one could do about him anyway, then you used him, shut your eyes, and held your nose.

How to assure the Russians that they were still considered to be worthy allies became the question. Roosevelt's answer was to indicate that rewards on the democratic side outweighed those available from the less trustworthy Axis powers and to remind the Soviets that Japan was still a threat to both American and Soviet interests in the Far East. Roosevelt knew that Germany was making economic demands of the Russians that might have been causing alarm in Soviet circles. If he offered the Russians attractive deals that augmented their security, they might turn in America's direction. It was a calculated gamble, but he was willing to count on a falling-out between Germany and Russia, based on his conviction that Hitler would prove to be too greedy for Stalin. This accounts for the president's decision to include the USSR among the nations qualifying for American aid and later for Lend-Lease assistance.

In October 1940, Roosevelt announced his intention to secure a defense perimeter for the United States in the Western Hemisphere and to provide aid to powers threatened by the Axis coalition. This was an extension of the

---

[27]Ibid., 16, no. 658, July 5, 1940, pp. 18–21, FDRL.

destroyers-for-bases deal made one month earlier with the British. The next logical step would be the Lend-Lease arrangement of early 1941. The president feared that if Hitler conquered Europe, he might attempt to seize or influence the Western Hemisphere possessions of the defeated European powers. If FDR could convince the English to cede him bases, or if he could provide Great Britain with the wherewithal to defend the United States by keeping Hitler as far away as possible, he would be serving U.S. security needs. Although the initial destroyers-for-bases deal was primarily aimed at aiding Britain, Roosevelt tried to identify any nation that might challenge or be attacked by the Axis powers as qualifying for assistance.

Under the definition of "threatened" powers, President Roosevelt could extend Lend-Lease to the Soviet Union, but he had to do this cautiously. How far FDR was prepared to go was revealed in a press conference on October 15, 1940. He had authorized the secretaries of war and navy to inventory military supplies and equipment and strategic materials to determine what was needed for national defense and to decide what was available to sell to other nations that might help to defend American national interest. A reporter immediately asked if this had any connection with conversations going on with Russia concerning the release of machine tools. FDR supposed so; it was "probably the same thing. I know those conversations are going on, and Russia wants tools. Yes." The question was posed again: "They will then be available for Russia?" He expanded on his answer: "In other words, the general idea is, if we don't need them for ourselves we turn them over to a friendly power."[28] The president had decided that he needed Russian assistance in defense of American interests, and the Soviets had not slipped so far beyond the pale that they were irretrievably lost to the democratic cause.

Having added the Soviets to the powers eligible for aid, the next step was to work on them as fellow conspirators against Japan's threatening policy in the Far East. Thus the president encouraged Secretary of the Treasury Henry Morgenthau to pursue a three-cornered deal with the USSR, the United States, and China in order to deliver a clear message to Japan. He gave the go-ahead signal in July, and the campaign intensified later in the year.[29] The United States was limited by the neutrality laws and by shortages of certain materials as to the type of aid it could provide to China, so Roosevelt encouraged Morgenthau to attempt to convince the Soviets to supply China's needs in these areas. This was to be the substance of the three-cornered deal.

Morgenthau met with some of his aides and reported that, on September 19, he had accomplished "the most important thing" he had done all year

---

[28]Ibid., no. 689, October 15, 1940, pp. 266–67, FDRL.
[29]Morgenthau Diaries, Book 307, September 19, 1940, p. 65, Henry Morgenthau, Jr., Papers, FDRL.

at a cabinet meeting: He had overcome the opposition of Cordell Hull and Sumner Welles to the deal with the Soviets. His plan for Sino-Soviet-American cooperation entailed buying manganese from Russia, with the understanding that the Soviets would sell some arms to China. The United States would give credit to China, the Chinese would give tungsten to the Russians, and the Russians would then receive the tungsten and transfer it to the United States. After considerable discussion by the cabinet, Roosevelt said, "Henry, I guess you had better get hold of the Russians and start your talk."

On September 20, Morgenthau and his aides Jesse Jones and Dr. Harry Dexter White met with the Russian ambassador, Konstantin Umanskii. The treasury secretary outlined the nature of his proposed arrangement and suggested that, since they all wanted Japan stopped and China strengthened, their quarrels should be set aside. Umanskii countered that there could be no cooperative program among the three of them unless there were "good relations between every two angles of the triangle." Morgenthau answered that there were common denominators: Both were friendly to China, and both desired peace in the Pacific.[30]

Morgenthau apparently called in Henderson to verify that the Treasury Department's "foreign policy" would enable Secretary of State Hull to stop Japan if he were really serious about it. Hull and Welles were indeed serious about blocking Japan, and even about using the Soviet Union in this ploy, but their approach was different. They wanted a trade agreement, but on their own terms. To some degree, each department knew what the other was doing, although neither understood why, and cooperation in their efforts was unlikely.

As Morgenthau maneuvered to consummate his Russian "deal," a report from Ambassador Steinhardt indicated that the Soviets thought that something significant might result from their talks with the Americans. They were pleased by "the 'intensification' of American policy in the Far East in opposition to Japan."[31] A conversation between Steinhardt and his Chinese counterpart in Russia illustrated that the Nationalist government of China was also excited about Washington's moves to cooperate with Moscow in blocking Japan. The Chinese ambassador expressed his "firm hope" that an improvement in American-Soviet relations would result in an increased flow of supplies, which in turn would aid in stopping Japan's aggression in China.[32]

While Morgenthau was initiating his contacts, Ambassador Steinhardt informed Secretary Hull that Stalin had given a frank assessment of Russia's position vis-à-vis Great Britain and Germany to British Ambassador Sir

---

[30]Ibid., September 20, 1940, p. 148, Morgenthau Papers, FDRL.
[31]Steinhardt to Hull, September 25, 1940, DSF 711.61/755.
[32]Ibid.

Stafford Cripps. Stalin had assured Cripps that his policy was designed to avoid the involvement of the USSR in the war "and in particular to avoid a conflict with the German army." Stalin was convinced "that Germany constituted the only real threat to the Soviet Union and that a German victory would place the Soviet Union in a difficult if not dangerous position but he felt that it was impossible at the present time to invite the certainty of a German invasion of the Soviet Union by an alteration of Soviet policy." Stalin then told Cripps that he preferred to run the risk of war with Germany without allies, because he believed that even a British defeat would not be disastrous for Russia. Germany would be so weakened and extended that it would be difficult "*for the Nazis to persuade the German people to launch a new aggression.*"[33]

Morgenthau discussed his "progress" with the president, who told him that Umanskii did not stand well with his own government so another route was being pursued: "We have decided to do half of our negotiations with the Russians through Steinhardt, and Steinhardt has just had a long talk with Molotov." Morgenthau asked if the talk was satisfactory, and FDR responded: "Not entirely." Morgenthau wanted to know if the Russians had a definite agreement with Germany and Japan. The president answered: "No. I think they will continue their mugwump policy of sitting on the fence." The treasury secretary then inquired if there was a chance to prevent Russia from getting closer to Germany and Japan, and FDR assured him there was.[34]

On October 17, Morgenthau again met Umanskii, who complained that negotiations over what Russia would purchase were not going well. In fact, the $22 million of machine tools the Soviets wanted had been cut back by more than $10 million. He reminded Morgenthau that "after all, we are the two biggest and most powerful nations in the world which are not at war, and I take it that you are interested in seeing that we stay friendly." Umanskii added that Soviet policy was to stay out of war. Morgenthau then asked if Umanskii would care to educate him on Soviet foreign policy. The Russian ambassador expressed concern over German machinations in the Balkans and in eastern Europe and concluded that, while the Kremlin was trying to deal with German advances through diplomacy, "of course we cannot let them get stronger in that territory."[35]

---

[33]Steinhardt to Hull, September 22, 1940, DSF 741.61/899 (author's italics added to emphasize Stalin's unusual statement that the Nazi government might respond to public opinion pressure).

[34]Morgenthau Diaries, Book 318, October 3, 1940, p. 165, Morgenthau Papers, FDRL.

[35]Ibid., Book 323, October 17, 1940, pp. 60–61, Morgenthau Papers, FDRL.

# V

On September 27, 1940, the United States and the Soviet Union became the object of an Axis plan to intimidate and isolate them. But the Tripartite Pact between Germany, Japan, and Italy signed on that date had the reverse effect. Hitler intended that the pact would make Roosevelt back off on aid to Britain and focus on new worries in the Far East. Hitler even planned to invite the Soviets into the agreement, believing that they would be so concerned about the combination of powers as to join them out of self-preservation. Hitler intended to isolate Britain and make Churchill realize that neither the United States nor the Soviet Union would risk coming to Britain's assistance. Roosevelt certainly did not act as predicted, and the Soviets immediately began to ask what was in it for them and continued their talks with the Americans. Aleksandra Kollantai, the Soviet minister to Sweden, told U.S. Minister Frederick A. Sterling that the Kremlin viewed the Tripartite Pact as a distinct threat to the USSR and to the United States.[36] Sterling wrote from Stockholm that it had become obvious over a month's time that the Soviet minister was under instructions from her government to establish closer relations with the American and British legations.[37]

Russian discussions with the Americans bothered both the Japanese and the Germans. German Foreign Minister Ribbentrop tried to explain that the Tripartite Pact was intended merely to stop the meddling of the war-mongering Americans by forcing interventionists in Washington to realize that, if the United States entered the war, it would face the combined force of the Axis powers. He assured the Soviets that they were in no danger from the agreement and that the squeeze on the Americans would mean an early peace.[38] Ribbentrop argued that it was questionable how much aid the United States could provide to England and how much of it actually could be delivered through the German submarine blockade. Even if the Americans decided to enter the war, it was "of no consequence," because Germany would never allow an Anglo-Saxon to land on the European continent. Germany was "indifferent" to what the Americans did.[39]

Hitler also tried to disabuse the Russians of any faith they might place in the Americans in a conversation, or perhaps monologue would be the better term, he had with Molotov on November 12. The Nazi leader said that the United States was pursuing an imperialist policy and certainly was not fighting for the British Empire but rather to secure the remnants of that

---

[36]Frederick A. Sterling to Hull, October 23, 1940, DSF 711.61/768.

[37]Sterling to Hull, October 28, 1940, DSF 711.61/766.

[38]U.S. Department of State, *Nazi-Soviet Relations, 1939–1941: Documents from the Archives of the German Foreign Office*, Raymond James Sontag and James Stuart Beddie, eds. (Washington, DC: Government Printing Office, 1948), pp. 195–96.

[39]Ibid., pp. 218–19.

empire for America. He saw no real danger from U.S. assistance, because it was merely intended to keep the British fighting long enough to rearm America and to augment its military power by acquiring British bases. Hitler told Molotov that this would do the Americans no good, because he would establish a Monroe Doctrine for Europe and Africa.[40]

In a further effort to attract the Russians away from any deals with the Americans, Hitler told Molotov that he proposed collaboration between Germany, Italy, and France to settle the problems of Europe and could offer assistance to settle Russo-Japanese differences in the Far East. The United States, he assured Molotov, had no business in Europe, Africa, or Asia.[41] An interesting aspect of this conversation is the degree to which the Nazis went out of their way to persuade the Russians that neither U.S. aid to Britain nor American interests outside the Western Hemisphere were of any consequence.

Molotov was unmoved by Hitler's assertions. He asked hard questions about what would happen to Finland, the Baltic States, the Balkans, and Turkey. Hitler tried to divert the commissar "to the south," presumably India, but Molotov pursued Russian interests in Europe doggedly. At this point the Nazi leader turned Molotov back to Ribbentrop, who attempted to convince him that Churchill and the British were finished and that the Soviets should make a deal while they could. Just then a British air raid forced them into the embassy's bomb shelter. Molotov asked: If the British were defeated, "why are we in this shelter, and whose are those bombs that fall?"[42]

The Russians continued to attempt at least a modicum of reconciliation with the Americans. Thus on November 27, 1940, Umanskii assured Welles that there was absolutely no conflict of interest between the United States and the Soviet Union in the Pacific. In other words, Japan was still potentially their common enemy.[43] Welles and Umanskii met again on December 16 and assured each other that their governments intended to increase aid to China.[44]

Beginning in August 1940, hard intelligence reached the State Department about the planning of Operation Barbarossa, the code name for Hitler's intended assault on the USSR. This allowed the Americans to hope that at last Russia would side with the democracies. The first inkling of the attack came from the U.S. commercial attaché in Berlin, Sam E. Woods.

---

[40]Ibid., p. 231.

[41]Ibid., p. 233.

[42]Quoted in James MacGregor Burns, *Roosevelt: Soldier of Freedom* (New York: Harcourt, Brace, Jovanovich, 1970), p. 17.

[43]Memorandum of conversation between Welles and Konstantin Umanskii, November 27, 1940, DSF 711.61/788.

[44]Memorandum of conversation between Welles and Umanskii, December 16, 1940, DSF 711.61/78071/2.

27An anti-Nazi friend of Woods, with close associates in the Reich's ministries and in high party circles, slipped notes into the American's pocket in a movie theater, informing him about a conference to plan an invasion of the USSR. Several weeks later the German reported that Hitler said he intended to have "only my soldiers from Vladivostok to Gibraltar."[45] Hitler might have aborted Barbarossa had the Russians conceded the further collaboration he wanted in both economic arrangements and division of territory. However, Commissar Molotov made an unprecedented visit to Berlin in the late fall, flatly refused to grant further concessions, and returned to Moscow. This left Hitler seething, and the order went out in November to speed up the preparations for Barbarossa.[46]

Roosevelt ended the year determined to ensure that the Axis powers would not prevail. In his "arsenal of democracy" address of December 29, 1940, he declared that "there can be no appeasement with ruthlessness." The United States therefore had no choice but to supply Britain with arms, airplanes, and ships. He said his speech was not a fireside chat on war but a talk on national security policy intended to prevent generations of Americans from having to fight a last-ditch defense of their homeland. He recalled his first fireside chat, in which he told his countrymen about the banking crisis, and played on their recollection of that day when he explained the nature and extent of the problem. Now he was forced to do it again. This was a far more menacing crisis, because it was an external threat and thus less under their direct control to meet and overcome.

He admonished his listeners not to be deceived as to the nature of the threat: "Never before since Jamestown and Plymouth Rock has our American civilization been in such danger as now." He told them that on September 27, 1940, the Tripartite Pact had been hurled directly at America by the Nazi masters of Germany, who "have made it clear that they intend not only to dominate all life and thought in their own country, but also to enslave the whole of Europe, and then to use the resources of Europe to

---

[45]Quoted in Cordell Hull, *The Memoirs of Cordell Hull*, 2 vols. (New York: Macmillan, 1948), 2:967.

[46]Bohlen, *Witness to History*, pp. 103–5. For a Soviet view of the events see Vladimir Petrov, *"June 22, 1941": Soviet Historians and the German Invasion* (Columbia: University of South Carolina Press, 1968), pp. 174–77. This is a translation of a study entitled *June 22, 1941*, by the Soviet historian Aleksandr M. Nekrich, who took advantage of the presumed thaw that permitted criticisms of Stalin's policies as long as they concentrated on the errors of Stalinism. This work was published in the USSR in 1965. By 1966, Nekrich was under attack for deviationism and other deficiencies in his scholarship and was expelled from the Communist Party in 1967. He later emigrated to the United States. Bohlen's interpretation of events in the period before the attack is in some degree corroborated by a Soviet diplomat who accompanied Molotov to Berlin as his translator. See Valentin Berezhkov, *History in the Making*, trans. Dudley Hagen and Barry Jones (Moscow: Progress Publishers, 1983), pp. 23ff. However, Berezhkov contended that Hitler already had determined to attack the USSR and the meeting with Molotov was merely a smoke screen, although the Soviet foreign minister did anger the Germans by his insistence on Soviet objectives in eastern Europe.

dominate the rest of the world." After this, Hitler had ominously threatened the United States when he defiantly replied to his opponents: "Others are correct when they say, with this world we cannot ever reconcile ourselves. . . . I can beat any other power in the world." "In other words," FDR explained, "the Axis not merely admits but proclaims that there can be no ultimate peace between their philosophy of government and our philosophy of government."[47] He castigated those who wanted to hide their heads in the sand and pretend that no threat existed.

Roosevelt told American citizens that the preceding two years had proved that Hitler could not be appeased; there could be "no reasoning with an incendiary bomb. We know now that a nation can have peace with the Nazis only at the price of total surrender." The best way to keep from having to send Americans to war was to provide every ounce of assistance that could be spared to the enemies of nazism. He ended his address with a passionate request for national effort and sacrifice to make up for lost time in facing the ominous threat posed by the Axis powers: "I call upon our people with absolute confidence that our common cause will greatly succeed."[48] President Roosevelt believed that he could be more forthright than he had been previously because of the desperate situation the United States would confront if Great Britain went down.

Rapprochement with the Soviets became more and more important to Franklin Roosevelt as the world crisis deepened. He had observed in 1939 that there were dark days ahead if all the armed powers were on the same side. In late 1940 he moved to prevent such an alignment.

---

[47]Roosevelt, *Roosevelt's Foreign Policy* (1941), pp. 310–17.
[48]Ibid.

# II

## The Soviet Factor in Roosevelt's Policy

AFTER THE FALL OF FRANCE, the threatened German invasion of Great Britain, and the occupation of strategic positions in Bulgaria and elsewhere in eastern Europe (which apparently neutralized the Soviets), FDR grew more fearful for the survival of the nations blocking Nazi expansion. Frances Perkins recalled that the president presented the cabinet with various plans to step up aid to the beleaguered allies or to any other possibly threatened power, including the USSR.[1] After the termination of the Russo-Finnish War, in March 1940, Roosevelt could begin to speak about aid to the Soviets. However, the climate still did not seem right to lift the moral embargo against Russia. Sumner Welles finally convinced Roosevelt to release a letter announcing the end of the embargo, in part because of Konstantin Umanskii's complaint that until this was done the Russians could not get badly needed supplies.[2]

FDR hoped that the Russians might swing their allegiance to the democracies because of a German threat. He had information from "a usually reliable source" in Switzerland that an invasion of Great Britain would be attempted "in the near future." If the invasion failed, Berlin might seek an "inconclusive peace" allowing the Germans to retain Belgium and part of the French coast. If England then refused this arrangement, "Germany will have to find food for the occupied countries and will move definitely into [the] Balkans and possibly into [the] Ukraine."[3]

Secretary of the Interior Harold Ickes passed on to the president some observations from Alfred Bergman, who had done business in the Soviet Union and was at one point suggested as a possible ambassador to the USSR. Bergman had recently discussed the European crisis with a representative of the "extreme Right" in France, Henri de Kerillis, who had served in the Chamber of Deputies. The Frenchman believed that Russia

---

[1]Frances Perkins interview.

[2]Sumner Welles to FDR with enclosures, December 9, 1940, OF 220, FDRL.

[3]Memorandum, FDR to Hull, January 16, 1941, PSF II, Departmental Files, State Department, 1940–1942, Box 22, FDRL.

was the main reason the British had chosen to replace Lord Halifax with Anthony Eden: "Eden realized that Russia must be brought into the struggle for the British Empire and by all means possible be weaned away from Germany. For a successful war, Russia is necessary." Kerillis contended that, no matter how much France, Great Britain, or the United States hated communism, Russian interests were tied to those of the United States and Great Britain because "she fears mostly Germany and Japan." He cautioned that history was on the march and that the United States had to understand Russia's value, "even at terribly great risks, which perhaps are not so great if we consider that all is lost if she is on the other side or not with us . . . we must be realistic now."[4]

President Roosevelt resisted pressure from within his administration to announce that the Soviet Union was eligible for Lend-Lease, although he had implied this earlier. He was reluctant to give his opponents in Congress any ammunition for their campaign against Lend-Lease, and he was content to have the Soviet Union included implicitly in nations qualifying for aid without making a public issue of it. If the predicted future falling out between the Nazis and the Soviets occurred, the machinery was in place to step up aid to the Russians. In the interim, they were able to buy whatever strategic materials they needed.[5]

## II

Because China was one of the threatened powers, FDR tried to arrange help for Chiang Kai-shek through the Soviets. This bothered Ambassador Joseph C. Grew, who tried to find out exactly what the State Department had in mind, as he feared that tightening the screws on Japan too firmly might backfire.

Grew suffered from a deficiency common among foreign service officers in the Roosevelt years: They often operated with limited knowledge of the administration's foreign policy. Aware of this problem, the ambassador asked Cordell Hull for some enlightenment regarding the broad outlines of policy so that he could do his own job more effectively. Grew reflected dejectedly that

> it must be difficult for the Administration to visualize just how much we feel out on a limb with regard to many matters of high policy, intelligence and tentative plans to meet hypothetical developments, and it would be simply silly to hold that hypothetical developments cannot be approached until they arrive. Naturally information along those lines might, and probably would, have an important bearing on

[4]Harold Ickes to FDR, January 28, 1941, PSF, Interior, Ickes, FDRL.
[5]Thomas R. Maddux, *Years of Estrangement: American Relations with the Soviet Union, 1933–1941* (Tallahassee: University Presses of Florida, 1980), pp. 138–39.

my work out here. If Ambassadors are something more than messenger
boys, they must be allowed to see behind the scenes.[6]

This was one of the shrewdest of Grew's observations in his long diplomatic
career, for he assessed precisely a major deficiency of American foreign
policy: Policymakers did not plan for alternatives. Herbert Feis also
identified the problem, when he contended that the nation's leaders pursued a
course of crisis-to-crisis diplomacy, hoping that each crisis would be the last
and that there would be no need to plan for contingencies.[7]

Grew asked the president for a clear definition of U.S. policy. FDR
rather bluntly informed the ambassador that the Far East was only part of
the wider world: "I believe that the fundamental proposition is that we must
recognize that the hostilities in Europe, in Africa, and in Asia are all parts
of a single world conflict. We must, consequently, recognize that our
interests are menaced both in Europe and in the Far East."[8] Grew had
suggested in his letter that embroilment in the Far Eastern war would so
handicap America's ability to aid England in Europe as to mean the
difference between Britain's defeat and victory. Roosevelt countered that, if
Japan gained possession of the Dutch East Indies and the Malay Peninsula,
"the chances of England's winning in her struggle with Germany would be
decreased thereby." American strategy "toward ensuring our own security"
had to be to give the British assistance by "both sending of supplies to
England and helping to prevent a closing of channels of communication to
and from various parts of the world, so that other important sources of
supply will not be denied to the British and be added to the assets of the
other side."[9] This is absolutely the clearest exposition of Roosevelt's
Europe-first orientation. Far Eastern affairs were secondary to taking care of
the Nazi threat to America's security and its political and social system.[10]

Japanese Foreign Minister Matsuoka Yosuke, fearful of joint U.S.,
British, and Soviet aid to China, tried to keep the Russians out of this
combination. He visited Russia and Germany in early 1941. Matsuoka
had lunch in Moscow with U.S. Ambassador Laurence Steinhardt, who
reported the conversation to Grew. The foreign minister told Steinhardt that
there had been little progress in Japanese-Soviet negotiations because the
Russians asked the Japanese to concede too many of their Far Eastern
ambitions. Matsuoka believed relations had to improve, because Japan's
choices were either to come to an agreement with Russia or to prepare to

---

[6]Joseph Clark Grew Papers, Houghton Library, Harvard College Library, Cambridge,
Massachusetts, bMS Am. 1687.5, Personal Notes, no. 413, January 1941, p. 4736. The
author is indebted to the Houghton Library for permission to cite the Grew Papers.

[7]Conversation with former Department of State official Herbert Feis, spring 1958,
National Archives, Washington, DC.

[8]FDR to Grew, January 21, 1941, Grew Papers, Personal Notes, no. 144, p. 4793.

[9]Ibid.

[10]Ibid.

fight. Concerning the reported invasion of Russia planned by Germany, Matsuoka insisted that it would not take place unless the Soviet Union seriously curtailed shipments of needed supplies and foodstuffs to Germany. He thought the Germans had intentionally circulated rumors of an attack in order to frighten the Russians into meeting German supply requirements.[11] Stalin came to believe this ploy by June 1941, with terrible consequences for the Russians.

On April 13, Matsuoka concluded the Japanese-Soviet nonaggression pact, thereby creating an opening for Japan's southern advance. The democracies feared that the pact might also clear the way to Singapore and Indochina. Hitler wanted the southward advance so badly that he had Joachim von Ribbentrop badger Matsuoka about it during the Japanese foreign minister's visit to Berlin.[12] He hoped to interdict the British supply route from the East.

Stalin was forced to accommodate Japan in part because of the German moves into Bulgaria. Soviet Foreign Commissar V. M. Molotov sent a sharp note to the German ambassador to the Soviet Union on March 1, 1941, warning the Germans that the USSR was not going to ignore this violation of Soviet security interests.[13]

In April, German State Secretary Ernst von Weizaecker wrote to his boss, Ribbentrop, expressing his fears that Germany might become embroiled in a war with the Soviet Union. He warned that the British would think that the Germans had turned east because they were not sure of winning in the west. This might stiffen British resistance and prolong the war.[14]

In the spring of 1941, Cordell Hull decided to tell Ambassador Umanskii about Operation Barbarossa, assuming that the ambassador would forward the information about the German attack to his government. The secretary of state hoped that revealing this plan would prove America's sincere desire to cooperate against the common enemy. He speculated that foreknowledge of Barbarossa influenced Stalin to hasten the signing of the pact with the Japanese and to take a stronger stand against German actions in the Balkans. However, Russia's failure to increase its defensive fortifications or to move more forces into the east European buffer zone was perplexing. Knowledge of Barbarossa certainly affected Hull's advice to FDR on Far Eastern policy. Hull asserted that the nearly certain prospect of a German-Russian war convinced him that the Russo-Japanese nonaggression pact could not possibly turn into an alliance between the two

---

[11]Grew Papers, Personal Notes, February 1941, pp. 4994–96.

[12]Gordon W. Prange et al., *Target Tokyo* (New York: McGraw-Hill, 1985), p. 357.

[13]Memorandum, V. M. Molotov to the German ambassador on the entry of German troops into Bulgaria, March 1, 1941, in Jane Degras, ed., *Soviet Documents on Foreign Policy*, 3 vols. (London: Oxford University Press, 1953), 3:483.

[14]U.S. Department of State, *Nazi-Soviet Relations*, pp. 333–34.

powers. The United States could take a stronger stand against Japanese aggression with the surety that Russia would soon be fighting on the Allied side.[15]

On May 8, Frederick Sterling, the U.S. minister to Sweden, informed Hull that he had heard that Molotov had been removed from the prime minister's post because of the American reaction to the Molotov-Matsuoka agreement.[16] The explanation reported by Arthur Schoenfeld, the U.S. minister in Helsinki, was more likely. He attributed the change to growing anti-German sentiments in Russia. His conjecture was corroborated by the Finnish foreign minister, who told the American that when the news of Molotov's removal reached the Finnish capital the German minister foresaw a possible change in Soviet policy that would not be to Germany's benefit. Schoenfeld agreed, based on his recent conversation with a Soviet colleague in Helsinki evidencing an increasingly candid anti-German spirit.[17]

Whatever the reasons for Molotov's dismissal the Russians wanted Hitler to believe that they were prepared for any move he might make on their western frontier. They were convinced that the Russo-Japanese agreement had freed them from concern to the east. *Pravda* reported a conjecture from the Japanese news agency Domei that the USSR was concentrating powerful armed forces on its western frontier, including significantly large elements from Soviet commands in the Far East and central Asia. The Soviet news agency Tass denied that there was any truth to the story, but the question remains: Why did Tass report this at all?[18] The answer is that the Russians wanted the foreign embassies in Moscow, and especially the Germans, to see it.

General Eugen Ott, the German ambassador in Tokyo, told the Soviet secret agent Richard Sorge that the pact "was a far from happy thing for Germany."[19] Sorge was one of the Soviet Union's most effective agents, and through his contacts at the German embassy he was able to piece together the complete story of Operation Barbarossa, although he blew his cover getting the information and transmitting it to Moscow. On May 19 he informed Moscow that "nine armies of 150 divisions will be concentrated against the U.S.S.R." Sorge waited for a response, and when he received it he could not believe it. A terse message informed him that "we doubt the veracity of your information." One of Sorge's Japanese agents recalled later the bitterness they felt after they had risked their lives and managed to get out so much detailed proof "only to have it rejected, and to see the Soviet Union simply sit there."[20] Perhaps the best explanation of why Stalin did

---

[15]Hull, *Memoirs* 2:968–69.
[16]Frederick Sterling to Hull, May 8, 1941, DSF 861.002/203.
[17]Arthur Schoenfeld to Hull, May 10, 1941, DSF 861.00/11885.
[18]Degras, *Soviet Documents* 3:487–88.
[19]As quoted in Prange, *Target Tokyo*, p. 359.
[20]Ibid., pp. 368–73.

not believe several reports of German treachery was that he did not want to believe it; he chose instead to think that the Germans wanted a provocation, and he was not going to give it to them.

In a message delivered to Matsuoka, with the assistance of the American embassy in Moscow, Winston Churchill tried to prove the folly of siding with the enemies of Britain and the United States. Churchill wanted the Japanese to ponder whether their adherence to the Tripartite Pact was more or less likely to bring America into the war. If the United States entered, "and Japan ranged herself with the Axis Powers, would not the naval superiority of the two English-speaking nations enable them to deal with Japan while disposing of the Axis Powers in Europe?" Churchill asked if Japan was prepared to face Great Britain and the United States when they defeated Germany. He told Matsuoka that steel production in the United States during 1941 would reach 75 million tons and in Great Britain about 12.5 million versus the 7 million produced in Japan. He suggested this would be inadequate for Japan to conduct a "single-handed war."[21] Churchill's ploy probably had an effect, but perhaps not the one he intended. It is possible that Japanese military leaders decided that it might be necessary to strike the United States before Japan was left alone to face the economic and naval power of the United States and Great Britain. Grew thought that Churchill's message had sobered the more responsible Japanese leaders and convinced them to try to seize foreign policy leadership from Matsuoka. He believed that the efforts to neutralize their antagonisms with Russia proved their caution.[22]

On April 14, Grew evaluated the intent and results of the Russo-Japanese nonaggression pact. He told the Department of State that the pact apparently had been signed "chiefly for the effect that each party believed it would exert on the other party and on third parties (on Germany from the Soviet point of view, and on the United States and Great Britain from the Japanese point of view)." This was an accurate assessment, but he was off base when he surmised that the treaty tended to help resolve Japan's conflict with China. His shrewdest observation foretold the freedom the pact would give to Japanese extremists who advocated a southward advance, "because it guarantees Soviet neutrality in case Japan gets into war with a third country (i.e., the United States)."[23]

Grew reflected that sometimes the affairs of the world hinged on the unpredictable, in this case on one too many vodkas.

> One of the most amusing episodes of the signing of the treaty was that after the signature everybody, including Stalin, proceeded to get tight and the farewells on the station platform were accompanied by back

---

[21]Grew Papers, Personal Notes, no. 144, February 1941, pp. 4996–97.
[22]Ibid., pp. 5014–15.
[23]Ibid., p. 4993.

slappings, bear-hugs and even kisses. . . . One cannot help wondering whether that last glass of vodka may not have been responsible for this startling demonstration of affection, with its marked psychological effect on international affairs.

Grew found the platform incident amusing, but not the final remark that Stalin reportedly made to Matsuoka: "The Soviet Union and Germany will take care of Europe while Japan will straighten out the East, and later, between them, they will take care of the Americans."[24]

## III

Raymond Gram Swing, writing for the London *Daily Express* on May 11, 1941, stated the clearest exposition that has ever been made of Roosevelt's strategy for confronting the aggressors. To avoid giving ammunition to his isolationist critics, Roosevelt could not be the one "to organize and educate, to cajole and threaten. This American decision, to be worth while, and to have historic justification, must be national first, before it can be Roosevelt led."[25]

Many believed that FDR should move boldly to meet the aggressors. W. Averell Harriman grew impatient with the policy of drift while FDR refused to "face an unpleasant decision."[26] William Bullitt informed the president that the people he had talked to in a recent swing through Kentucky, Tennessee, Massachusetts, New York, New Jersey, and Pennsylvania had told him that they accepted the president's leadership because they believed he knew more about the situation in foreign policy than anyone else. Bullitt surmised, "You could, I think, even reverse your entire policy and be followed by a vast majority. In other words, your personal prestige has never been higher and you have only to lead. The moment seems to be ripe for bold action,—and it is 11:59."[27]

Secretary of War Henry L. Stimson also urged Roosevelt toward action and with a similar rationale: "From what has come to me on all sides I feel certain the people of the United States are looking to you . . . to lead and guide them in a situation in which they are now confused *but anxious to follow you.* Under these circumstances I think it would be disastrous for

---

[24]Ibid., p. 4994.

[25]Memorandum, Harry L. Hopkins to Grace Tully (one of FDR's secretaries), enclosing a copy of Raymond Gram Swing's editorial from the *Sunday Express*, May 15, 1941, PPF 1820, FDRL. Special Presidential Assistant Hopkins asked Tully to put this article in a folder with other materials for the president's next speech.

[26]W. Averell Harriman and Elie Abel, *Special Envoy to Churchill and Stalin, 1941–1946* (New York: Random House, 1975), p. 19.

[27]Bullitt to FDR, May 21, 1941, PPF 1124, William C. Bullitt Folder, 1933-1944, FDRL.

you to disappoint them." Stimson wanted the president to declare the United States to be a belligerent, because the decision for war should not await a chance sinking or a shot fired by the enemies of civilization.[28]

In response to these proddings, Roosevelt began to measure the public pulse. On May 20, Hadley Cantril of the Princeton Public Opinion Research Institute sent Anna Rosenberg of FDR's staff the latest results of his surveys on foreign policy. Cantril had posed this question: "Which of these two things do you think is the more important for the United States to try to do—to keep out of war ourselves, or to help England win, even at the risk of getting in the war?" Thirty-five percent wanted to keep out, 62 percent wanted to help, and only 3 percent had no choice.[29] Even more significant were two questions about defeating Germany. One asked: "If in trying to defeat Germany it becomes necessary to send a large army to Europe, would you favor this step?" Forty-seven percent answered yes, 44 percent said no, and 9 percent were undecided. The other question asked whether the respondents believed that FDR had gone too far in opposing Germany or not far enough. Only 22 percent thought he had gone too far, while 46 percent thought he had gone about his task at just the right pace, 8 percent had no opinion, and 24 percent thought he had not gone far enough.[30]

Perkins recalled that FDR assigned a number of people in the administration the task of educating the public. In speeches, they were to insert something about preparedness and aid to Great Britain in order to "test the wind."[31] One of those who had been asked to feel out the Midwest was Secretary of Agriculture Claude Wickard, Jr. After his return to Washington, he reported to FDR that three thousand farmers in Hutchinson, Kansas, applauded all statements concerning the need for national defense. The audience was less enthusiastic when he indicated that Britain was standing between the United States and Hitler. Only attentiveness without applause greeted him when he talked about the need to see that American materials were delivered to Britain. He advised that the most effective approach was to emphasize that the United States was aiding Great Britain in order to make it the first line of American defense and not because of any sentimental attachment. Wickard also sent along the results of a poll taken at a Kiwanis meeting in St. Paul, Minnesota, after a debate between two local residents on the international situation. The audience favored aid to Britain by 90 to 11; convoys to ensure delivery of goods were favored by 57 to 49; even if the convoying were to result in war, the audience favored convoying by 51

---

[28]Henry L. Stimson to FDR, May 24, 1941, PPF 1820, FDRL (emphasis in original).
[29]Hadley Cantril to Anna Rosenberg, May 20, 1941, PSF, Princeton Public Opinion Folder, FDRL.
[30]Ibid.
[31]Frances Perkins interview.

to 49; but they opposed Secretary Stimson's idea that there should be an immediate declaration of war by 83 to 14.[32]

Although President Roosevelt was not prepared to go as far as he was urged by Stimson and others in the administration, he did accept the idea that it was time to announce to the world America's intent not to be taken unaware by the aggressors. In a radio address of May 27, 1941, FDR meant to prepare Americans for a crisis situation and to garner support for his next steps by declaring the existence of "an unlimited national emergency" that required strengthening of the nation's defenses "to the extreme limit of our national power and authority." On May 31 he issued a statement thanking all of those who sent him letters and telegrams of congratulations on the speech. However, according to one of the writers of this speech, it was intended "to scare the daylights out of everyone, but it did not do much else."[33]

# *IV*

James P. Warburg, who had been among the first of the New Deal diplomatic appointments, warned FDR that there was not much time left before British morale failed and urged him to lead the United States to Britain's aid.[34] President Roosevelt continued to wait. He was rewarded by Adolf Hitler, who came directly to Britain's aid when he decided against all logic to loose his wehrmacht on the Soviet Union. Hitler explained his reasoning behind Operation Barbarossa in several ways to his generals, his foreign office, and his ally Benito Mussolini. One constant remained in each rationalization: Knocking Russia out of the war either would force the British to give up or would leave the Germans free to attack the British Isles at their leisure. He asserted to Mussolini that it made no difference whether the Americans actually entered the war as belligerents because they were already supporting Germany's enemies. Britain, on the other hand, lived on the twofold hope of help from Moscow and from Washington. "We have no chance of eliminating America. But it does lie in our power to exclude Russia. The elimination of Russia means, at the same time, a tremendous relief for Japan in East Asia, and thereby the possibility of a much stronger threat to American activities through Japanese intervention."[35] Thus the United States, if this rationale is believed, played a role in the decision to attack the Soviet Union.

---

[32]Claude Wickard to FDR, May 24, 1941, OF 1, FDRL.

[33]Roosevelt, *Roosevelt's Foreign Policy* (1941), p. 395. See also Robert Dallek, *Franklin D. Roosevelt and American Foreign Policy, 1932–1945* (New York: Oxford University Press, 1981) p. 266, for this quote.

[34]James P. Warburg to FDR, June 6, 1941, PPF 540, James P. Warburg Folder, FDRL.

[35]Department of State, *Nazi-Soviet Relations*, p. 351.

Churchill's address to the British nation after the Nazi attack on Russia was repeated in the United States and, according to Ralph B. Levering, won more approval for the Soviet cause than anything else could have done at the time.[36] Levering argued convincingly that FDR no longer had to step forward on the Russian issue. Churchill, because of his immense popularity in the United States, had done this for him, allowing Roosevelt the leisure of dealing with the isolationists and the Communist haters with slight parries and thrusts while he went ahead with tentative plans to provide aid to the Soviet Union.

When news of Hitler's attack on the USSR reached the United States, Roosevelt responded cautiously. At his press conference of June 24, a reporter asked him if he would comment on Welles's statement that although the Soviet Union was a dictatorship, and the United States did not approve of this form of government, it was now aligned with the democracies.[37] Roosevelt reaffirmed that the United States would "give all the aid we possibly can to Russia." When asked if the aid would come under Lend-Lease, FDR laughed, a gesture which the press understood from long experience; they might as well give up asking, because he was not going to tell them. A reporter wanted to know if the defense of Russia was essential to American security. Roosevelt deflected the question by asserting that it was the kind of query he did not answer.[38] He did not have to answer, because Churchill had already done so by saying that "the Russian danger is . . . our danger and the danger of the United States."[39]

William Bullitt advised Roosevelt on how to deal with the Soviet question and informed the president that he agreed with the initial press release concerning the assault: "The line you took when the Germans attacked the Soviet Union—that of giving support to anyone (even a criminal) fighting Hitler—was, of course, sound." Roosevelt had not used the analogy Bullitt ascribed to him, but Bullitt often put his own words into others' mouths and then lauded their obvious agreement with him. He thought that Roosevelt should use his next press conference to tell the American people that they needed to produce defense materials with even greater speed, as Germany might soon have all of Russia's vast resources to draw upon. Bullitt cautioned that the Russians were as untrustworthy as ever and that FDR should keep this in mind.[40] This was certainly not the sort of advice FDR was looking for at a time when he believed that the

---

[36]Ralph B. Levering, *American Opinion and the Russian Alliance, 1939–1945* (Chapel Hill: University of North Carolina Press, 1976), pp. 39–41.

[37]*FRUS: Diplomatic Papers*, vol. 1, *General, Soviet Union, 1941* (Washington, DC: Government Printing Office, 1958), pp. 767–68.

[38]Press Conferences, June 24, 1941, no. 750–4, p. 408, FDRL.

[39]As quoted in Levering, *American Opinion*, p. 40.

[40]Bullitt to FDR, July 1, 1941, PPF 1124, General Correspondence, Drawer 3-41, FDRL.

USSR might be the most important factor delaying a German assault on England.

A more accurate reflection of Roosevelt's position came from W. T. Stone, who attempted to explain Welles's announcement that the United States would provide all possible aid to Russia. Despite earlier pronouncements that the USSR was a totalitarian dictatorship, there was a new set of circumstances. Although Great Britain was the first line of defense, now that Germany had attacked the Soviet Union material assistance should be given to Russia "as long as it resists Germany."[41] It was almost as though Stone had been briefed on administration policy, which perhaps was indeed the case.

Adolf A. Berle, Jr., feared that the British would seize the initiative and determine a course for the postwar world together with the Russians. He asked permission to begin to plan for the postwar era. FDR told him to go ahead, but he cautioned that "for Heaven's sake don't even let the columnists hear of it." The assistant secretary of state was told to keep in mind "that the elimination of costly armaments is still the keystone—for the security of all the little nations and for economic solvency." He admonished: "Don't forget what I discovered—that over ninety percent of all national deficits from 1921 to 1939 were caused by payments for past, present, and future wars."[42]

Roosevelt, concerned about pressures from the opponents of aid to Britain and the USSR, warned Churchill on July 14, 1941, against making any deals with anyone about the postwar era. This concern stemmed from FDR's recollection of the public response to the release of the secret treaties at the end of World War I.[43] Part of his concern was alleviated when Berle informed him that apparently the Russians were perfectly willing to acknowledge the need to restore those areas of eastern Europe that had been victimized by the German invasion. Berle noted that the USSR already had recognized the Czech government-in-exile resident in London and had pledged restoration of the prewar borders for Czechoslovakia, doing so without consulting with anyone insofar as he knew.[44] FDR was still concerned about Churchill, and he asked him to clarify his position: "I am inclined to think that an overall statement on your part would be useful at this time, making it clear that no post-war peace commitments as to territories, populations or economies have been given. I could then back up your statement in very strong terms."[45]

---

[41]W. T. Stone, "Washington Newsletter," *Foreign Policy Bulletin* 20 (June 27, 1941).

[42]Adolph A. Berle, Jr., to FDR, June 21, 1941, and Roosevelt's response of June 26, 1941, PSF II, Departmental Files, State Department, 1940–1941, Box 22, FDRL.

[43]FDR to Winston Churchill, July 14, 1941, PPF, Churchill, FDRL.

[44]Berle to FDR, July 17, 1941, PSF II, Departmental Files, State Department, 1940–1941, Box 22, FDRL.

[45]FDR to Churchill, July 14, 1941, Map Room Papers, FDRL.

The British were not dissuaded from discussing territorial settlements, and at the end of the year Foreign Secretary Eden intended to speak to the Russians about spheres of influence on a visit to Moscow. The president did not appear to consider that it might be helpful to have Russian claims limited in advance by firm decisions about borders and spheres of influence, but this did occur to Churchill and Eden. Cordell Hull suspected that the British wanted to make territorial deals with the Russians, and he wished to hamstring them from the outset.[46] He, too, remembered Woodrow Wilson's embarrassment by the devious plans of his allies.

# V

Certainly one reason Roosevelt was reluctant to identify too closely with the Russian war effort was the information already conveyed to him by Secretary of War Stimson and Secretary of the Navy Frank Knox. On June 23 they conjectured that Russian chances for survival against the German onslaught were slim to none. At the outside they gave the Russians three months before the Red Army collapsed, and more probably it would be four to six weeks.[47] FDR reflected this assessment when he wrote to his ambassador to Vichy France, Admiral William D. Leahy. "Now comes this Russian diversion. If it is more than just that it will mean the liberation of Europe from Nazi domination—and at the same time I do not think we need worry about any possibility of Russian domination."[48] It is possible that this letter to Leahy, whose anti-Soviet attitude was known to FDR, was an attempt to point out how important the Russian resistance was to the Allied powers and to prepare at least one important navy man for the need to help the Soviet Union if indeed the Russians proved to be capable of resisting the German blitzkrieg.

During the early days of the fighting in Russia, Washington debated whether and how much aid the Soviets should receive. Some administration officials argued against aid, fearing that the Soviets might make a deal with Hitler again; others contended that it would be like sending matériel to the Nazis because Russia's collapse was imminent, still others were simply anti-Soviet, some doubted the wisdom of concentrating on anything but aid to Britain, and some thought that supplying Russia would detract from the building of American defenses in the Far East.[49] Even Joseph E. Davies, the

---

[46]Memorandum, Cordell Hull to FDR, February 5, 1942, Footnote Folder, Papers of Harry L. Hopkins, FDRL.

[47]Stimson to FDR, June 23, 1941, PPF 20, FDRL; Frank Knox to FDR, June 23, 1941, PSF, Knox File, FDRL.

[48]Admiral William D. Leahy, *I Was There* (New York: Whittlesay House, 1950), pp. 37–38.

[49]For a detailed discussion of all of these positions and their advocates see Dwight William Tuttle, *Harry L. Hopkins and Anglo-American-Soviet Relations, 1941–1945* (New York: Garland, 1983), pp. 82–86.

pro-Soviet former U.S. ambassador to the USSR, did not discount the possibility that Stalin might coldly assess his position and decide to strike a deal with Hitler. "Stalin is oriental, coldly realistic and getting on in years. It is not impossible that he might even 'fall' for Hitler's peace as the lesser of two evils." This meant that Stalin had to be convinced that he was not "pulling the chestnuts out of the fire" for allies who he knew had no use for him.[50]

Roosevelt's troubleshooter, Harry L. Hopkins, was unenthusiastic at first about aiding the Soviet Union. Hopkins feared that aid to Russia would divert badly needed supplies from Great Britain to a country that he did not find attractive as an ally.[51] This counsel from FDR's most trusted adviser was reinforced by a report from Hadley Cantril on his survey taken after the attack on Russia. An overwhelming majority of Americans wanted it to win against Nazi Germany; however, "a majority of people opposed helping Russia the way we are helping Britain."[52]

Lowell Mellett, director of the Executive Office of the President's Office of Government Reports, informed Hopkins that public support for aid to Britain was such that even if it meant going to war the public wanted Britain to get American assistance. Furthermore, "in spite of initial bewilderment, public opinion is reported gradually coming around in favor of aiding Russia."[53] Hopkins was among those "gradually coming around." When he returned to London, he "moved closer to the President's view that Russia was essential to America's security both as a deterrent to Japan and as a foe to Hitler." Hopkins's son Robert asked him why he was willing for the United States to have anything to do with such a "dangerous bunch of people" as the Russian Communists, and Hopkins told him: "They're fighting the Nazis. That's the only thing you have to worry about."[54]

Hopkins decided, with Churchill's urging, to go from London to the USSR, and he got FDR's permission to do so.[55] When he met with Stalin, Hopkins shrewdly presented Roosevelt's reasons for opposing Hitler and cleverly placed Russia on the side of the angels fighting the Devil, contending that there was a need in the world for a minimum moral standard which the Nazis did not meet. The Germans, he continued, were a people who would sign a treaty one minute and break it the next, and "nations must

---

[50]As quoted in ibid., p. 85. See also Joseph E. Davies to Hopkins, July 8, 1941, Hopkins Papers, FDRL.

[51]Tuttle, *Harry L. Hopkins*, pp. 81–86.

[52]Cantril to Rosenberg, July 3, 1941, PSF, Princeton University Folder, FDRL.

[53]Lowell Mellett to Hopkins, July 26, 1941, Hopkins Papers, Box 304, Footnote Folder, FDRL.

[54]Tuttle, *Harry L. Hopkins*, p. 97.

[55]FDR to Hopkins, July 26, 1941, Hopkins Papers, Box 304, Footnote Folder, FDRL.

fulfill their treaty obligations, . . . or international society could not exist."[56]

Stalin rationalized his pact with Germany in the Soviet journal *Mirovoe Khoziaistvo* on July 3. He asked whether it was a mistake to have signed an agreement with the likes of Hitler and Ribbentrop, and he answered "of course not." Even though the German government was headed by "monsters and cannibals," any nation would want a treaty with its neighbor so long as it "did not encroach either directly or indirectly on the territorial integrity, independence, and honour of the peace-loving States."[57] The brazenness of this whitewash of Soviet policy is breathtaking. Stalin's plan to divert the German menace had gone awry, and the best light had to be put on that embarrassing episode. His rationalization of the Nazi-Soviet pact and the treachery of Germany prevailed in the USSR until long after de-Stalinization began to create a climate for reexamining the origins of the war and Stalin's role in failing to prepare for it. Then the door to criticism was opened only a small crack.[58] When Aleksandr Nekrich went too far and questioned the nonaggression pact and the behavior of those responsible for defense, he was forced to seek asylum in the United States in order to continue his career as an historian. Part of Nekrich's crime was indirect; his book encouraged others to ask why there was not a deeper probe into who was responsible for the lack of preparation for the attack and the failure to respond to it. His most serious misstep was questioning the very foundation of Soviet historiography, historical determinism.[59]

Berle sent Hopkins some advice on how to deal with the USSR. Since the Russians believed that they had no real friends, only temporary allies, they could turn back and make a deal with Hitler as quickly and completely as they had done in 1939. Berle reminded Hopkins that the USSR had signed a treaty with Germany when they left the war in 1917, releasing German

---

[56]Memorandum of conversation between Hopkins and Joseph Stalin, July 30, 1941, Hopkins Papers, Box 303, H. L. H. to Moscow Folder, FDRL.

[57]"Extracts from a Broadcast Speech by Stalin on the German Invasion of the Soviet Union," *Mirovoe Khoziaistvo*, July 3, 1941, in Degras, *Soviet Documents* 3:491–93.

[58]The author participated in the First Colloquium of a series titled "The Soviet-American Coalition in World War II" held as a part of the Soviet-American project on "The History of the Second World War." This took place in Moscow, USSR, October 19–23, 1986, where ten American and ten Soviet scholars discussed Soviet-American relations between 1939 and 1942. The Soviet scholars differed over the wisdom of Stalin's strategy, and at least two of them noted that Stalin and others bore the blame for Soviet unpreparedness for the attack by Hitler on the date it occurred. There was no dissent, however, on the subject of Soviet efforts to uphold the peace through collective security arrangements, and the Soviet papers were clearly defensive on the subject of the Nazi-Soviet pact, which most of them contended resulted from the failure of the democracies to uphold the principle of collective security.

[59]See Petrov, "*June 22, 1941*," pp. 14–15, 28–29, 167, 172–73, 176–83, 193, 197–98, 201, 203, 205, 210, 254–55, 258–59, 278–79. That Soviet scholarship has swung back to a more critical evaluation of the reasons why the USSR was caught unaware by the invasion was illustrated by some of the papers and commentary at the October 1986 colloquium (author's notes on the Moscow Colloquium).

troops to fight in the west, and there could easily be another such treaty. He cautioned that the Russians hated Great Britain even more deeply than they hated Germany, "though Fate put them on the same side for the moment." Soviet perfidy was apparent; American intelligence reports indicated that the Germans believed that "they had bought certain Russian officials, but we do not know who." Therefore, the British reliance on Soviet support might be ill founded. "Eastern Europe is looking out for itself; not for the British or for us. We can be of help to each other now and will do so. But we cannot bet our whole shirt on the continuance of the relationship."[60]

Hopkins ignored Berle's memorandum, probably because he was persuaded by Churchill that Great Britain badly needed its alliance with the Soviet Union if England was not to lose the war. The president's special assistant also changed his mind about Russia's ability to withstand the German onslaught as a result of his talk with Stalin, Molotov, and the Soviet generals. He convinced Roosevelt to have more hope for a sustained Soviet effort against the Nazis.[61] Perhaps this change of attitude partly stemmed from Stalin's repeated reference to the importance of FDR's moral influence as well as the material power of the United States being thrown into the crusade against the Nazis. Stalin argued that American participation might as well come at this juncture because it was going to have to come anyway, for Great Britain and Russia could not stand alone against the material strength Germany had gained from its conquests. Stalin went so far as to promise that American troops would be welcome on the Russian front.[62] Hopkins learned firsthand that Stalin held all the reins of Soviet authority, and he told Hull that it was necessary to send an American military and diplomatic mission to Moscow for a top-level conference with Stalin personally.[63]

Lend-Lease expediter Oscar Cox insisted that Russian orders be handled through his organization. If the Lend-Lease mechanism were not utilized, those who opposed delivery of the materiél would find a variety of legal devices to slow it up. Edward R. Stettinius, Jr., referring to Army Chief of Staff General George C. Marshall's testimony before the House Subcommittee on Appropriations that aid to Russia was aid to American defense, argued that "there now does not any longer seem to be as much reason for holding back from lend-lease aid to Russia." Stettinius recommended that the best way to make assistance to Russia palatable would be to proclaim the success of Harriman's conference in Moscow and then release the news that aid would come via the Lend-Lease program. To

---

[60]Memorandum, Berle to Hopkins, July 30, 1941, Hopkins Papers, Box 303, Book 4, Harriman-Beaverbrook Mission, FDRL.

[61]Tuttle, *Harry L. Hopkins*, pp. 99–107.

[62]Hopkins to FDR, July 31, 1941, Hopkins Papers, Box 304, Footnote Folder, FDRL.

[63]Hopkins to Hull, July 31, 1941, DSF 740.0011 EUROPEAN WAR 1939/15578.

make sure that Americans would not think that the Russians were getting something for nothing, it also could be announced they would pay in manganese and other strategic materials that the United States needed.[64]

FDR was concerned about whether the deliveries could be made in time to prevent a Russian collapse. He was convinced that, if Russia could withstand the German onslaught until October, the rains, snow, and severity of a Russian winter would keep the country safe until spring.[65] Thus preparations began for the First Protocol, as the formal agreement on aid was called; it was followed by several others. While some deliveries were made, they were not nearly in the amount or of the specific items the president and his envoys Hopkins and Harriman had promised. Sufficient supplies simply were not available, but further delays were caused by people in the government and in the military who still were not convinced that supplies should be sent that might fall into German hands. Still others thought that supplies should not fall into Russian hands.

FDR, angry at the failure to meet the Soviet requests, spoke sharply to Stimson, who seemed embarrassed. During a cabinet meeting Roosevelt looked directly at Stimson and charged that "the Russians have been given the runaround. . . . I am sick and tired of hearing that they are going to get this and they are going to get that. . . . Whatever we are going to give them, it has to be over there by the first of October, and the only answer I want to hear is that it is under way." He then turned to Henry Morgenthau, who told him: "The trouble, Mr. President, is that with Harry Hopkins away Oscar Cox tells me that he just hasn't got enough authority to get anywhere or any place and that he does get the run-around all the time." The president responded, "Well, I am going to put one of the best administrators in charge, Wayne Coy, and his job will be to see that the Russians get what they need."[66]

After his cabinet meeting, Roosevelt ordered Coy to cut the red tape expeditiously because practically nothing the Russians had asked for had been delivered. He understood Soviet suspicions: "Frankly, if I were a Russian I would feel that I had been given the run-around in the United States." He authorized Coy to get out the list of Russian requests and to "use a heavy hand—act as a burr under the saddle and get things moving!"[67]

Harriman's assessment of Roosevelt's motivations was that the decision was purely pragmatic: "Ideology had little or nothing to do with the President's decision to help the Russians. It was simply a matter of American self-interest, as Roosevelt saw it: he supported the Russians, as

[64]Memorandum, Edward R. Stettinius, Jr., to Hopkins, undated, Hopkins Papers, Box 303, Russian Aid Folder, 1941, FDRL.

[65]Memorandum, FDR to Wayne Coy, August 2, 1941, PSF, Russia, 1941, FDRL.

[66]Morgenthau Diaries, 1941, August 4, 1941, pp. 0952–53, Morgenthau Papers, FDRL. Morgenthau dictated this entry two days after the cabinet meeting.

[67]Memorandum, FDR to Coy, August 2, 1941, PSF, Russia, 1941, FDRL.

he had earlier supported the British in the hope that whenever America entered the war (as he believed she inevitably would) it might not be necessary to send large ground forces into battle." Harriman also believed that Roosevelt, who had been very much affected by World War I and its terrible cost in human lives, hoped that "if the great armies of Russia could stand up to the Germans, this might well make it possible for us to limit our participation largely to naval and air power." He was determined to give every possible bit of help to keep Russia in the war, and he would rather err on the side of generosity than skimp on the aid sent, even when Harriman and others thought "that particular Russian requests were not necessary or had not been justified."[68]

Davies, Morgenthau, and others who supported FDR's decision to aid the Soviets extensively were desperately afraid that Stalin still might find a way to back out of the alliance with Great Britain, which would mean losing the war. It was important to send the Soviets planes, tanks, and trucks rather than to keep them in the United States, because the Russians were fighting the battles and the Americans were not. General Marshall agreed, and on August 2 he reported to President Roosevelt on the intensification of aid to the Russians.[69]

## VI

As the German drive into Russia gained ground in the fall of 1941, Roosevelt recognized the seriousness of the situation and directed his subordinates to get the flow of military supplies moving. He wanted to make sure that "all reasonable munitions help be provided for Russia, not only immediately but as long as she continues to fight the Axis powers effectively." For this reason, he needed detailed information on what could be provided and when. He ordered the War Department, in cooperation with the Navy Department, to submit to him by September 10 recommendations for distribution of U.S. production of munitions for Great Britain, the United States, and the Soviet Union "for the period from the present time until June 30, 1942." He would discuss with Churchill the aid that the British would provide, and after that he would be able to inform the Russians of specific items to be supplied from both sources.

President Roosevelt wanted his military mission to know what they could offer. If after the meeting in Moscow adjustments were necessary, they could recommend changes "after due consultation with the Russians and the British on the spot."[70] Roosevelt's intent was clear: The War Department was to provide information about what was available; it was not to

---

[68]Harriman and Abel, *Special Envoy*, pp. 73–74.
[69]Memorandum, George C. Marshall to FDR, August 2, 1941, OF 220, FDRL.
[70]Memorandum, FDR to Stimson, August 30, 1941, OF 220, Russia, FDRL.

determine how much would be provided. The president would be advised by his own military mission in coordination with the Russians and the British as to when and how much aid would be given. Roosevelt attempted to eliminate in advance any obstructionism from the War Department bureaucracy. On September 3 the White House released the names of the members of the president's mission to Moscow. W. Averell Harriman was to chair the group, which was to consist of experts on the production and distribution of military equipment, men who either were known to agree with Roosevelt's priorities or who owed primary allegiance to the president.[71]

When Harriman's mission reached Moscow, he discovered the low esteem in which the Soviets held Ambassador Steinhardt. Stalin told Harriman on September 30 that the American ambassador was too receptive to rumors he picked up from other embassies, including absurd stories about the fall of Moscow. Stalin complained, somewhat contemptuously, that Steinhardt "came to the Soviet Government in terror and demanded a place for the embassy on the Volga. He sent a number of his people to Khazan. Twice in the first six weeks he became panicky and thought there was no hope for Moscow." According to Stalin, Steinhardt's attitude made the ambassador of little value in the relationship between the two countries. Harriman countered that he was surprised, for he had "found the Ambassador calm and ready to be helpful in every direction."[72] Considering Stalin's own decision to move the Commissariat of Foreign Affairs and other government offices to Kuibyshev on October 16, this attack on Steinhardt was strange.[73]

Stalin then invited Harriman to evaluate Umanskii. The Soviet ambassador received low marks for his "excessive enthusiasm." He bothered too many people about the supply question and so irritated them that they were reluctant to be of help to him. Protocol dictated that, since Hopkins was the president's assistant on supply questions, Umanskii should follow Hopkins's guidance and work with his staff. Harriman did not want his remarks to seem unfriendly, so he complimented Umanskii's helpfulness in explaining the problem of American financing for the USSR.[74]

During his discussions with the Americans and the British, Stalin asked Lord Beaverbrook to evaluate Ambassador Ivan Maisky, "whom Beaverbrook then extolled indicating his only difficulty was the persistence and force of his presentation of Russia's needs. Stalin asked whether he didn't lecture him on doctrine and Beaverbrook smilingly replied he didn't

---

[71]White House press release, September 3, 1941, OF 220-D, FDRL.

[72]Memorandum of comments regarding Ambassadors Steinhardt, Cripps, Umanskii, and Maisky during third meeting with Stalin at the Kremlin, September 30, 1941, Hopkins Papers, Book 4: Beaverbrook-Harriman Mission, no. 39, FDRL.

[73]Berezhkov, *History in the Making*, pp. 153–56.

[74]Memorandum of comments regarding Ambassadors Steinhardt, Cripps, Umanskii, and Maisky during third meeting with Stalin at the Kremlin, September 30, 1941, Hopkins Papers, Book 4: Beaverbrook-Harriman Mission, no. 39, FDRL.

give him a chance." Then Beaverbrook requested Stalin's reactions to Ambassador Stafford Cripps. Stalin responded, without enthusiasm Harriman thought, "Oh, he's all right." Beaverbrook called Cripps a bore; Stalin interposed, "Like Maisky?" Beaverbrook said, "No, like Mrs. Maisky." Harriman remembered the whole conversation as "frank and informal and joking."[75] Harriman may have thought that the talks were "frank"; blunt would be a better description of Stalin's probings. Obviously he wanted to get rid of Steinhardt and was neutral on Cripps, but he also wanted to know whether his men in Washington and London were effective. Shortly after this discussion Umanskii was replaced by Maxim Litvinov, but Maisky stayed on in London until he was promoted to a new post in the Commissariat of Foreign Affairs in 1943.

Stalin asked the British to accede to Soviet claims "to the 1941 frontiers, excluding those with German-occupied Poland." Beaverbrook urged his government to support this request but found continuing "hostility to the 1941 frontiers project of a determined and extreme character." Furthermore, the reluctance of British military officials to deliver supplies to Russia caused Beaverbrook "to become a protagonist."[76]

While the Soviets complained about British and American attention to their supply requirements, Roosevelt, Hull, and the State Department grew more and more concerned about what the Russians were doing with the Polish forces in Russia. Hull told Harriman to try to get them into battle or at least out of Russia. Stalin should be approached with the assurance that the United States understood that there was perhaps not enough spare equipment in Russia for retraining these forces. Therefore, they should be sent to Iran, where the Americans and the British could do the job and return them to fight on the Russian front. Stalin responded:

> An opportunity has not yet presented itself to me to make myself acquainted with details concerning the question of Poles in the Soviet Union. Information concerning the Soviet Government's position in the matter will be given to you by me in two or three days after I have given the matter some study. There is no doubt in my mind that the Soviet Government will take into consideration definitely the Polish desires and the interests of Soviet-Polish friendly relations.[77]

He was not about to release the Polish soldiers for training in Iran, as many of them might have known that the Soviets had killed more than ten thousand of their officers in the massacre in the Katyn Forest near Smolensk

---

[75]Ibid.

[76]Ibid.

[77]Hull to Harriman, November 7, 1941, and response for Harriman by Steinhardt enclosing Stalin's answer, November 14, 1941, Hopkins Papers, Box 303, Book 4: Harriman-Beaverbrook Mission, FDRL.

when Soviet troops occupied that area from 1939 to 1941.[78] Stalin tried to appear to be working cooperatively with the Poles, and he agreed to a meeting with the head of the Polish government-in-exile, General Wladyslaw Sikorski. Andrei Vyshinski, acting on Molotov's authority, informed the Polish ambassador to Moscow that Sikorski would be received.[79]

## VII

After the German attack on Russia, Roosevelt instructed Joseph Grew to deliver a message to Prince Konoye Fumimaro, the Japanese prime minister, asking what Japan's plans were vis-à-vis the Soviet Union. Grew was to inquire about rumors that Japan intended to attack Russia as part of its Tripartite Pact agreement with Germany. FDR hoped that these stories were not true, because this would "upset the hopes of the American Government, which it understood were shared by Japan, that peace in the Pacific area might be rendered more secure and strengthened." He wanted an assurance from Konoye.

Konoye responded through Foreign Minister Matsuoka Yosuke that "the Japanese Government had not so far considered the possibility of going to war with Soviet Russia." He added that future developments would largely decide Japan's policy. When Grew asked what he had in mind, he responded that possibly a Soviet alliance with Great Britain or an attempt by the United States to supply the USSR with strategic material through Vladivostok for use against Germany could change Japan's policy. Matsuoka contended that he was under great pressure from powerful groups in Japan to go to war with Russia, and the hands of these extremists would be strengthened by either of these occurrences.

Matsuoka could not resist asking Grew if the rumors that the United States would enter the European war had any foundation. Grew was instructed to answer Matsuoka's question with the assertion that American entry into the European war "would be purely of a defensive character and that Mr. Hitler could best furnish information on this point by revealing his future contemplated steps of aggression." Matsuoka's hand was visible in the blustering formal response that rejected the idea that the United States

---

[78]For a detailed account of this incident see Janusz K. Zawodny, *Death in the Forest: The Story of the Katyn Forest Massacre* (Notre Dame, IN: University of Notre Dame Press, 1962). At the time this book appeared there was considerable debate as to the accuracy of its premises, and some American scholars still believe this story was a Nazi propaganda effort. However, it was credited by Robert Dallek in his study of Roosevelt's foreign policy as having been believed by Churchill and by FDR, who felt hamstrung by the need to avoid giving the Germans any credibility and especially not at the expense of an ally. See Dallek, *Franklin D. Roosevelt and American Foreign Policy*, p. 400.

[79]Telegram, Thurston to Hull, November 12, 1941, Hopkins Papers, Box 303, Book 4: Harriman-Beaverbrook Mission, FDRL.

had carte blanche to decide when its rights were violated and complained about the American "indictment of Germany." This was Matsuoka's last communication with Grew before he was booted out of the cabinet, and Grew judged it appropriate that the Japanese foreign minister died politically as he had lived, going out with an aggressive, vitriolic, bellicose blast at the United States.[80]

Neither Roosevelt nor Hull wanted war with Japan. They hoped that tough sanctions on oil and gasoline shipments would show the Japanese how serious the Americans were, and they thought that the Japanese might decide that it would be better to sit on the fence until the situation in the European war became clearer. Nor did war between Japan and the Soviet Union fit into Hull and Roosevelt's strategy; they wanted the Russians to be able to devote their whole effort to the war against Hitler.

Secretary Hull tried to force Japan to back away from its alliance with Germany. In a conversation with Ambassador Admiral Nomura Kichisaburo and Ambassador Kurusu Saburo, the secretary detailed the problem of Americans accepting an agreement with a country that maintained an alliance with Hitler. Nomura responded that it would not be easy for Japan to back out of the treaty, and he brought up what he thought was a similar situation, that the United States abhorred communism but nonetheless aided the Soviet Union. Hull then took a somewhat threatening posture, saying that he "frankly did not know whether anything could be done in the matter of reaching a satisfactory agreement with Japan; that we can go so far but rather than go beyond a certain point it would be better for us to stand and take the consequences." Nomura pleaded with the secretary to understand that Japan was hard-pressed, and surely Hull was well aware of Japan's desire "to reach some agreement with the United States." Hull then lectured the Japanese on their policy of moving toward rather than away from empire, rejecting the modern direction which the United States was pursuing. He pointed out that the United States was trying "to induce the British Empire to reduce its Empire preferences." Why could Japan not do the same?[81] The answer was that the Japanese Imperial Conference, going on at that very time, had already rejected this course on the grounds that the years of conflict in China would then have been for nothing. Hull did not want a showdown yet; he was stalling for time. This sort of appeal, however, was unlikely to slow the wave of Japanese aggression.[82]

---

[80]Grew Papers, Personal Notes, 1941, pp. 5339–41.

[81]Memorandum of conversation between Hull, Nomura Kichisaburo, and Kurusu Saburo, with Joseph W. Ballantine present, November 18, 1941, memoranda of Conversations, Japan-Peru, Box 60, Folder 232, Japan, October-December 7, 1941, Cordell Hull Papers, Library of Congress, Washington, DC.

[82]Concerning the desire to stall for time and the spiral of events toward war in Japan see Burns, *Soldier of Freedom*, pp. 154–59.

Certainly one impediment to the president's and Hull's efforts to prepare the nation for war was Congress's reluctance to help educate the public. FDR wanted congressmen to speak out in favor of his policy, but few did so. Archibald MacLeish, who wrote speeches for the president, complained to Grace Tully that he needed FDR's help with getting more congressmen on the road, as "senators Pepper and Lee, and particularly Senator Pepper, have carried most of the load."[83]

A note from Hadley Cantril dated December 5 illustrated that public opinion was ahead of Congress in supporting the president. Cantril's most recent poll had asked if the United States should take steps to keep Japan from becoming more powerful even if this meant risking war. Sixty-nine percent answered yes, 20 percent said no, and 11 percent had no opinion.[84] This documented the firm belief among Americans that war with Japan had become virtually unavoidable. Pearl Harbor may have been a shock in terms of the nature of the attack and its cost in ships and manpower, but it was no shock that war had begun with Japan.

---

[83] Archibald MacLeish to Tully, December 2, 1941, OF 3575, Foreign Policy, 1939–1945, FDRL.

[84] December 5, 1941, PSF, Public Opinion Polls, FDRL.

# III

## Alliance by Necessity

JAPAN'S ATTACK ON THE U.S. fleet at Pearl Harbor on December 7, 1941, changed the entire complexion of the war. Attempts to keep Japan on the fence had failed, leaving Cordell Hull and Roosevelt perplexed by their misjudgment, chagrined at the losses, but relieved of doubts concerning when or if the United States would become directly involved in World War II. Franklin Roosevelt no longer had a choice concerning commitment of troops and matériel. As to whether the USSR might be a suitable ally, Japan's leaders had mooted that question for the American president. All that remained to be settled were the nature and objectives of the new anti-Axis coalition.

Eleanor Roosevelt reflected that after the years of tension and uncertainty her husband was relieved. Both of them had decided by this time that the defeat of Hitler was an absolute necessity, if there was to be any hope for a democratic world order. Victory was unlikely without some form of American participation beyond simply aiding Britain and Russia.[1] Frances Perkins made a similar judgment of the president's response. She recalled that FDR had warned the cabinet for more than four years of the Axis menace to America but had been prevented by the isolationist climate from confounding Hitler's plans for conquest. December 7, she judged, had removed the burdens of restraint and indecision.[2] All of those who spoke to or met with Franklin Roosevelt on that first day were of a similar mind. Although Japan had instigated the attack, nearly everyone's thoughts immediately turned to Hitler and the European war. Harry Hopkins instantly stated that they all knew that the main enemy was Hitler. Henry Stimson and others wanted to declare war immediately on Germany, but Roosevelt resisted in the name of national unity.[3]

Maxim Litvinov, who by a twist of fate was received as the new Soviet ambassador to the United States on the very day that Hitler declared war on

---

[1] Eleanor Roosevelt interview.
[2] Frances Perkins interview.
[3] Dallek, *Franklin D. Roosevelt and American Foreign Policy*, p. 312.

the United States, told Secretary Hull that there was no chance of Russia declaring war on Japan until things were under control on the German front. Hull told the Soviet ambassador that Americans would wonder why they aided Russia and received nothing in return in their war with Japan.[4] When Litvinov was commissar of foreign affairs, he would not have let pass this opportunity to remind Hull that the fighting in Europe was, after all, aiding the Americans in defeating the main enemy. Friendly relations were too important to bring up this sort of argument at that time. Litvinov faced his new assignment with certain misgivings. His orders were to press the Americans for goods and for an immediate second front, and he found the task disagreeable. When news of the Japanese attack reached the Soviet capital, the Russians judged that "one of the main events of the Second World War" had just taken place because this would bring American entry into the war against Hitler.[5]

Some members of Roosevelt's staff worried about opposition to a Soviet-American alliance. Joseph Davies suggested that Roosevelt should clarify the issue of continuing cooperation on a global scale with Great Britain, the USSR, and China to defeat the common enemy. In this same vein, Archibald MacLeish urged Steve Early to have the president assert that the American people were heartened by Litvinov's statement that the United States and the Soviet Union "have a common cause and a common enemy." Then the president could say "with equal firmness that the United States will carry on its program of furnishing the tools of victory to the Soviet armies without let up. We will proceed to double and quadruple our shipments and continue them, until the common enemies of mankind are annihilated."[6] Early sent this message over to Sumner Welles and received a courtly rebuff for his efforts. Welles said that the only way the president could be properly served was "for the State Department to issue statements of this character or to have the opportunity of advising the President . . . should it be thought best for the White House to issue them."[7]

---

[4]Memorandum of conversation between Cordell Hull and Maxim Litvinov, December 11, 1941, "Soviet Policy in [the] United States-Japanese War," Memoranda of Conversations, PHILIPPINES-YUGOSLAVIA, Box 61, Folder no. 250, 1934–1942, Hull Papers.

[5]Maxim Litvinov, *Notes for a Journal* (New York: William Morrow, 1955), p. 310. This book was introduced by E. H. Carr with a cautionary note that not everything in this volume was fully reliable and that even its authenticity had been called into question. Carr said that the early part of the volume seemed to correspond with the interview given by Litvinov to Richard C. Hottelet of CBS Radio in Moscow in 1946, which was printed for the first time in the *Washington Post* in 1952. Actually, it is more the mood and bluntness that are similar rather than the contents. The statements about Stalin, Soviet policy, and other aspects of the American-Soviet relationship do correspond, however, with the very straightforward and pessimistic final interview Litvinov had with Sumner Welles before the Soviet diplomat left the United States for the last time in 1943.

[6]Telegram, Joseph Davies to Steve Early, December 11, 1941; memorandum, Archibald MacLeish to Early, December 12, 1941, OF 36, FDRL.

[7]Memorandum, Welles to Early, December 12, 1941, ibid.

At this stage the State and War departments still were hoping to encourage Russian entry into the Pacific war. Hull outlined the scenario of pressure, including the threat of curtailing shipment of Lend-Lease supplies if Russia should decide not to participate in the war on Japan. Gradually, however, the secretary realized that the Soviets might indeed be unable to carry the brunt of the war against Hitler and be of real assistance against the Japanese at the same time. Hull was convinced that the USSR would enter the Far Eastern war shortly, based on his information about Japan responding to a German request to attack Russia. Stalin encouraged this expectation by saying that it probably would be sometime the following spring when the Russians would enter the war against Japan.[8]

Roosevelt laid out for Cordell Hull items to include in a war aims message. He wanted the United States, Great Britain, the USSR, and China to be listed at the top of the declaration to illustrate that they were together in this as aligned Great Powers. The British were to be prodded to include India among the signers; FDR's anticolonialism already had appeared. He took another position that would irritate Churchill: He saw no reason why the Free French should be included. He thought of the statement as a supplement to the Atlantic Charter, and he wanted the language concerning war objectives to be quite specific.[9] Roosevelt proposed a Supreme War Council responsible for establishing war plans and distributing supplies.[10]

FDR gave the joint declaration draft to Ambassador Litvinov, who went to discuss it with Hull. The secretary thought that Litvinov seemed surprised when he was told that the declaration had not been submitted to other powers pending Soviet approval of the draft. In fact, Litvinov gave him a proposal that the Russians had prepared, assuming that the other allies already had signed their own. Hull found nothing objectionable in the Soviet draft except that the Soviet Union had stated the war's purpose as defeating Hitlerism, whereas the American draft stated it as defeating the signatories of the Tripartite Pact, which, of course, would include Japan. Litvinov was not about to announce directly that Japan was a Soviet enemy, but he assured Hull that the Japanese were included as adherents to the Soviet definition of "Hitlerism."[11]

Quickly the Russians proved that they were anxious to establish their devotion to the alliance. They extolled America's power to counteract Axis resources and expressed their sincere appreciation for the president and his

---

[8]Hull, *Memoirs* 2:1111–12.

[9]FDR to Hull, December 27, 1941, Hopkins Papers, FDRL. See also *FRUS: Diplomatic Papers*, vol. 1, *General, British Commonwealth, Far East, 1942* (Washington, DC: Government Printing Office, 1960), p. 13.

[10]Draft Joint Declaration on War Aims, December, 27, 1941, DSF 740.0011 (European War 1939)/12-2741. See also *FRUS: General, 1942*, pp. 6–18.

[11]Memorandum of conversation between secretary of state and Ambassador Litvinov, December 29, 1941, DSF 740.0011, European War 1939/18038. See also *FRUS: General, 1942*, pp. 18–20.

aid. *Izvestiia* published an editorial birthday greeting to President Roosevelt. It stated that the United States, under Roosevelt's vigorous leadership, had met the greatest ordeal of the century and a half of American history, and the Americans, like the Russians, were determined to achieve final victory "over Hitlerism and its allies."[12]

Collaboration in winning the war was less wholehearted than President Roosevelt wanted or the Russians expected. The American military attaché in Moscow reported on January 15, 1942, that the absence of close cooperation among the three major allies in the conduct of the war against the Axis powers was a subject "about which volumes could be written." He added that the Russians charged that they were not getting what they had been promised in the Moscow protocols arranged by Ambassador Harriman.

The question was: Did the Americans really want to fulfill those promises? The attaché noted that the alliance had been forced on both sides against their will by the common enemy in Germany; there never had been and never could be any mutual interest beyond that. He also asked: "Is it desirable to have a Red Russia with too much to say? Shall our aid, therefore, be free and all out, or shall it be carefully gauged—so carefully that both Germany and the Soviet Union will find themselves completely exhausted and neither can be a dominant factor after the war?" He assumed that real aid had been intended, but, if this were true, "we have failed; if our aid is being gauged, we are successful."[13] Obviously, the writer was not sympathetic to the USSR, but he assumed that the policy being pursued was not the one that had been intended, and he thought that his superiors needed to understand what was happening. The military attaché in Moscow accurately identified the indecision and confusion of those who were responsible for deciding whether to aid the Russians fully or to hold back on assistance.

Nor were the Americans the only ones who were guilty of hedging on promised aid. An unsigned memorandum sent to Harry Hopkins contended that the British had no Russian policy and charged that the initial burst of enthusiasm over helping the USSR had suffered a relapse in Britain. The lack of military aid from Great Britain made it appear to Russia that the Neville Chamberlain policy of playing the Germans and the Russians against one another had not been supplanted and that the British were husbanding their strength so as to take advantage of the exhaustion of German and Russian power on the Continent. The writer warned that this problem had to be dealt with immediately. "Delay in making decisions, and

----

[12]Dispatch from Henderson, January 31, 1942, PSF, Unindexed Safe File, Russia, FDRL.
    [13]Military attaché report, January 15, 1942, Moscow, EE 246, U.S. Department of State, Foreign Service Post Files, Record Group 84, Federal Records Center, Suitland, Maryland (hereafter cited as Post Files). The report, according to a marginal comment, may have come from a Captain Schuster.

procrastination in all our proceedings have almost destroyed the hope of effective collaboration with Russia."[14]

FDR and Hull wanted a cooperative relationship with the USSR. They realized that, if they wanted a smooth-running embassy in Moscow able to deal effectively with the Soviets, Laurence Steinhardt would have to go. They prepared the groundwork for this by asking the Turks if they would find Steinhardt an acceptable ambassador. They responded that they would be happy to receive him.[15] Among those seriously considered in January to replace Steinhardt was General James H. Burns, who had been used by FDR and Harry Hopkins as a troubleshooter, but the president did not want to remove Burns from his position of expediting Lend-Lease. He asked Hull what he thought of sending Joe Davies back to Moscow because he "would really be persona grata, would have access to Stalin, and in a couple of weeks could get into complete touch with the airplane and tank situation. If you think well of this will you speak to him?"[16] That nothing came of this is not surprising. If Hull knew anything about the attitude of the professional diplomats assigned to Moscow, he knew that Davies well might be persona grata with the Soviets, but he was persona non grata with the embassy staff. Hull might have had wholesale requests for transfers, if not actual resignations, if he sent Davies back to Moscow.

In March the prime minister of the Polish government-in-exile, General Wladyslaw Sikorski, urged the United States to bring up the question of the position of smaller nations in the postwar structure. Roosevelt suggested to Acting Secretary of State Welles that Sikorski should be "definitely discouraged," because "it would cause serious trouble with Russia."[17] This is another example of the president's desire to postpone vexing problems until the war was over.

From the beginning of the alliance between the Soviet Union and the United States, the second front issue emerged as a point of controversy. There was a sense of déjà vu in the way the Americans and Russians parried and bickered on the subject. They behaved much as they had in the 1930s when the debt question had been constantly brought up by the Americans as a reason for lack of further cooperation, and the Russians threw back at them the U.S. failure to sign a nonaggression pact promised during Litvinov's visit with FDR in November 1933. Litvinov must have thought that he was watching a remake of an earlier movie in which he had played a role as he asked the Americans to open the second European front, and they in turn asked when were the Russians going to prove that they were real allies by

---

[14]Unsigned memorandum of March 25, 1942, Hopkins Papers, Book 4: Beaverbrook-Harriman Mission, Russia, FDRL.

[15]Dispatch from Ankara, Turkey, to Hull, January 3, 1942, DSF 123, STEINHARDT, LAURENCE A./437.

[16]Memorandum, FDR to Hull, January 17, 1942, FSF, State, Hull Folder, FDRL.

[17]Memorandum, FDR to Welles, March 7, 1942, FSF, State, Welles, FDRL.

opening a second front against the Japanese. Welles confronted the Russian ambassador with a request for a quid pro quo. Litvinov told Welles that it was imperative that a new front be created and that the British were wasting valuable time by refusing to consider establishing one in western Europe. Welles countered: "I said it was obvious that one of the chief problems at the present moment was the fact that Japan was able to concentrate all of her strength in one area in the Pacific." Then he presented Litvinov with his counterproposal: the Russians could have their second front, but it required mutual efforts to defeat the Axis powers, including Japan. As the undersecretary of state put it, if a new front were created against Japan, "particularly that front which Japan dreaded most, namely, the possibility of air attacks from Siberia against her naval bases and her munitions factories, a very great deal of strain would be taken off the British and American forces in the Pacific and consequently make it far easier for them to consider favorably the undertaking of some other front in Europe."[18] This was the stalemate: America would risk attacking the Continent if Russia relieved the pressure in the Far East, but Russia would risk attacking there only after the question was no longer in doubt in the West.

## II

Secretary Hull was decisive about British and Russian discussions on postwar boundaries and spheres of influence. He wrote a memorandum to President Roosevelt on February 5, 1942, with enclosures that he had sent to the U.S. ambassador to Great Britain, John G. Winant, reminding FDR that U.S. policy opposed any predetermined spheres of influence in eastern Europe. Hull had told Winant that American postwar policies were clearly stated in the Atlantic Charter, which also represented the positions of the British and Soviet governments. The charter guaranteed people the right to approve territorial changes that would affect them directly as well as the right to choose the form of government under which they would live.[19] In view of this, if any of the three governments entered into agreements in conflict with these principles, "they were in violation of solemn pledges." Secret agreements especially were to be avoided. Hull told the president that this communication had been sent to Winant so that Anthony Eden, who was about to talk to Stalin, would understand fully the American position.[20]

---

[18]Memorandum of conversation between Welles and Litvinov, February 23, 1942, DSF 861.24/845. See also *FRUS: Diplomatic Papers*, vol. 3, *Europe, 1942* (Washington, DC: Government Printing Office, 1961), pp. 693–95.

[19]Winston S. Churchill, *The Second World War*, vol. 3, *The Grand Alliance* (Boston: Houghton Mifflin, 1950), pp. 443–44.

[20]Memorandum, Hull to FDR, February 5, 1942, with enclosures of a memorandum of February 4 and a dispatch to John G. Winant of December 5, 1941, Box 304, Footnote Folder, Hopkins Papers, FDRL.

In his message to Roosevelt, Hull also expressed his opposition to Stalin's suggestion to Eden of a secret protocol concerning Soviet frontiers and new territorial divisions for eastern Europe. The Soviet leader wanted Russia's frontiers of June 22, 1941, to be recognized, which meant that the Baltic States and one third of Poland would be permanently incorporated into the Soviet Union. He also desired incorporation of Bessarabia and other parts of Romania. Furthermore, Stalin wanted the British to agree to restore Austrian independence, detach the Rhineland from Germany, create an independent Bavaria, transfer East Prussia to Poland, transfer the Sudetenland to Czechoslovakia, give the Dodecanese and parts of Bulgaria and northern Syria to Turkey, and make certain territorial adjustments in favor of Greece. Hull stated that Eden had resisted these suggestions on grounds that he had promised the United States that no such agreements would be made. The secretary wanted FDR to hold firm against territorial redistribution, for once the dike was breached a flood of demands would follow.

Two passages were marked in the margin of the text by either the president or someone in his office. The first called attention to the reasons for Hull's opposition, based on U.S. policy:

> If the principle is once admitted that agreements relating to frontiers may be entered into prior to the Peace Conference, the association of nations opposed to the Axis, which thus far has been based upon the common aim of defeating the enemy, may be weakened by . . . mutual suspicion and by efforts of various members to intrigue in order to obtain commitments with regard to territory at the expense of other members.[21]

In the second marked passage he observed that firmness would be needed because the British would be pressured by Stalin. Hull warned the president about the tricks the Russians would try (and had tried) on Eden to get their way. They had implied that a separate peace might be necessary if these agreements were not made. Surrender to Soviet demands would have an especially deleterious effect on the smaller nations looking to the United States and England for protection, and it would add fuel to Axis propaganda.[22]

Hull made some significant assumptions concerning American policy. He assumed that the United States would not consider the kind of secret treaties that had caused trouble at the end of the Great War. Although he implied that there might have to be concessions to Soviet demands, they could not be made "in advance."[23] There was some logic to Hull's arguments, given traditional U.S. policy and the general tenor of the

---

[21]Ibid.
[22]Ibid.
[23]Ibid.

administration's attitude toward foreign policy: Do not plan ahead, meet the crisis of the moment, and do not make any commitments that would preclude later adjustments.

Hull already had been charged with the responsibility of planning for the peace conference at the end of the war, and possibly he thought that, given time and room to maneuver, he could arrange a better treaty. The victorious allies might be able to persuade the Soviets that they did not need, for protection, control of the smaller states around them. If Hull believed this, his Russian experts were not giving him the benefit of their knowledge of Russian history and the centuries-long Russian quest for secure borders safe from an assault, particularly an assault from Germany. Nor, at this juncture, could he know that policy decisions that might alter Soviet suspicions would not be made by the Department of State at the latter stages of the war; instead, they would be taken over by the War and Navy departments in the name of wartime expediency. The military and other close advisers to the president would make the decisions and would ignore most of the State Department's advice.

Cordell Hull's fears concerning a British-Russian deal prior to the peace conference seemed well founded. Sumner Welles recorded a conversation he had on February 14, 1942, with the British ambassador, Lord Halifax, concerning recent negotiations between the British and the Russians. According to Ambassador Halifax, Winston Churchill, while visiting FDR, received an urgent cable from Anthony Eden suggesting that Stalin's requests for immediate recognition of the Soviet Union's 1941 boundaries should be met. These boundaries would incorporate in the USSR the Baltic States, the province of Bessarabia, and the part of Finland that had been ceded to the Russians in 1941. Stalin had not mentioned the inclusion of any part of Poland as an essential point. Churchill knew that the Americans were not amenable to these delineations, and he responded, "expressing indignant disapprobation of the points mentioned and saying that he felt that Mr. Eden should reply that a decision on questions of this character should wait until the war was over."[24] Halifax then wrote to Churchill, dissenting from the prime minister's instructions to Eden, and he let Welles know about his dispatch. He reminded Churchill that British opposition to the incorporation of the Baltic States in 1939 had been one of the prime causes for the breakdown in negotiations with the Soviet Union at that time and also had been a significant factor contributing to the Soviet decision to sign the agreement with Germany.

Halifax and Welles attempted to define wartime and postwar Anglo-American-Soviet policies and to persuade one another of the correctness of their positions. Welles was aghast when he looked at a British Foreign

---

[24]Memorandum of conversation between Welles and Lord Halifax, February 18, 1942, *FRUS: Europe, 1942*, pp. 512–13.

Office telegram that asserted that "a simple refusal to meet [Stalin's demands] would involve the risk that Anglo-Soviet relations would deteriorate and that cooperation between Great Britain and Russia and between the United States of America and Russia both during and after the war may be seriously endangered."[25] Welles said he raised the Anglo-American commitment to self-determination expressed in the Atlantic Charter against Halifax's views. Halifax countered with the plebiscites in the Baltic States: The Latvians, Estonians, and Lithuanians had voted in Soviet-supervised plebiscites to merge with the USSR. Welles thought that his discussion would have been "even less profitable" had he used the argument he really wanted, "that these 'plebiscites' were faked."[26]

Halifax suggested an alternative policy for the Americans. Instead of agreeing to Soviet incorporation of the Baltic States, Anglo-American policy would guarantee at least Soviet military bases in these states and would assure the Russians that they would not be precluded "from putting forward at the Peace Conference their claim to absorb the Baltic States, Bessarabia and Northern Bukovina and parts of Finland." This would disarm Soviet suspicions while they all got on with the business of defeating the enemy. The Lend-Lease arrangement with the British and the U.S. lease of the Guantanamo naval base in Cuba provided a precedent for leaseholds. Thus the principles of self-determination would not be violated.[27]

According to Halifax, Britain and the United States should tell Stalin that the concessions he desired required specific guarantees on his part if they were to be validated, guarantees that would make it difficult for him to press for further concessions. Stalin would have to reaffirm his statement of November 6, 1941, that the Soviet government "had no intention of interfering in the internal affairs of other people." He would also have to acquiesce in a confederation plan for the weaker countries of Europe, especially those in the Balkans, Poland, and Czechoslovakia. The United States and Great Britain also would insist that Stalin cooperate with them in preparing for the reconstruction of Europe with full regard for all of their interests. Halifax told Welles that he had discussed his proposals with FDR the day before, but Welles responded that the president had not mentioned any of these ideas to him.

Halifax tried to influence Welles by handing him a telegram from the Foreign Office, dated February 15, which expressed British fears about the postwar world if the Russians were not pinned down in advance. A weakened France meant a power vacuum in Europe, and a revived Germany might try to fill the gap via another deal with the Russians, who might be tempted to collaborate with the Germans for historical and economic

---

[25]Ibid., p. 514.
[26]Ibid., pp. 514–15.
[27]Ibid., pp. 515–16.

reasons. Another fear was that, before the British and Americans could enter the war on the Continent, Russian prestige would become enormous, thus tempting the USSR to try to create Communist governments in the majority of Europe's nations. At the very least, if the Russians succeeded in conquering Germany without British and American assistance, they might then "be in a position to denude German factories of the equipment needed to restore Russian industry," in which case they would become "to a considerable extent independent of British-American assistance, [and] might no longer desire to adapt themselves to policies which we and the United States may wish to pursue." The Foreign Office warned that "it would be unsafe to gamble on Russia emerging so exhausted from the war that she will be forced to collaborate with us without our having to make concessions to her." The memorandum urged the Americans to remember that "there is also the important point of particular and immediate interest to the United States that our present answer to Stalin's demand may later on affect the Russian decision whether or not to make war on Japan."[28]

Welles blasted the British proposals presented to him by Halifax; he labeled them "a complete repudiation of the principles for which this Government stood." This was certainly true, but perhaps it was time to reconsider some of those principles in light of the alternatives that the world would face if the war ended with the Soviet Union both convinced its security was threatened by the peace and in possession of major portions of central and eastern Europe. What would the United States do if the Russians were able to affect the future of those areas in such a way as to provide them with either nominal independence or virtually no independence at all? Welles apparently did not conceive of the possibility that American principles could not be maintained in total and the Soviet Union could not or should not be persuaded to accept American guarantees of Soviet security. He also failed to consider that Stalin would not place much confidence in the assurances of capitalist statesmen that they would protect Communist Russia from a resurgent Germany. After all, Stalin was already convinced that the British had tried to take care of both nazism and communism by letting the Germans and Russians exhaust themselves in a struggle against one another. It was not likely that he would forget this and believe that at the end of the war they would treat him any differently than they had when they rejected Russian proposals for collective security in the 1930s.

Halifax must have been despondent, and perhaps a little angry also, as Welles accused the British and French of having failed in the interwar years to make the Versailles settlement work. He contemptuously told the British ambassador: "I could not conceive of this war being fought in order to undertake once more the shoddy, inherently vicious, kind of patchwork world order which the European powers had attempted to construct during

[28]Ibid., pp. 517–18.

the years between 1919 and 1939. . . . If that was the kind of world we had
to look forward to, I did not believe that the people of the United States
would wish to partake therein."[29] Welles's threat was that his government
would leave the British to fend for themselves if they made any deals with
the Russians that violated American principles. Halifax refrained from
reminding Welles that the bad peace and the Treaty of Versailles, which he
castigated, had been forged in part by the United States. Europeans believed
that the Versailles peace had failed, at least in some measure, because the
Americans had refused to help enforce a treaty that they had imposed on
Europe in the first place.

On April 2, 1942, Walter Thurston, the chargé in Moscow, also
reported to Hull on "the apparent determination of the Soviet government to
obtain recognition by the British and American governments of its 1941
frontiers." He noted their ambitions for retaining the Baltic States, the
territory conquered from Finland and Poland, and parts of Bessarabia and
Bukovina.[30]

Adolf A. Berle, Jr., who participated in the discussions with Lord
Halifax, decided to set down for the record a memorandum of the British
requests and the American response. For the most part Berle supported
Welles's views of both traditional U.S. policy and opposition to any deals
with the Russians and British. He referred to "the repeated attempt by the
British to secure our consent to a proposed British-Russian treaty by which
the British would assent to the taking over by Soviet Russia of the Baltic
Republics." What bothered Berle most was that this apparently would be a
secret treaty. He recorded "the almost frantic pressure by the British upon us
to secure our assent to this."[31]

British diplomats wanted an agreement to declare the Baltic States part
of Russia and to let residents there, and in other Soviet-occupied areas, who
wished to leave do so. Given the American penchant for worrying about the
little guy, Berle's reaction was perfectly understandable. However, when one
examines what happened to expatriates from eastern Europe at the end of the
war, perhaps it would have been better for all concerned if the decision to
allow them to leave had been made then. Instead, they were turned over to
the Russians for repatriation. Many were sent off to serve various penalties
in Russia, including work in the gulags. Some were summarily shot.
Humane intentions often do not bring humane results. In a sense, Berle
admitted this when he observed that the United States had best not agree to
emigration arrangements, because the Americans were not "even in a
position to say that [refugees] will be granted free immigration into the

[29]Ibid., pp. 519–20.

[30]Walter Thurston to Hull, April 2, 1942, Box 1346A, Moscow 711.2 811.11, Post
Files.

[31]Memorandum, Berle to Acting Secretary of State Welles, April 3, 1942, DSF
741.61/782. See also *FRUS: Europe, 1942*, pp. 513–16.

United States." In other words, it worried Berle that the United States either would feel responsible for these people or would get the blame for what happened to them, and in either case the Americans would be expected to do something about it. Congress already had proved to be unwilling to change immigration legislation to accommodate the Jews fleeing from Europe, even though their plight had gained sympathy in the United States, so there was little hope that the immigrants from the Balkan and Baltic states would receive any better treatment.[32]

Although Hull, Welles, and Berle were unable to prevent the British from negotiating a treaty recognizing expanded Soviet borders, they did force the arrangement to be public, to be limited to the areas incorporated between 1939 and 1941, and to exclude other possible annexations that might occur as a result of the successful conduct of the war against Germany. The State Department received the British draft of the treaty wherein Eden "explicitly reserved Polish rights as to her frontiers and . . . inserted a specific provision which would permit all inhabitants of the Baltic republics to emigrate . . . if and when the Soviet Union claimed sovereignty over those regions. . . . [Ivan] Maisky had apparently indicated no objection to these two points."[33] Welles was not satisfied with the inclusion of any territorial settlement, but he must have been pleased by the limitations that the British accepted, based on the American complaints.

## *III*

President Roosevelt, aware of the wrangling with the British over their proposed treaty with the USSR, decided to try the direct approach with Stalin. Perhaps a face-to-face meeting could assuage Soviet fears, or possibly getting V. M. Molotov to come to the United States might clear the air. Roosevelt regretted the geographical distances that made it impossible to meet with Stalin at that time, for he thought that personal conversations would be greatly useful in arranging the conduct of the war against Hitler. He proposed a meeting off Alaska for the following summer, if all went well in the war. For the interim, he urged that they try to arrange strategy by close communication that should include sending Molotov to Washington to discuss military strategy "involving the utilization of our armed forces in a manner to relieve your critical western front. This objective carries great weight with me."[34]

In April 1942 the new American ambassador to the Soviet Union, Admiral William H. Standley, met with Stalin and Molotov. He delivered a

[32]*FRUS: Europe, 1942*, pp. 513–16.
[33]Memorandum of conversation between Welles and Halifax, April 22, 1942, ibid., pp. 544–45.
[34]FDR to Stalin, April 4, 1942, ibid., pp. 541–43.

message from FDR appealing for an early meeting with Stalin. He told them that his mission was to sustain and foster the "traditional friendly relations existing between our two countries; and to further in every way possible the policy of President Roosevelt . . . to seek out and remove obstacles to the flow of supplies to Russia."[35] Later, when Ambassador Standley's resignation was accepted, it was partly on the grounds that his work assignment, to expedite supply deliveries to the Soviet Union during the severest phase of the war, had been completed. He knew that this was why he had been selected; nonetheless, he resented petulantly the special missions of Averell Harriman, Davies, Hopkins, and others who left him out of what was going on.

At the beginning of his assignment Standley apologized to the Russians for delays in delivery of supplies and told Stalin that he hoped the Americans could rectify this by the end of April. He asserted that the president had ordered the highest priority for the delivery of materials of war to Russia.[36] The Americans believed they were showing the Russians that they were sincerely trying to meet their commitments and that if there were delays they did not result from lack of effort. The Russians viewed matters differently; if promises were not delivered upon, there had to be some deeper motive, probably one related to an Anglo-American scheme to make them pay a higher cost in the war so that they would not be able really to win it. Certainly they thought the failure to deliver a second front, the failure to send the quantity or quality of supplies needed on the Russian front, and the American obstreperousness in opposing Soviet security demands relating to postwar territorial settlements all were related to American objectives for the postwar world.[37]

Negotiations about postwar arrangements did not go as smoothly as the British thought they might. Anthony Eden reported that the discussions had stalled over Soviet demands concerning the borders of Poland, which contradicted British guarantees to the Poles in 1939. The Russians flatly refused the arrangement suggested by the Americans concerning emigration of residents of the Baltic States and their right to remove personal and other possessions. In addition, the Russians wanted the treaty to keep secret their claims to Finnish and Romanian territory. Eden finally suggested that no mention of this territory should be made, and the Russians modified their extreme demands and withdrew their claims relating to Poland. Concerning

[35]Memorandum of conversation between Standley, Molotov, and Stalin with Soviet interpreter Pavlov, April 23, 1942, Box 1345 A, Moscow 125-704, 1941–1942, 700-1942, Conversations with Soviet Officials, Post Files.

[36]William H. Standley to Hull, April 24, 1942, DSF 740.0011, European War, 1939/212111/2.

[37]This suspicion persists and is still brought up by some Soviet scholars who insist that FDR desired a weakening of Russian power in order to pursue imperial objectives at the expense of the USSR after the war; however, other Soviet scholars disagree with this perspective. Author's notes of the Moscow Colloquium, October 21–23, 1986.

other territories under their domination, only minorities were to be permitted to withdraw to other areas, not the indigenous population; Poles from Lithuania, for example, would be allowed to emigrate. They abandoned their insistence on a secret agreement but asked for a clause stipulating British recognition that Russia had special interests in Finland and Romania. Eden still hoped that this might be avoided. According to Ambassador Winant, it was clear from the outset that Molotov had two interests in mind:

> First, a second front, and second, the treaty proposals. I understand that the British have told him that we (the United States and Great Britain) stand together on the second front issue. . . . I also told them very frankly that I did the best I could to present the Russians' point of view to you and to Mr. Hull, but that you were both definitely opposed to a British-Russian treaty containing agreements on frontiers. . . . [Molotov] told me that he would reconsider the draft treaty and perhaps refrain from making any decision until after he had talked with the President. This was a definite concession, as Molotov had intended to return directly to Moscow from Washington and up to this point they had shown no interest in the draft treaty.[38]

Molotov communicated with his government, that is, with Stalin. In view of the strong American protest against a territorial settlement, he was prepared to discuss Eden's draft treaty excluding those provisions, and he recommended this in light of the president's position.[39] The Russians might abandon the demands made in the treaty for security provisions in Europe only because they believed that this would hasten the opening of the second front on the Continent. The Russians expected quid pro quos to be delivered, or all bets were off.

---

[38]Winant to Hull, May 24, 1942, *FRUS: Europe, 1942*, pp. 559–60.
[39]Winant to Hull, May 25, 1942, ibid., p. 564.

# *IV*

## *Searching for Victory: Demands for a Second Front*

WITH THE STALEMATE OVER the Anglo-Soviet treaty apparently resolved, the Russians and the Americans looked forward to ensuring the settlement of the war with Germany on grounds that would secure an early Allied victory. V. M. Molotov went eagerly to Washington to arrange the opening of a second front, and Roosevelt awaited his arrival as an opportunity to make clear Russia's importance in defeating Hitler. The results were not to be satisfactory for either the Russians or the Americans.

Molotov arrived in Washington on the afternoon of May 29, 1942. He was an unusual guest even for the Roosevelts, who entertained an odd assortment of kings, princes, actors, authors, and other people whom Eleanor or Franklin found interesting. Perhaps the commissar had heard the tales of terrible cuisine served by the president's cook, as he carried a suitcase containing brown bread and sausages. He also carried a pistol; trust in others' security measures was obviously not one of his strong suits. Nor was he all business; Molotov announced immediately that after his meetings he wanted to go on a sight-seeing tour of the Luray Caverns in Virginia.[1]

On the evening of Molotov's arrival, just before dinner, President Roosevelt mixed some of his famous cocktails for the commissar, Harry Hopkins, and the translators, V. N. Pavlov and Professor Samuel Cross from Harvard. They then settled back for a lengthy discussion that included considerations of a postwar order. Winston Churchill had brought up the subject of a postwar association, in effect a revival of the League of Nations, and FDR had told him that this idea was impractical because too many countries would be involved. Instead, it should be the duty of the United States, the Soviet Union, Great Britain, and China (provided the latter achieved a unified government) to act "as the policemen of the world." First, they would have to achieve a general disarmament, but the four of

---

[1]David Brinkley, *Washington Goes to War* (New York: Alfred A. Knopf, 1988), p. 220.

them would retain sufficient armed forces to impose peace and would arrange adequate inspection agreements to prevent secret rearmament such as Hitler had managed.

President Roosevelt laid out his plans in simple terms. If any nation menaced the peace, it could be blockaded; if it still did not acquiesce, it would have to be bombed. FDR wanted a peace that could be guaranteed for twenty-five years. In an unfortunate choice of words, reminiscent of Neville Chamberlain's assertion when he returned from Munich, Roosevelt said that his aim was "peace in our time." The president further explained that other nations might be accepted by the Big Four as fellow guarantors of the peace as they proved their reliability.[2]

Molotov's thoughts on the president's proposals must have been mixed incredulity and happy anticipation. The Russians did not trust international organizations to guarantee their security. Certainly their experience with the League of Nations had not been conducive to such faith. Roosevelt's suggestion of a simple power bloc of victors to ensure their safety from future aggressors had to be appealing. Concerning general disarmament of all except the Big Four, Molotov "observed warmly that the President's ideas for the preservation of mutual peace would be sympathetically viewed by the Soviet government and people." This was certainly an understatement, as the "Soviet government," meaning Stalin, would have welcomed any arrangement that so severely restricted the power to determine world affairs.

Roosevelt cautioned Molotov to remember that there should be no public statements on the Four Policemen concept until after the war, but they and the British should decide among themselves in order to have a policy then. Molotov wondered aloud whether this was Roosevelt's final judgment, and when FDR responded affirmatively Molotov was enthusiastic: The president's proposal was "quite realistic [and] he was in sympathy with it." Roosevelt wanted to have a brand-new approach to world peace, as "the old balance of power theory did not work."[3]

When the president first met with Molotov, they took up immediately the subject that the Russians most wanted to have verified by the Americans, that Hitler was the chief enemy. Roosevelt agreed and recalled his own repeated assertion that it was necessary to remain on the defensive

---

[2]For a discussion of Roosevelt's Wilsonian perspective and his idea for creating a world where popular decisions for peace would replace the selfish government ambitions that led to war see Edward M. Bennett, *Recognition of Russia: An American Foreign Policy Dilemma* (Waltham, MA: Blaisdell, 1970), pp. 133–34.

[3]Conversations at the White House between Roosevelt, Harry Hopkins, and V. M. Molotov, with their interpreters present, Friday, May 29, 1942, *FRUS: Europe, 1942*, pp. 573–74.

in the Pacific until the situation in Europe was under control. Americans had been difficult to persuade, but they had accepted this.[4]

Molotov switched to another item of concern to the Russians, the provisions of the Anglo-Soviet treaty. Roosevelt acknowledged that he was familiar with the treaty and that it was all to the good. He expressed satisfaction that the frontier problem had been left out of the document. He knew that this would have to be dealt with eventually, but there would be better times to present it. Although Molotov and his government disagreed with this perspective, they had bowed to the preferences of the British and Americans. The commissar then broached the Soviet quid pro quo for its agreement to postpone the territorial boundaries issues: the second front. He asserted that the Allies would benefit from launching the second front immediately. If Hitler could be distracted from the Russian front, the Soviets would be able to prepare for a major offensive and strike a decisive blow that would crush the Nazi forces.

Molotov painted a bleak picture of the Russian front, where the balance of forces was "too precarious for comfort." The Germans' mechanized equipment and aviation were superior, and Molotov was not sanguine concerning the summer campaign then under way. If Hitler were permitted to concentrate on the Soviets, he might be able to take Moscow and Rostov and thus control the great resources in food, raw materials, and oil of central Russia. This would mean that the USSR could not continue to exert such pressure as it had on Hitler, and thereafter the brunt of the war would fall on the United States and Great Britain.[5] Obviously, Molotov hoped that the Americans would be fearful enough of the possibility of a Russian collapse that they would rush the second front at all costs. Molotov's approach nearly worked, but, as FDR explained, there simply was not enough materiél or transportation to undertake such an invasion without incurring totally unacceptable losses.[6]

Molotov met with Roosevelt again at the White House, this time accompanied by Ambassador Maxim Litvinov. The president must have shocked Molotov and Litvinov when he asserted that all over the world there were many islands and colonial possessions "which ought, for their own safety, to be taken away from weak nations."[7] He proposed that three to

---

[4]Ibid., p. 567.

[5]Hopkins Papers, Book 5: Molotov Visit, 1942, Hopkins Box 311, Sherwood Collection, FDRL. Hopkins recorded some other points in a separate set of minutes which did not appear in the *FRUS* volume. According to these notes, not only did Molotov spend most of his time at dinner urgently pushing the second front but later he also did the same in greater detail in conversations with General George C. Marshall and Admiral Ernest J. King.

[6]PSF, Diplomatic, Russia, 1942–1943, Box 68, FDRL.

[7]Conversations at the White House between Roosevelt, Hopkins, Molotov, and Maxim Litvinov with their interpreters present, June 1, 1942, *FRUS: Europe, 1942*, pp. 579–80.

five countries should supervise them under the auspices of an international committee. The idea for such "trusteeships" had come from Chiang Kai-shek, and FDR thought it was a good one. Colonialism was dead, and the white nations would not be able to hold nonwhite areas in colonial subjugation; thus, the best thing to do was to move these islands toward nationhood as quickly as possible, as soon as twenty years for some.[8]

On May 31 the president had met with General George C. Marshall, Admiral Ernest J. King, and Harry Hopkins to discuss a final statement that he would make to Molotov. FDR thought that the dangerous situation on the Russian front "required that he . . . make a more specific answer to Molotov in regard to a second front." He had drafted a cable to send off to Churchill proposing an August date for the invasion of France. Marshall said that this "would arouse great resistance on the part of the British," and Hopkins agreed with him. They discussed at length the convoying of equipment to Russia via the northern route and the possible effects of cutting down on these shipments, which would result from preparations for opening the second front.

Hopkins proposed that if the Russians could get the necessary munitions for that year, "such as tanks, airplanes, spare parts, guns and ammunition, that they probably would be quite satisfied if they had definite assurances of 'Bolero' in 1942."[9] To have enough ships to prepare for Bolero, they would have to drop the Archangel supply route to Russia. According to Admiral King, this withdrawal would also then "very substantially relieve the pressure on the British Home Fleet and make more destroyers available for the Atlantic convoy." Hopkins thought that General Marshall believed that Bolero was "inevitable sometime in 1942 merely by the force of circumstances." FDR told Hopkins to draft a cable to the "Former Naval Person," as Churchill sometimes signed himself, and it was then sent.[10]

Roosevelt told the Russians that they could still expect the second front in 1942. Molotov had apparently asked for more supplies, and FDR wanted him to know that the Russians could not have both a second front and increased shipments. The Soviets "could not eat their cake and have it too." Molotov responded, with what Cross described as "deliberate sarcasm," that the second front would be stronger if the first front held fast. Molotov wondered what would happen to the Soviet Union if it cut down its requirements and no second front opened.[11]

---

[8]Ibid.

[9]"Bolero" was the code name given to the planned buildup of American forces and supplies in Great Britain in preparation for Operation Roundup, the name given initially to the planned attack on the French coast commencing the second front.

[10]Memorandum, May 31, 1942, Hopkins Papers, Box 136, Molotov File, FDRL.

[11]Ibid.

On June 11, 1942, a joint communiqué avoided naming a specific date but did confirm that "full understanding was reached with regard to the urgent task of creating a second front in Europe in 1942." There it was in writing, a promise to deliver the second front in 1942, which the Russians were not going to let the Americans forget. Postwar security was mentioned only vaguely, in a discussion of "fundamental problems of co-operation of the Soviet Union and the United States in safeguarding peace and security to the freedom-loving peoples after the war." The signatories of the communiqué assured the world that the two governments were interested in pursuing "the common objectives of the United Nations."[12]

Harry Hopkins assessed the results of the meeting for Ambassador John G. Winant the day after the press release. The Russian had gotten along "famously" with the president, "and I am sure that we at least bridged one more gap between ourselves and Russia." There was still a long way to go, "but it must be done if there is ever to be any real peace in the world." The United States and Great Britain could not organize the world between themselves "without bringing the Russians in as equal partners." If things went well for Chiang Kai-shek, then China also must be included. "The day of the policy of the 'white man's burden' are [*sic*] over. Vast masses of people simply are not going to tolerate it and for the life of me I can't see why they should." Concerning the second front, Hopkins thought that some of the British were holding back a bit, but it was moving along as well as could be expected.[13]

Despite Molotov's pessimistic report on the desperate situation on the Russian front, FDR's optimism returned. In a conversation with Henry Morgenthau on June 16, FDR explained that "the whole question of whether we win or lose the war depends upon the Russians." If they held out that summer, tying down 3.5 million Germans, victory was probable. He thought Japan would definitely attack the USSR in Siberia within a few weeks, but this would not disturb him if the Russians handled the situation properly by giving up Vladivostok and gradually withdrawing. "Siberia is a big country and supposing they do retreat 500 miles or more, what of it?" Japanese forces had just attacked the Aleutian Islands, but he was convinced this had less to do with an assault on Alaska than with a drive on Siberia.[14]

FDR tried to convince Stalin that the Aleutian campaign was directed against the Russians and that perhaps they should pay more attention to the Pacific war. The Americans wanted access to Siberian air bases, where it would be easier for them to strike at Japan's productive capacity, but the

---

[12]Press release, June 11, 1942, Hopkins Papers, Book 5: Molotov Visit, FDRL.

[13]Hopkins to John G. Winant, June 12, 1942, Hopkins Papers, Book 5: Molotov Visit, no. 13, FDRL.

[14]Morgenthau Diaries, June 16, 1942, p. 1131, Morgenthau Papers, FDRL.

Russians had resisted these requests on grounds of their neutrality agreement
with Japan. If they could be convinced that Japan was about to violate that
treaty, then the Siberian bases might be opened, providing an alternative
route to get equipment to the Red Army for its drive against the Germans.[15]

A threat from Japan was still not of uppermost concern to the
Russians, and if Roosevelt thought that a possibility of an attack would
cause any change in Stalin's strategy he was mistaken. Ambassador
William H. Standley made this quite clear in a dispatch of June 22, 1942.
The Soviet press was harping on the second front issue, and Soviet citizens
persistently reminded Standley and his staff that there was a definite
commitment to cross the Channel during the current year. Standley
cautioned that

> in view of the manner in which the Soviet Government and people have
> accepted what would appear here to be a solemn obligation on the part
> of the United States and Great Britain to create a second front in 1942, I
> feel convinced that if such a front does not materialize quickly and on a
> large scale, these people will be so deluded in their belief in our
> sincerity of purpose and will for concerted action that inestimable harm
> will be done to the cause of the United Nations.[16]

This may have been the most perceptive dispatch Standley forwarded during
his tenure in Moscow. Despite all of the reasons against launching an attack
on the Continent, the Russians placed their faith in the pledge for an
invasion in 1942, and future cooperation from them might depend on
whether the invasion materialized.

In London, Ambassador Winant asked the British if their negotiations
with the Soviets had improved their relations. Their replies were
emphatically affirmative. Clark Kerr told Winant that Molotov had returned
to Russia "apparently a 'new man.' " The deputy undersecretary of state in
the British Foreign Office, Sir Orme Sargent, was convinced that much of
the Russians' suspicion resulted from their ignorance of the outside world.
He touted the "educational value" of Molotov's trips to London and
Washington. The "reception accorded him in both capitals must prove
helpful in dissipating Russia's anti-foreign complex." The marked change
in the attitude of the Russian military authorities toward the British military
mission was a clear example of this beneficial effect: The Russians began
"to lift the veil of deep secrecy with which they have hitherto shrouded
practically every military problem in which the British have shown
interest."[17]

[15]FDR to Stalin, June 19, 1942, *FRUS: Europe, 1942*, pp. 598–99.
[16]William H. Standley to Cordell Hull, June 22, 1942, ibid., p. 598.
[17]Winant to Hull, June 23, 1942, ibid., pp. 598–99.

## *II*

Roosevelt prepared a memorandum for Hopkins, General Marshall, and Admiral King that laid out the items to be considered at the conference in London at which they were to discuss the second front and other issues. They were to investigate carefully the prospects for beginning Operation Sledgehammer, the cross-Channel assault, before the end of the year. The negotiators should "strongly urge immediate all-out preparations for it, that it be pushed with utmost vigor, and that it be executed whether or not Russian collapse becomes imminent." In fact, the disintegration of the Russian front would be all the more reason to put Allied troops in action on the Continent. The prime purpose of the operation was to divert German air forces from the Russian front.[18]

Roosevelt ordered his emissaries to inform him immediately if they thought that Operation Sledgehammer would be impossible to implement in 1942. If this were the case, they were to ensure that American troops were committed somewhere else before the end of the year. Whatever happened, they must remember the importance of the Middle East (that is, Egypt and the Suez Canal, Syria and the Mosul oil fields) and access to Persian Gulf oil. If Germany controlled the Middle East, the Nazis and the Japanese together could cause the loss of access to the Indian Ocean and the interdiction of trade in vital materials through Tunis, Algiers, Morocco, and Dakar, which would cut off ferry traffic through Freetown and Liberia.

Hopkins, Marshall, and King were to resist pressure to pursue an all-out attack in the Pacific to defeat Japan as quickly as possible. The main front was still in Europe, and they were not to forget this. Defeating Japan would not mean the defeat of Germany, but if Germany were to go down Japan would follow. He reminded them whom the order was from in his broader capacity: His signature line was "COMMANDER-IN-CHIEF."[19]

President Roosevelt was obviously impressed by the Russians' assertions that their ability to stay in the war depended on relief from the pressure on their front. Ambassador Standley reinforced this perception; contrary to the situation two months earlier, when the Soviet press had asked where the vaunted German spring offensive was, "now the press stresses the seriousness of the military situation, and states that it is a matter of the life or death of the Soviet state."[20]

---

[18]FDR to Hopkins, Marshall, and King, July 16, 1942, Hopkins Papers, Sherwood Collection, Book 5: London Conference, FDRL. Sledgehammer was the name given to the plan for a hastily assembled force of about 150,000 men who would be thrown into France in 1942, and probably sacrificed, in order to prevent a Soviet collapse.

[19]FDR to Hopkins, Marshall, and King, July 16, 1942, Hopkins Papers, Sherwood Collection, Book 5: London Conference, FDRL.

[20]Memorandum, Recent Trends in the Soviet Press, July 24, 1942, Box 1347B, Moscow, 880-121.8, Public Press, Post Files.

Stalin was furious at the curtailment of deliveries because of heavy shipping losses and the delays in opening Sledgehammer, and he expressed his feelings bitterly to Churchill. The prime minister became so worried about Stalin's attitude that he felt that he should go to Russia and speak to Stalin personally. Roosevelt, unable to make the trip himself, sent W. Averell Harriman along, perhaps to keep Churchill from doing anything that might undermine American policy (as the British had attempted in the issue of territorial settlement with the Russians). FDR also sent Churchill some galling advice on how to get along with the Soviet dictator. The prime minister should remember Stalin's personality and the dangers he confronted: "I think we should attempt to put ourselves in his place, for no one whose country has been invaded can be expected to approach the war from a world point of view."[21] This was rather like a new recruit telling his sergeant how to drill the troops.

Churchill, accompanied by Harriman, Ambassador Sir Stafford Cripps, and the interpreters, met with Stalin, Molotov, and Marshal Klementi Voroshilov for four hours on August 12. The prime minister pronounced the first two hours "bleak and sombre." He asked for plain speaking between friends, and that is what the Russians gave him. They assailed the British for their reluctance to begin Operation Sledgehammer. Churchill explained with maps and with arguments why they could not launch the assault. After two hours of wrangling, Stalin "finally . . . said he did not accept our view but we had the right to decide." Churchill tried to get the Soviet leader to focus on Operation Roundup, the larger invasion plan for the Continent, which Stalin "passed over too lightly because it was remote and there were great difficulties in landing anywhere outside fighter cover." They then switched to the "ruthless bombing of Germany." Stalin wanted the morale of the Germans to be struck hard.[22]

Churchill next discussed Operation Torch, the planned attack in North Africa. This operation was meant partly to bring Vichy France to its senses and partly to swing the Free French forces in Africa into genuine action.

---

[21]Quoted in Burns, *Soldier of Freedom*, p. 236.

[22]Stalin and his generals desperately wanted air attacks on Berlin. They were so concerned about this that the first Russian military mission, in Washington to order Lend-Lease equipment in August 1941, put a few B-17 bombers first on their priority list. G. F. Bajdukov, a member of the mission, said that FDR was surprised and wanted to know why they made such a request when strategic bombers would be less helpful to them than fighter aircraft. Bajdukov answered that they would raise Russian morale and demoralize the Germans by hitting Berlin, and the Russians had no planes capable of doing this. Author's notes, Moscow Colloquium, October 21–23, 1986. This was the Soviet flyer's second visit to the White House; he had been copilot on the Tchkalov transpolar flight, which landed at Vancouver, Washington, on June 21, 1937. Roosevelt received the crew in order to imply an improvement in U.S.-Soviet relations. General George Marshall was commander at the military base, and the Russian fliers stayed with him. See Edward M. Bennett, "The Diplomatic Significance of the Trans-Polar Flight from the Soviet Union to the USA, of June 1937," *Soviet Journal of Modern and Contemporary History* 3 (1988): 42–46.

The Russians seemed more interested than might have been expected, and, according to the interpreter, Stalin said: "May God prosper this undertaking." Stalin warmed to the subject and expressed four positive reasons for launching this campaign: It would hit Rommel in the rear, impress the Spanish, set the Germans and the French to fighting in France, and "expose Italy to the whole brunt of the war." Churchill was pleased by Stalin's instant grasp of the importance of the invasion, but he added a fifth reason: to shorten the supply route through the Mediterranean.[23]

Despite efforts to persuade Stalin that a second front unsecured by adequate transport and air cover would be more harmful than helpful, the Soviet leader was not convinced. In an aide-mémoire handed to the Americans and the British, the Russians again accused them of downgrading the Russian front and not living up to their commitments. The British countered with their own note assuring their ally that this was not the case. It would be foolhardy to waste 150,000 or more troops and attendant supplies on a Sledgehammer adventure that was sure to fail, while the much safer North African campaign could relieve the German pressure on Russia.[24] They parted with unaltered mutual suspicions concerning motives and sincerity.

## III

Polish Americans and the Polish government in London inundated the British and U.S. governments with requests for action to force the Kremlin to release Poles in Russian-occupied territory for combat duty or for emigration to Iran or South Africa. The Americans and British tried to convince the Russians to let the Polish military forces in Russia join the fighting, but the Kremlin countered that, although these troops had been armed and trained by the USSR, they seemed reluctant to enter the war actively. According to a memorandum from the American embassy at Kuibyshev, the Polish government-in-exile contended that the Russians were keeping these units from fighting, the Poles were being mistreated, and Polish officials were being prevented from maintaining contact with their citizens. The author of the memorandum asserted that the Russian government had indeed prevented such contact and had attempted to wreck the Polish organization in Russia set up for purposes of maintaining the liaison. He agreed with the Polish ambassador to Russia, however, that protests only made matters worse.[25]

---

[23]"Former Naval Person" to FDR, August 14, 1942, Hopkins Papers, Sherwood Collection, Book 5: Harriman, Churchill in Moscow, August 1942, Box 311, FDRL.

[24]Ibid.

[25]Unsigned memorandum, "Steps taken by the American Embassy in Kuibyshev with view towards Improving Soviet-Polish Relations," 1942, after September 10 and before September 16, Box 1346A, Moscow, 711 Polish-Soviet Relations, Post Files.

This pressure only made Stalin more suspicious of American objectives. The Russians viewed the Poles in light of their refusal to accept any arrangements in the late 1930s that might have allowed the Soviet Union to come to Czechoslovakia's aid during the Munich crisis. They also remembered Colonel Joseph Beck's fraternization with the Nazis when Beck headed the Polish foreign office. Although the execution of thousands of Polish officers in the Katyn Forest was not revealed until April 1943, if the Soviets perpetrated this atrocity (as has been commonly accepted in the West), they were not likely to allow too much Western contact with Poles in Russia.[26]

A virtual parade of Roosevelt "troubleshooters" passed through Moscow in 1942, including General Patrick Hurley, the U.S. minister to New Zealand, in October. Soviet suspicions and anger about Roosevelt's special emissaries became evident when Hurley called on Litvinov before his departure for the Soviet Union. Hurley found Litvinov in "a rather truculent and critical mood, pointing out that Mr. Willkie,[27] Ambassador Standley, the Military Attaché, and the Naval Attaché to Moscow were all coming home and wondering why, with all this wealth of reporting imminent, anyone else should have to go to Russia." Litvinov wondered what else about Russia the Americans might need to know. Hurley reported that he gave as good as he received and left Litvinov in a better mood.[28]

After the successful launching of the North African campaign, Stalin seemed to let up a little on the second front issue. He sent congratulations to FDR for the success of the effort and commented on his meeting with Hurley: "I had with General Hurley a long conversation regarding questions of strategy. It seemed to me that he understood me and was convinced regarding the correctness of the strategy now followed by the Allies."[29] This probably referred to Roosevelt's explanation to Stalin that he wanted Hurley to visit so that Stalin could make him understand the Europe-first orientation of Allied strategy. In another dispatch of the same date, Hurley related Stalin's effort to soft-pedal his previous obstreperousness on the

---

[26]For details of the Soviet response to the German charges that the Russians had perpetrated the massacre at Katyn Forest and the effect of the affair on Polish-Soviet and Allied-Soviet relations see Harriman and Abel, *Special Envoy*, pp. 199, 200, 206, 301–2, 318, 349.

[27]Wendell Willkie went to the USSR in September 1942 to act as a goodwill ambassador and got in trouble by accepting Soviet tales of a British plot to delay the second front, which he repeated when he arrived home. See memorandum, Isador Lubin to Harry Hopkins on Willkie's trip, October 30, 1942, Hopkins Papers, Sherwood Collection, Book 5: Lubin, FDRL; Loy W. Henderson to Hull, October 19, 1942, Box 1345B Moscow 711, Post Files; memorandum by Standley attached to a cover letter to Hull, October 24, 1941, *FRUS: Europe, 1942*, p. 639.

[28]Memorandum by William Moreland, Jr., of the office of the Secretary of State, October 8, 1942, *FRUS: Europe, 1942*, p. 654.

[29]Molotov to Henderson, November 15, 1942, ibid., p. 660.

second front issue, perhaps fearing that there was some plan afoot to shift emphasis to the Pacific:

> His first sentence on the subject under discussion was to the effect that you had adopted the correct and the most effective strategy. He stressed the imperative need of creating a reserve in Russia to justify Russia in assuming the offensive. He referred again to the necessity for a second front in Europe *eventually*, but agreed fully on the effectiveness of the opening of what he referred to as another front in Africa.[30]

Whatever Stalin's motive for telling Hurley that he appreciated Roosevelt's grasp of the necessary strategy, the Soviet leader had not changed his mind on the need for a second front. He simply accepted that there was not going to be one in 1942; the next step would be to arrange for it as soon as possible.

## *IV*

President Roosevelt decided that long-range communication with Stalin had its uses, but a face-to-face meeting might better disabuse the Russian leader of his suspicions concerning Allied sincerity in helping Russia to defeat Hitler. Therefore, in a dispatch of December 5, Roosevelt proposed an early meeting with Stalin, "sometime around January 15."[31] Although Roosevelt certainly had considered such a meeting before, the trigger for this decision was a memorandum written by General James H. Burns summarizing the importance of the relationship with Russia: "We not only need Russia as a powerful fighting ally in order to defeat Germany but eventually we will also need her in a similar role to defeat Japan. And finally, we need her as a real friend and customer in the post-war world."[32] Burns tried to convince Harry Hopkins, to whom the memorandum was addressed, that the United States needed Soviet help in the Pacific war. The step-by-step plan for reaching Tokyo required not only the capture of the Pacific islands along the way but also "large scale bombing attacks . . . which will have as their target the very heart of the Japanese Empire and the source of its strength."[33] Bombing raids from Siberia were the most direct way to hit Japan. This was one of the few times that Burns's views corresponded with Department of State policy.

---

[30]Henderson to Hull, personal to the president from Patrick Hurley, November 15, 1942, ibid., p. 657, emphasis added.

[31]Henderson to Molotov, December 5, 1942, transmittal of a message from FDR of December 2, 1942, ibid., p. 666.

[32]Memorandum, James H. Burns to Hopkins, "Importance of Soviet Relationships and Suggestions for Improving Them," December 1, 1942, Hopkins Papers, Sherwood Collection, Book 5: Russia, FDRL.

[33]Ibid.

The remainder of his memorandum, however, was less likely to gain agreement in the State Department. Burns reminded Hopkins that after victory over the Axis powers the Soviet Union would emerge as one of the three most powerful nations in the world. If there were to be peace in the postwar era, "we should be real friends so that we can help shape world events in such a way as to provide security and prosperity." How to achieve all of these aims was the question, and Burns tried to answer it. First, it would be necessary to "arrange for a conference between the President and Mr. Stalin at some appropriate time and place." Next, he thought that the top military leaders of the United States—Marshall, King, and Henry H. "Hap" Arnold—should go to Russia and "discuss freely our plans, our capabilities and our limitations." This would establish a "better spirit of 'Comrades-in-Arms.' "[34]

In a direct slam at Ambassador Standley, Burns suggested that the United States should send to the Soviet Union "an ambassador of top rank as to national standing, vision, ability and willingness to serve the country first." And, with an eye toward stopping some obvious caviling about the Russians, he suggested that a general policy should be established and enforced "throughout all U.S. departments and agencies that Russia must be considered as a real friend and be treated accordingly and that personnel must be assigned to Russian contacts that are loyal to this concept."[35]

Stalin's response to Roosevelt's invitation was that a meeting was impossible at that time, because the winter campaign would probably not diminish in January: "More probably the contrary will be true."[36] Stalin, however, did raise the hopes of the Americans that their efforts to win his confidence might be succeeding. Loy Henderson informed the Department of State on the first anniversary of Pearl Harbor that the tone of the Soviet press and radio during the preceding month was such "as to influence the Soviet population to have a more friendly feeling towards the United States and Great Britain, in particular toward the United States." In a speech of November 6, Stalin emphasized the importance of the "fighting alliance" between the United States, Great Britain, and the USSR and that he was pleased with the new front in Africa which, while it was not *the* second front, was nonetheless a prelude to it.[37]

Henderson complained to Cordell Hull about the dangerous precedent being established, of bypassing the department in important matters relating to the ongoing role of the foreign service in America's Russian policy. The embassy learned what FDR's special missions were doing and saying only indirectly, and it had no control over their approaches to the Russians.

[34]Ibid.
[35]Ibid.
[36]Stalin to FDR, December 5, 1942, *FRUS: Europe, 1942*, p. 666.
[37]Henderson to Hull, December 7, 1942, DSF 861.9111/369.

Because of this, the embassy did not know what it should report concerning the Churchill-Harriman mission or the Willkie visit. Henderson cautioned that

> since some of these missions negotiate or discuss matters which may vitally affect present and future relations between the United States and the Soviet Union, it would appear that unless [you are] informed of what they are doing the Department may have difficulty in making decisions with regard to current problems of American-Soviet relations in full consonance with the activities in which some of these special missions are engaged.[38]

The chargé reminded Hull that President Roosevelt and Stalin were exchanging messages about American-Soviet relations through the naval attaché, who gave the embassy paraphrases of these communications for transmission to Stalin via Molotov. Stalin's replies were sent through Molotov to Litvinov for transmission to FDR. Molotov then gave the embassy copies of his communiqués to Litvinov. The Department of State was informed so indirectly of what was going on that perhaps Hull did not know at all.[39]

FDR responded to Stalin's refusal to meet with him by expressing his "deep" disappointment that such a meeting could not take place, because there were many matters of "vital importance" which they should discuss. These matters included what should be done when German defeat permitted considerations of the "future policies about North Africa and the Far East which cannot be discussed by our military people alone." FDR proposed that they should try to meet in North Africa around March 1.[40] On December 13, Stalin suggested that they set an agenda of items that might be important to deal with in an exchange of letters. He wanted Roosevelt to follow up on the promises "with regard to the opening of the second front in Europe which were given by you, Mr. President, and by Mr. Churchill in relation to the year 1942, and now in any case with respect to the spring of 1943." In contrast to his earlier position, Stalin agreed with the Allied policy of trying to bring the Vichy French into line against the Axis forces. He wanted to discount rumors concerning Soviet opposition to such plans.[41]

Litvinov and Standley engaged in a sparring match concerning both strategic planning for the remainder of the war and the prospects for postwar cooperation between the two powers. Standley promised that when he returned home he would devote his time "to the further development of the

---

[38]Henderson to Hull, December 8, 1941, *FRUS: Europe, 1942*, p. 667.
[39]Ibid., pp. 667–68.
[40]Henderson to Molotov, December 10, 1942, transmittal of a message from FDR to Stalin, ibid., p. 675.
[41]Stalin to FDR, December 13, 1942, ibid., pp. 675–76.

existing friendly relations between our countries with the idea that that was necessary to the winning of the war and that I thought that the cooperation of our two countries when this war was over was one of the most vital matters in post-war readjustment." Litvinov asked the ambassador what he thought would be the most important obstacles in American-Soviet relations. Standley said that Soviet territorial objectives, including claims to the Baltic States and parts of Romania and Poland, comprised a major obstacle, and Soviet reluctance to enter the Pacific war was another. Litvinov reiterated Stalin's statement that the Russian people wanted to cooperate with the peoples of the rest of the world, and he did not bother to respond to the gibe about fighting Japan. Ambassador Standley was sure that Stalin's assurance was sincere "and that any differences could be ironed out around the conference table, provided of course the countries went into the conference with a cooperative spirit, making satisfactory concessions."[42] What the Soviet perception of "cooperation" and "concessions" meant and what Standley thought they meant were worlds apart.

Quid pro quos abounded in the efforts of the Russian and American leaders to fathom each other's wartime and postwar policy positions during 1942. Obviously, the Russians perceived the second front as the basic guarantee of the "sincerity" of their allies, while guarantees of their borders were preeminent among their considerations for postwar "cooperation." The Americans desired Russian trust, but they were not inclined to commit themselves to an operation in continental Europe that they considered suicidal and nonproductive. They wanted the Soviet Union to prove its loyalty to the cause of victory by making a commitment to enter the Pacific war, if not immediately, then as soon as German defeat was assured. They prodded the Russians to show good faith by postponing territorial considerations until a postwar peace conference.

President Roosevelt, in his final dispatch to Stalin of 1942, reiterated his main considerations. He desired Russian military planning cooperation, promised delivery of aircraft to the Caucasus front, and assured Stalin that General Omar Bradley would be authorized to deal with military coordination. Roosevelt again tried to convince the Russians that they were not immune to a Japanese attack, which the president was sure would come sooner or later, and he offered Bradley's assistance to arrange delivery of aircraft and supplies for this eventuality. The president did not respond at this time to Stalin's appeal to name a date for launching the second front.[43] Suspicions and charges of bad faith declined toward the end of the year, but

---

[42]Standley memorandum of a luncheon interview with Litvinov, December 14, 1942, Box 1345A, Moscow, 700-1942, Conversations with Soviet Officials, Record Group 84, Post Files, National Archives and Federal Records Center, Suitland, Maryland.

[43]FDR to Stalin, December 30, 1942, transmitted via a dispatch of January 1, 1943, *FRUS: Europe, 1942*, pp. 683–84.

they were still under the surface, ready to reemerge if mutual promises remained unfulfilled.

# V

## Soft Promises and Hard Lines: American-Soviet Sparring

ALTHOUGH FDR PREFERRED to meet with Stalin and worried about alienating him if the president got together with Winston Churchill, Roosevelt agreed to meet with the British prime minister when Stalin once again declined. Churchill was convinced that the Russians had only one conference subject in mind: a cross-Channel invasion of France. He did not want the military staffs of the three powers to decide this issue without a meeting between himself and Roosevelt.[1] The meeting at Casablanca thus was arranged, without Russian participation.

At a conference with the Joint Chiefs of Staff at the White House on January 7, 1943, the president asked George Marshall if he did not believe that it would be a good idea for the general to go to Moscow. Marshall, puzzled, asked what he might be expected to accomplish there. Roosevelt responded that such a visit would lift Russian morale. Because Stalin had been unable to accept the two invitations to consult with Churchill and Roosevelt, the Russian leader "probably felt out of the picture . . . and . . . has a feeling of loneliness."[2]

With Harry Hopkins in tow, Roosevelt left Washington for Casablanca, where he and Churchill intended to plan the next phase of the war with their military and political advisers. After extensive meetings among Roosevelt, Churchill, and their staffs, the president and the prime minister sent the bad news to Stalin. The second front would be delayed once again. Roosevelt commented prophetically: "To win this war, we have been forced into a strategic compromise which will most certainly offend the Russians."[3] They

---

[1]Winston Churchill to FDR, December 12, 1942, *FRUS: Diplomatic Papers, Conferences at Washington, 1941–1942, and Casablanca, 1943* (Washington, DC: Government Printing Office, 1968), p. 500.

[2]Joint Chiefs of Staff minutes of a meeting at the White House, January 7, 1943, ibid., pp. 506–7.

[3]Elliott Roosevelt, *As He Saw It* (New York: Duell, Sloan, & Pearce, 1946), p. 109.

thought that they might mollify Stalin with the announcement at Casablanca of the unconditional surrender principle.[4]

On March 16, Stalin wrote them that Operation Husky, the planned invasion of Sicily, was not an adequate substitute for the frontal attack on the Continent. He warned "of the grave danger with which delay in opening a Second Front is fraught."[5] Shortly thereafter, the Red Army began to curtail its offensive operations, and Churchill feared the possibility of a separate peace.[6] Stalin further showed his displeasure by "curtly" informing Marshall that he "would not be welcome" in Moscow after the Casablanca Conference.[7]

# II

Joseph Davies met with Elbridge Durbrow, a Soviet expert in the State Department, to explain his concern over a possible disintegration of American-Soviet relations. Davies worried that the British were trying in every way to win Soviet favor. They even were willing to make territorial concessions which, if the United States opposed them, would leave the Americans facing the combined power of their two allies. This may have been Roosevelt's fear as well, and it might account for the posture he assumed later, when he, Churchill, and Stalin met. The president often sided with Stalin and used the British prime minister as his foil. In FDR's view, this had two advantages: It would persuade Stalin that there was no Anglo-Saxon combination against him, and it would prevent the Russian-British united front that Davies feared.

Davies reminded Durbrow that the Russians considered certain east European territories vital to their security and would not back down on their demand for them. Durbrow disagreed with Davies's analysis. Although the Russians emphasized their strategic importance, he dismissed these areas cavalierly: There were no strategic frontiers of significance to the Russians between the Rhine and the Ural Mountains, and the same was true of the Baltic ports, which after all provided access to an inland sea.[8] Davies sought

---

[4]Hopkins Diary, January 24, 1943, Hopkins Papers, Box 330, Casablanca File, FDRL.

[5]Stalin to Churchill and Roosevelt, January 20, 1943, Union of Soviet Socialist Republics, Ministry of Foreign Affairs, *Correspondence between the Chairman of the Council of Ministers of the U.S.S.R. and the Presidents of the U.S.A. and the Prime Ministers of Great Britain during the Great Patriotic War of 1941–1945*, 2 vols. (New York: E. P. Dutton, 1958), 1:89 (hereafter cited as *Correspondence*); Stalin to Churchill and Roosevelt, March 16, 1943, 2:59, ibid.

[6]Vojtech Mastny, *Russia's Road to the Cold War* (New York: Columbia University Press, 1979), pp. 74–85.

[7]Leonard Mosley, *Marshall: Hero for Our Times* (New York: Hearst Books, 1982), pp. 229–30.

[8]*FRUS: Diplomatic Papers*, vol. 3, *British Commonwealth, Eastern Europe, Far East, 1943* (Washington, DC: Government Printing Office, 1963), pp. 500–505.

an arrangement that was unavoidable if the United States wanted to get along with the USSR after the war. Durbrow and the group he represented opposed this kind of realism, unless it could be arranged within the bounds of the principles that had always underlain American foreign policy. If the Russians could not accept this, then security was not really their objective; they must be bent on expansion. These conflicting points of view were not confined within a single executive department of the government; soon they would crop up everywhere.

The struggle in the United States over the nature of Soviet territorial claims was recognized in the Soviet Union. On February 9, Ambassador William H. Standley relayed a *Pravda* story attacking an American journalist, Constantine Brown, for "playing into the hands of German propagandists." Brown had charged in an article in the *Washington Star* that the Soviet Union intended after the war to launch an annexationist policy in both the Far East and Europe. Brown identified Soviet expansionist interests in Bulgaria, Yugoslavia, and Czechoslovakia, as well as a sphere of influence reaching through Iran to the Persian Gulf and a desire to retake Bessarabia. David Zaslavski, who wrote the *Pravda* article, compared the statement about Bessarabia to someone saying that the United States claimed the right to retake California, as the territory was, like the Baltic States, already a part of the USSR. Zaslavski reasserted Stalin's statement of November 9, 1942, that Russia had no interest in taking other's territory.[9]

The U.S. military attaché in Moscow, Brigadier General Joseph A. Michela, conjectured that "the Soviets intend to push their claims in Europe, even to the extent of resorting to armed force, the day the war with Germany ends." To prove his point he cited several indications that the Russians planned to continue military action after the Germans were defeated. All the evidence pointed to Soviet intentions to exercise "as much influence and control as possible throughout the world and definitely in Europe." The time had come to get tough with the Russians.[10]

On February 24, Michela pursued this theme further. He called the attention of his superiors to a series of press articles, emanating from the Ukraine, attacking Polish writers abroad who demanded wider Polish boundaries after the war, including areas already taken by the Russians inside their 1941 borders. "They have great significance and indicate quite clearly that the Soviets will permit no free Baltic States; there will be no release of Polish territory occupied as of June 1, 1941; no release of Bessarabia. We might well add that there will be no withdrawal of troops from Iran, and that

---

[9]William Standley to Cordell Hull, February 9. 1943, Box 1350B, Moscow 710-1943, Post Files. November 9, 1942, was the date mentioned in the dispatch, although in fact he said this on November 6, 1941.
[10]Military attaché report, "Comments on Current Events No. 105," February 18, 1943, EE 273, ibid.

there will be strong demands against Finland."[11] Michela played a role in determining the attitude of his superiors in the army, or at least reflected an attitude common to many of them. They opposed cooperation on the supply issue, development of the second front at an earlier date, and any effort to reach accommodation on Soviet security needs.

Averell Harriman thought that postwar Russian economic requirements could be used to make the Russians conform to American expectations. Economic aid should be used to influence political action "compatible with our principles." If the Russians balked, there should be no compunction about cooperating with Great Britain without the Soviet Union.[12] This very clear exposition of the advantages of dollar diplomacy was similar to Charles Evans Hughes's idea during the 1920s that America need not engage in entangling alliances to have its way in the world; it had the economic power to influence political events. In a sense this idea was a precursor of the Marshall Plan.

## *III*

While certain army officers and some members of the Department of State suspected Russian objectives and schemed to thwart their plans, Franklin Roosevelt, Anthony Eden, and Harry Hopkins discussed the prospects for getting along with the Russians after the war at dinner in the White House on March 14. As Hopkins recalled it, the conversation centered around a detailed assessment of the postwar geographic problems of Europe. Eden surmised that the Russians were central to postwar policies and that they had two different plans up their sleeves: The preferred course was to cooperate with the Americans and the British; the other required going it alone in an adversary role. They probably leaned toward cooperation, because Stalin was not prepared to face the implications of Russian control over Europe. Hopkins asked what the Russians would demand at the peace conference. Eden said that the minimum demands would include incorporation of the Baltic States to ensure Soviet security. The Russian leader would use the plebiscites of 1939 to legitimize incorporation of Estonia, Latvia, and Lithuania.

Roosevelt feared that this would "meet with a good deal of resistance in the United States and England." He realized that the Russian armies would possess the disputed territories and that "none of us can force them to get out." It seemed to FDR that the only course was to ask the Russians for a new plebiscite. Eden presumed, correctly, that this would be unacceptable to Stalin. Roosevelt countered that he knew the Allies might have to agree to

---

[11]Military attaché report, "Comments on Current Events No. 107," February 24, 1943, EE 274, ibid.
[12]W. Averell Harriman to Hull, March 13, 1943, DSF 861.01/2320.

absorption, but they should use their acquiescence to gain other concessions from the Russians. Eden turned to Finland, where the boundary drawn up at the end of World War I would approximate Russian territorial demands. Roosevelt agreed that this was not unreasonable. They also affirmed that Bessarabia was traditionally Russian, so there should be no argument about Soviet demands there.[13]

Concerning Poland, Eden guessed that Stalin would ask only for the Curzon Line as the Soviet boundary and that he wanted a strong Poland, provided that the right people were in control there. Roosevelt saw problems with this, as there might be a liberal government in Poland at the time of the peace, but it could be thrown out within a year. Eden predicted that the Poles would create problems in part because they had large ambitions which they did not attempt to hide, and their leadership in London was not easy to deal with in this regard. The Poles were convinced that Russia would be weakened by the war and that German power would be virtually eliminated; as a result, Poland would emerge as the most powerful state in that part of the world. Eden condemned this dream as unrealistic. Roosevelt, Hopkins, and he agreed that Poland should have East Prussia. The Russians acknowledged this privately but would not say so to the Poles, who would then want to use it as a bargaining instrument at the peace table. Roosevelt decided that the big powers would have to determine what Poland would get; he did not intend to go to the peace table and bargain with it or the other small states. Polish borders would have to satisfy the Russians on the one hand and keep Germany under control on the other.[14]

According to Eden, the most important thing they had to agree on was Germany. Would they deal with the country as it existed, or would they break it up into smaller states? Eden contended that Stalin's deep-seated distrust of the Germans would lead him to insist on a divided Germany. FDR did not want to make the same mistake that French Premier Georges Clemenceau had made at Versailles by supporting an arbitrary division; instead, they should encourage the ambitions that would spring up within Germany for a separatist movement "and, in effect, approve of a division which represents German public opinion." Hopkins interrupted: What would they do if there were no separatist movement? Roosevelt and Eden agreed that then Germany would have to be divided in such a way as to ensure that Prussia was a separate state. "The Prussians cannot be permitted to dominate all Germany." Eden proclaimed that, despite the feelings of some of the Russians, Stalin wanted both British and American troops to be present in large numbers in Europe when the collapse came.[15]

---

[13]Memorandum of March 15 by Harry Hopkins of dinner conversation at the White House, March 14, 1943, *FRUS: British Commonwealth, 1943*, pp. 13–14.
   [14]Ibid., pp. 14–15.
   [15]Ibid., pp. 16–17.

When Eden, Lord Halifax, and Sumner Welles met on March 16, the British foreign secretary wanted to discuss Russia more specifically. President Roosevelt had asked him if there were anything to William C. Bullitt's thesis that the Russians were determined to dominate all of Europe by force of arms or by Communist propaganda. Eden did not think that this was the Soviet plan, and he had told the president that the wisest course was to cultivate Soviet friendship and confidence in the Allies in order to pave the way for postwar international cooperation and to avoid "in every way possible" hostility toward the USSR. He reiterated this position to Welles.[16]

Obviously, the Americans understood Soviet ambitions and tried to discover a means of satisfying them within a collective security arrangement that would allay Russian fears of again being encircled by unfriendly states. What they did not understand was the degree of paranoia they would confront if they proposed any plans for eastern Europe that did not take into account Stalin's concerns about a resurgent Poland or a German state system free from Soviet supervision. The absolute minimum Soviet demands would include the Baltic States, eastern Poland, part of Finland, supervision of Romania, punishment of Hungary, and no plebiscites. If Roosevelt continued to insist on plebiscites, the Russians would see this as anti-Soviet, because they had clearly announced that such a policy would work against their interests and security.

On the same day that Welles met with the British, Harry Hopkins called on Soviet Ambassador Maxim Litvinov and frankly asked what he believed the Russian demands would be at the peace table. Litvinov affirmed that the Baltic States had always been part of Russia and that they were essential to Soviet security. Litvinov denied that Russia coveted Finland, except for what had been gained at the end of the Russo-Finnish War. Poland would get East Prussia as compensation for surrendering eastern Poland to Russia. He did not expect any real trouble in this regard, although the Poles would make outrageous demands. The Americans and the British "should decide what was to be done about Poland and 'tell them' rather than ask them." He claimed that everyone would agree that the USSR should have Bessarabia. Hopkins then posed an important question: What were Soviet ambitions in the Far East? Litvinov changed the subject and proclaimed that he was sure Russia would like to see Germany dismembered, Prussia cut off from the rest of Germany, and at least two or three other German states created.[17]

In a conversation on March 17 involving Hopkins, FDR, and Cordell Hull, the secretary of state made clear his position on the question of German leadership after the war: There should be no long-winded trials of

---

[16]Conversation between Sumner Welles, Anthony Eden, and Lord Halifax, March 16, 1943, ibid., p. 18.

[17]Memorandum of conversation between Harry Hopkins and Maxim Litvinov, March 16, 1943, ibid., p. 25.

Hitler and his principal associates. These people should be collected and shot, "and do it quietly." He opposed a public trial; Hitler should be dealt with in just the way he would deal with his enemies if he won the war. Hopkins avowed that there was no understanding about what should be done in Germany immediately after the war and that there should be. Unless the Allies acted promptly, "either Germany will go Communist or [an] out and out anarchic state would set in; that, indeed, the same kind of thing might happen in any of the countries in Europe and Italy as well." Roosevelt agreed that the State Department should get together with the British and work out some sort of formal plan and then present it to the Russians. Possible Soviet influence would be constrained if the British and American armies were present heavily in France and Germany at the time of the German collapse, but, if they were not, having the Russians committed to an agreement would be crucial.[18]

## *IV*

Eden met with Hopkins and Roosevelt on March 22 and delicately questioned Roosevelt's ability to proceed with peace agreements before submission of a treaty to the U.S. Senate. He wondered whether FDR's commitment to restoring Austrian sovereignty could be acted upon without congressional involvement. The British remembered that they had believed Woodrow Wilson's assurances of American commitments at the Paris Peace Conference only to find that America would not live up to Wilson's promises. Eden presented a stickier question: How about an agreement to turn over East Prussia to Poland and eastern Poland to Russia? How would Congress and the American press receive such a fait accompli? The president was not prepared to answer this at that time. Roosevelt tried to pin Britain down on who would participate in making and keeping the peace. The president wanted the United States, Great Britain, the Soviet Union, and China to preside over arranging both the war and the peace as "the Big Four." In a recent speech, Churchill had excluded China from the powers that would be in a responsible position at the end of the war, and both Hull and FDR complained about the omission. Eden doubted China's ability to organize itself, believing that it might have to go through a revolution before this was possible. He was not happy at the thought of China "running up and down the Pacific." Eden was pleased when FDR assured him that the United States fully intended to maintain troops in Germany and probably in Italy until such time as there was no longer any need to police the former aggressor nations and that, insofar as the strategic areas of the

---

[18]Memorandum of conversation between Hopkins, Roosevelt, and Hull, March 17, 1943, ibid., pp. 25–26.

world were concerned, they should split up the responsibility of policing them.[19]

On March 29, Cordell Hull delivered one of his famous sermons to Anthony Eden. This tirade should have been directed toward the Russians, but Eden was at hand. The United States had not assisted the British and the Russians to ensure that they emerged in control of the world to the detriment of American principles. He conjured the image of many Americans who were "stating that Russia is saying almost nothing about her future plans and purposes and that, in fact, Russia will at the end of the war do as she pleases, take what she pleases and confer with nobody." These unnamed people were concerned because the United States was spending billions of dollars providing the Russians and the British with military supplies. It would be unlikely, if the war went on much longer, that they would be willing to continue their generosity "unless Russia shows some appreciation and speaks out in the spirit of teamwork and cooperation more fully both now and essentially after the war."[20]

Certainly, FDR would not have countenanced Hull's threat to curtail aid while the war was still in progress merely to win support for American policy. But neither the president nor Hull wanted premature Anglo-Soviet territorial settlements, and both still opposed postwar deals with the Russians, who were not gaining favor by their refusal to yield to such American principles as self-determination of peoples. Wilsonianism was not dead in the hearts of Cordell Hull and the unnamed critics of Anglo-Soviet policy objectives.

Hull summoned Litvinov and tried obliquely to deliver the same message, emphasizing the all-important need for the Big Four nations to stand together, for if any two governments attempted to control the world, they would meet with failure in a few years. Such ambitions would require permanent supplies of armaments "on such a vast scale as to overburden their own people and hopelessly handicap their whole social and industrial progress." Litvinov agreed, for he thought that in all probability Hull was assuring him that Great Britain and the United States recognized that they could not control events without Russian support. Actually, the secretary of state was trying to warn Litvinov that Great Britain and Russia could not control the world against American opposition, but this is not the way Litvinov understood it. Hull finally turned to the question of dependent peoples or, in the more popular American vernacular, self-determination of peoples. Although he had made some telling points about India to the British, this principle applied to all subject peoples everywhere and would

---

[19]Memorandum of conversation between Hopkins, Roosevelt, and Eden, March 22, 1943, ibid., pp. 35–36.

[20]Memorandum of conversation between Hull, Eden, and Halifax, March 29, 1943, ibid., pp. 40–41.

have to be considered at the peace conference.[21] Hull did not mention peoples
under Soviet dominance, but he clearly thought that he had delivered a
message to the Russians. Litvinov probably perceived this as one of Hull's
anticolonial sermons, and he did not consider his own country as
participating in colonization. Hull needed to be more direct if the Russians
were to understand that this was a warning concerning the Baltic States and
eastern Europe.

Hull was not alone in worrying about Soviet postwar ambitions.
Assistant Secretary of State Joseph Grew was impressed by a summary of
Soviet policy prepared by William Howard Gardiner, a former president of
the Navy League and an expert on military affairs. On April 8, Grew
forwarded Gardiner's assessment to FDR, with the notation that Sumner
Welles agreed that it should be brought to Roosevelt's attention. Gardiner
couched his evaluation in geopolitical terms. Using Karl von Clausewitz's
definitions of limited and unlimited war, he contended that the United States
was fighting Japan to secure total victory, and Great Britain and the Soviet
Union fought Germany with similar intent. Americans knew that neither
enemy could fight an unlimited war against them, and they might tire of
carrying on such a war against both Japan and Germany.

Russia might enter Berlin before U.S. or British troops arrived and
dictate peace terms, "whereupon the major problem of western Europe would
be: How to halt the Westward and Southwestward drive of Russia?"
Gardiner's solution was to defeat Japan first by pouring all of America's
resources into that battle and, if necessary, to stall the conclusion of the war
in Europe. He was convinced that Great Britain was finished as a great
power; the mantle of Pax Britannica would pass to the United States, and
future peace and security would depend on Pax Americana.

Gardiner foresaw the USSR as a future enemy who had to be contained:

> It is rumored that, after the Germans have been driven out of Russia,
> [Stalin] will move in Eastern Asia with forces already in reserve for
> operations there. Russia's immemorial trends there support the surmise
> that his first aim will be to drive the Japanese out of the Continent of
> Asia, north of China proper, and to take over their present holdings in
> Mongolia, Manchuria and, perhaps, in Korea—after we have put more
> pressure on the Nipponese.

This virtual elimination of Japan as a great power would free Russia to
move into East Asia. Stalin might provide base sites for the Americans to
attack Japan and seal off imports, but he would only commit a minimum of
manpower and resources. America should ensure "future control over the

---

[21]Memorandum of conversation between Hull and Litvinov, March 31, 1943, ibid.,
pp. 44–46.

Pacific and its shores, and our future political standing and commercial opportunities in Asia and Australasia."[22]

Gardiner foresaw a geopolitical division of the world. The United States was the inheritor of the British world position and the defender of the faith in maintaining the future security of the democracies. The opposing geopolitical force was the Soviet Union, and Gardiner's plan was to prepare for a future confrontation with the Russians. He wished to conduct the remainder of the war in Europe and the Pacific with the idea of containing the continental power of the USSR with the sea power and geographic position of the United States. Gardiner not only anticipated the Cold War, but he also judged it virtually inevitable. He capsulized the positions advocated by such diverse figures as General Michela, William Bullitt, Colonel Ivan D. Yeaton, Admiral William D. Leahy, and Assistant Secretary of State James C. Dunn. President Roosevelt did not comment on Gardiner's letter; instead, he forwarded it to the State Department.


# V


Problems with the Russians became even more apparent in April 1943. From the Division of European Affairs, Elbridge Durbrow related a conversation with the British indicating the deepening rift between Russia and Poland resulting from the Polish response to the Smolensk affair, also known as the Katyn Forest massacre.[23] The U.S. ambassador to Poland, Anthony J. Drexel Biddle, corroborated this information. Stalin had given an ultimatum to General Wladyslaw Sikorski: Unless he publicly denied the German allegations that Russians had killed the Polish officers in the Katyn Forest and withdrew his request for an International Red Cross investigation, the Soviet government would break relations with the Polish government-in-exile. Sikorski told Churchill that he could not comply totally with those conditions. He would promise to soft-pedal the Polish press stories on the missing officers and withdraw the request for a Red Cross investigation if the Russians would permit the evacuation of certain categories of Poles from the Soviet Union.

Russia demanded a retraction of the whole story, and Biddle hypothesized accurately that this might be a calculated move to force the Poles in London to pay a stiff price for resumption of relations. The Russians might instead grant recognition to their own Poles-in-exile, a move to be followed by the creation of a Polish-Communist armed force

---

[22]Joseph Grew to FDR cover memorandum and enclosed letter from William Howard Gardiner, April 8, 1943, and March 12, 1943, PSF, Departmental, State Department, January 1942-May 22, 1943, Box 90, FDRL.

[23]Memorandum of a telephone conversation by Elbridge Durbrow, April 26, 1943, *FRUS: British Commonwealth, 1943*, p. 396.

under General Konstantin Rogoszowski. In any case, the Soviet decision to suspend relations was prompted by a belief in Moscow that an offensive rather than a defensive posture would divert attention from the massacre.[24]

President Roosevelt attempted to smooth over the Polish-Russian controversy. He sent a message to Stalin, following an appeal by Ambassador Standley to V. M. Molotov. Standley beseeched Molotov to withhold issuance of a note to Poland until FDR could contact Stalin, but his entreaty was in vain. The intent of the Russians, according to some observers, was to create on Soviet soil the Soviet Union's own Polish government, which would exclude the reactionary elements in London and elsewhere. Standley rejected this assessment, because the Russian attempt to install a Communist regime in Finland during the Winter War had been a fiasco. The Soviet leaders were too realistic to try this approach again. In addition, there were not enough Poles of sufficient stature in Russia to make this attempt viable. Even so, the United States should be prepared for this possibility and realize such a government would not be really Polish but would be made up of Russian puppets.

Standley then contradicted himself. The State Department should be aware that if any successor governments of the nations bordering the pre-1941 boundaries of the USSR did not vouchsafe the policy of the Kremlin, they might be pressured to accept a government organized inside Soviet borders: "The nucleus of any European Government can be found in the Soviet Union and especially those governments in which the Soviet Union has geographic or strategic interests." The United States might face a turnabout in European history: "In 1918 West Europe attempted to set up a cordon sanitaire to protect it from the influence of bolshevism. Might not the Kremlin envisage the formation of a belt of pro-Soviet States to protect it from the influence of the West?"[25] Standley accurately predicted the ultimate fate of eastern Europe; the question was whether this was an irreversible Stalinist plot or an alternative depending on the development of Russia's relationship with its allies.

Stalin tried to allay suspicions arising in the West concerning his attitude toward Poland. He told a *New York Times* correspondent that the Soviet Union desired a strong and independent Poland after the war. Concerning the question of the postwar relationship between Poland and Russia, Stalin contended that it should be based on "good neighborliness and mutual respect, or, if the Polish people so desire, an alliance of mutual assistance against Germany, the chief enemy of both countries."[26]

On May 3, Ambassador Standley informed President Roosevelt that he had had enough of his Moscow assignment. His health was not up to

---

[24] Anthony J. Drexel Biddle to Hull, April 27, 1943, ibid., pp. 399–400.

[25] Standley to Hull, April 28, 1943, ibid., pp. 400–402.

[26] W. H. Lawrence to Steve Early, May 10, 1943, OF 220, Russia, 1941–1945, Box 2, Folder 1943, FDRL.

another Russian winter, and the original purpose of sending him there had been fulfilled. When he accepted the assignment, it was with the understanding that his talents were needed for the job because of its military requirements "and that diplomacy would remain in the background for the duration of the war." That phase of the Russian mission either was passing or had passed, and "plans will be in the making for peace discussions and the post war period." This would require a change at Moscow to someone "who does not only enjoy your complete confidence but who is also skilled by training and long experience in the field of diplomacy and international affairs." He did not feel that he had the required expertise, and time and circumstances dictated that the job could not be done by "special representatives."[27]

While the guard was changing in Moscow, Maxim Litvinov was being replaced in Washington as well. Litvinov called on Sumner Welles, and their conversation was frank and to some degree pessimistic. The Soviet ambassador wanted his remarks to be completely off the record, but Welles recorded them nonetheless. Two weeks earlier, Litvinov had told Welles of the difficulties he had had in carrying out his mission in Washington, not because of the Americans but because he lacked effective contact with his own government. This stemmed in part from the fact that the very confidential and intimate relationship he had enjoyed with Stalin until 1939 no longer existed. He did not say that this had resulted in part from his failure to carry through on the collective security policy he advocated with the West, but this was an underlying cause of his fall from grace. He complained that Molotov had removed everyone from the foreign office who had experience with the outside world or who had any personal knowledge of the United States or the Western democracies.[28] At about the same time, Ivan Maisky was recalled from London and "promoted" to an assistant's position in Narkomindel.[29]

Litvinov was convinced that none of his messages reached Stalin; or, if they did, they had no effect since none of his recommendations was accepted. He had, in fact, been forbidden by his government to appear or speak in public. He complained that this led to the Soviet Union being misinterpreted by the people of the United States, and he was powerless to remedy the situation. Because he was cut off from Stalin, the Soviet leader was completely unaware of the extent to which public opinion in the United States determined foreign policy. Time and again he tried to persuade Stalin that American public opinion had to be reckoned with, "but Stalin

---

[27]Standley to FDR, May 3, 1943, *FRUS: British Commonwealth, 1943*, p. 521.

[28]Memorandum of conversation between Welles and Litvinov, May 7, 1943, ibid., p. 522.

[29]Narkomindel is an acronym for Narodnaia Kommissariat Inostrannikh Del, the People's Commissariat of Foreign Affairs.

apparently paid no attention whatever to the recommendation which he had sent in this regard."[30]

Prophetically, Litvinov told Welles that the future peace of the world depended largely on the Soviet-American relationship. Without their cooperation there was no hope for development of an international organization with sufficient power to deal with the world's problems, and "the way things were now going, he did not see any prospect of the achievement of that kind of understanding and cooperation." This was the reason he had asked for recall to Moscow,[31] "where he intended to do his utmost to persuade Stalin that the policy which [he] had in mind should be followed in the interest of the Soviet Union itself." He also was resigned to the fact that this was probably a task doomed to failure. Welles was deeply impressed by this blunt talk, and he told Litvinov as much. President Roosevelt, he said, hoped to strengthen Soviet-American relations by meeting personally with Stalin. Litvinov doubted that such a meeting would take place, because Stalin could not afford to be absent from Russia while all the responsibility for the conduct of the war rested on his shoulders alone.[32]

Litvinov confessed to Welles that he was not privy to any information concerning Russia's plans for the postwar world or what territorial demands might be made. In his own view, if there were to be an effective United Nations Organization after the war, it would have to insist from the outset that there be no fascist-minded regimes in Europe and no antidemocratic individuals involved in any European governments. Welles reacted negatively, because this would require intervention of the United Nations in the affairs of the smaller powers, and this would never be approved by American public opinion. He immediately added that certainly the kinds of governments then in power in Germany, Italy, and Japan could not again be permitted, but there were ways to achieve this other than intervention. For example, the Four Freedoms would guarantee the salvation of democratic systems of government. If the people were allowed freedom of expression, in Woodrow Wilson's phrase, "the world would be made safe for democracy." Litvinov parted with a reference to the truly democratic nature of the Soviet constitution, but he probably thought that his hope for the

---

[30]Memorandum of conversation between Welles and Litvinov, May 7, 1943, *FRUS: British Commonwealth, 1943*, p. 522.

[31]If he did ask to be recalled to Moscow, the timing was certainly unexpected. When Litvinov's orders to return reached him, he was playing bridge at the Soviet embassy. He told a friend later, "I had just put my hand down as the dummy, and my partner was at a doubled and redoubled grand slam." His friend asked if they had made the hand. Litvinov said he had left the room, packed, and never went back to see what happened. His partner made the slam. See Alfred Sheinwold, "The Fruits of Research," *Contract Bridge Bulletin*, March 1988, p. 59.

[32]Memorandum of conversation between Welles and Litvinov, May 7, 1943, *FRUS: British Commonwealth, 1943*, pp. 522–23.

USSR to get along with the Americans was even more forlorn than he expected, for Stalin would never accept the worldview of Sumner Welles.[33]

Litvinov conjectured accurately that his task of persuading Stalin to consider American public opinion and closer cooperation with the United States was doomed to failure. His attempts to enlighten Stalin, if they were made, proved futile, and Litvinov's loyal service to his country was rewarded with humiliation. Ambassador Standley recalled his last meeting with Litvinov and his secretary at Narkomindel in an office so small that Edward Page, the American ambassador's interpreter, and the others had to remain standing during the entire discussion because there was not room enough for four chairs. Standley asked Litvinov what he would be doing, and Litvinov told the ambassador that he was waiting for an assignment.[34] It was to be a long wait.

William C. Bullitt added his to the voices warning the president that the time was at hand to prepare to confront the duplicitous Russians. On May 12, he instructed FDR that he was pursuing a completely incorrect strategy in the prosecution of the war. His analysis was nearly identical to that of William Howard Gardiner: Defeating Germany first was wrong; it played into the hands of Stalin and his minions. After the defeat of Germany, neither Great Britain nor the Soviet Union would live up to its promises to immediately make a full effort to defeat the Japanese. Only when Japan was on its last legs would Russia enter the Pacific war and demand a share in the Far Eastern peace settlement, with the intent of invading and annexing Manchuria. The war aims of the British and the Russians were far from identical to those of the United States. FDR should bluntly tell Stalin and Churchill that if they did not agree to his conditions America would shift its total effort to defeating its primary enemy, Japan. The United States could promise that if the war in Europe was still in progress after Japan was defeated it would then return to the task of defeating the Germans. He also subscribed to Churchill's "soft underbelly" thesis, that the best place to attack the Continent was through the south. This would cut off the possibility of Russia securing a foothold in central and eastern Europe.

Bullitt concluded his advice with a lecture to FDR on presidential responsibility: "We are losing our world leadership because we do not realize that we have won power over the world. We are not exercising OUR will to achieve OUR aims—which happen to give the world a better chance of peace than the aims of any of our Allies. We can achieve OUR aims in OUR way —if YOU WILL."[35] This was not the first time that Bullitt had written to Roosevelt suggesting a line of policy that the president obviously did not wish to follow; it was, however, nearly the last time. After 1943,

---

[33]Ibid., pp. 523–24.
[34]William H. Standley and Arthur A. Ageton, *Admiral Ambassador to Russia* (Chicago: Henry Regnery, 1955), pp. 471–72.
[35]William C. Bullitt to FDR, May 12, 1943, PSF, Department of the Navy, FDRL.

Bullitt no longer had the ear of the president. His anti-Soviet posture was too strident at a time when the president was trying to fathom a policy that would permit him to get along with Stalin.[36]

Cordell Hull was less belligerent toward the Russians than was Bullitt. He was still willing to try to deal with them, but he was closer to Bullitt's views on American-Soviet relations than he was to FDR's. Hull told Churchill, on the prime minister's visit to Washington in May 1943, that there should be a clearing of the air with the Russians. Hull proposed that carefully selected representatives try "to talk Mr. Stalin out of his shell, so to speak, away from his aloofness, secretiveness and suspiciousness until he broadened his view and visualized a more practical international cooperation in the future, at the same time indicating Russian intentions East and West." Churchill believed that Stalin would enter the Far Eastern phase of the war immediately upon the defeat of Germany. Hull saw no indication of this intent. He suspected that if Russia entered the war against Japan it would be two to three weeks before the end for the purpose of spreading out over Manchuria and other areas and to sit in on the peace conference. Hull scored Soviet secretiveness and lamented that the Russians, except for certain territorial demands on their European borders, would not reveal their plans for the postwar world.[37]

## *VI*

During the third week in May, Joseph Davies arrived in Moscow to carry out a special mission for the president with Stalin. It was not a happy experience for Ambassador Standley, who reported that Davies immediately held a press conference in which he lectured the correspondents on the disservice they would render to their country if they criticized the Soviet Union. Davies had created an unfortunate incident. After a question about whether he had discussed with Stalin the failure of the Russians to supply information to the American military attachés, Davies exploded when Quentin Reynolds disagreed with his statement that all of the military information that the Allies requested was given to the president and the

---

[36]Bullitt's stridency on the Russian question was proudly established by his brother when he edited the Bullitt correspondence. Orville Bullitt recalled the "wide divergency of opinion" between the British ambassador and his brother, quoting from the Earl of Birkenhead's *Life of Lord Halifax*. Bullitt and Halifax walked for a half hour together, and Lord Halifax found his companion excited and vehemently anti-Soviet. He told Halifax that the American government was blind to what he clearly perceived as Stalin's objectives, including absolute control of the governments in central and southeastern Europe. Bullitt warned of the Soviet threat to democracy. Halifax disagreed, which failed to impress Bullitt. The British diplomat thought him odd and did not believe that judgment was his strong suit. Orville H. Bullitt, ed., *For the President: Personal and Secret* (Boston: Houghton Mifflin, 1972), pp. 594–95.

[37]Hull-Churchill conversation, May 1943, *FRUS: Diplomatic Papers*, vol. 2, *Europe, 1943* (Washington, DC: Government Printing Office, 1964), p. 115.

prime minister. When Reynolds asserted that Generals Dwight Eisenhower and Henry Arnold had told him that they were not getting adequate military intelligence from the Russians, an acrimonious debate ensued between Davies and the correspondents in which "remarks were made and tempers lost."

According to Standley, Davies adopted "a violently pro-Russian attitude and as much as accused the correspondents of treason to their country and playing into the hands of Hitler by their 'picking up pins, by their criticizing the Soviet Union, by their listening to criticism from subordinate officials.' " He "sermonized" to the newsmen on the necessity to have more faith in the Soviets and maintained that Russia could make "countless complaints" against the United States. The upshot of the interview was that most of the correspondents "are up in arms against Davies and are questioning the wisdom of sending here a man with such intolerant views."[38]

Davies had a completely different view of his "mission," which he reported to the president from Moscow on May 29. Soviet suspicions of American objectives had to be overcome, and he believed that he had helped in this regard. He urged the launching of the second front during the next summer lest the appeasers in Russia gain the upper hand. He feared that certain elements in the Kremlin wanted Stalin to sit back after driving the Germans from Russian soil and let the Western powers bleed in their war with Germany. This group was convinced that the intent of the delay of the second front was to let Russia exhaust itself, and they thought that turnabout was fair play. The Russians would claim their right to their lost territories, and this had to be accepted. He praised the British diplomats and their dealings with the Russians but said nothing about the American embassy personnel. He smugly announced: "As to the particular mission I was engaged upon, I believe that the result thereof has been completely successful."[39]

By mid-1943 the lines had been drawn in the contest between the pro- and anti-Russian forces in the Roosevelt administration and the American military. The pros had the upper hand in their contacts with the president, but the antis were in place in the Department of State and the military missions. Cooperation or conflict with the Soviet Union for the remainder of the war and the following peace was still doubtful, when a new ambassador to Moscow was selected. Averell Harriman was willing to give the Russians the benefit of the doubt, but he was not committed to Davies's style of sycophancy.

---

[38]*FRUS: British Commonwealth, 1943*, pp. 651–53.
[39]Davies to FDR, May 29, 1943, ibid., pp. 657–60.

# VI

## Fathoming America's Russian Policy

SOME PRACTITIONERS OF foreign policy believe that power is its most important ingredient, while others opt for finesse. The extremists in these groups quote Karl von Clausewitz in support of power and Niccolo Machiavelli as a guide to manipulation. James MacGregor Burns in his study of Roosevelt, *The Lion and the Fox*, depicted FDR as embodying both characteristics. To exercise either style of diplomacy, however, a leader must be in control of all the mechanisms through which foreign policy functions. Concerning America's wartime Russian policy, the president was unable to completely establish his authority. This was not for lack of intent; he thought of himself as a strategist, maneuvering for position. One reason for his failure to maintain full control of policy was his leadership style. General James H. Burns and others warned him that he needed to determine clearly what course he wanted the nation to follow and lay down the law to those responsible for carrying out the policy. Obstructionists of his Russian policy occasionally heard him roar like a lion, but more often he behaved like a fox. The president inserted special envoys into the foreign policy process with the vague objective of improving relations with the Soviet Union without removing the considerable number of subordinates who the president knew were convinced that no such amicable relationship could or should prevail.

FDR suspected the devotion of his own State Department to his Russian policy and refused to appoint any ambassador to the USSR from the foreign service list; instead, he secured an ambassador, Averell Harriman, from among those known to share his own position on American-Soviet relations. Harriman was a man of enormous wealth and seemingly unbounded energy. He told FDR what he thought, and he disagreed with the president when he believed that it was necessary. If Harriman were to assume a pro- or anti-Russian position, it would be based on a very careful analysis of the evidence at hand. His selection must have initially pleased the Russians, because he was a known troubleshooter for the president and certainly had the confidence of his chief.

Harriman referred to himself as a confirmed optimist concerning the relationship with Russia because of his conviction that Stalin's desires for Russian reconstruction and security were based on getting along with the United States. Stalin was "a man of simple purposes and, although he may use devious means in attempting to accomplish them, he does not deviate from his long run objectives." Therefore, if he thought it was important to get along with the Americans, he would do so whatever the costs. Harriman was willing, but not eager, to serve in Russia. "I have thought a good deal about it since you talked with me and have some definite views as to how the situation might be handled. If you consider sending me, I would respectfully suggest that you recall me to Washington and give me an opportunity to put my ideas before you. You could then decide whether I should go. Real accomplishment by an Ambassador in Moscow is a gamble with the odds against success but the stakes are great both for the war in Europe and in the Pacific—and after."[1]

He was so keen about his position in London (expediting Lend-Lease materials as the preparations for the invasion of France progressed) that he wanted to go back to that post if Moscow proved to be a failure for him. Harriman made it clear that he did not want the assignment in Moscow if he were to be merely a clearinghouse for special emissaries from Washington, as had been too often the case with his two immediate predecessors. He wanted to be a genuine agent of his government and its chief, not an errand boy. "I am sure I can be of more use to you and the war in London than to remain in Moscow as a glorified communications officer."[2]

In late July, Ambassador William H. Standley reported on a disturbing series of articles in the Russian newspaper *War and the Working Class*. They appeared in this paper rather than in *Pravda* or *Izvestiia*, because they were trial balloons that the government did not wish to raise in the official publications. These articles spoke harshly about plans that FDR had already approved for postwar reconstruction in eastern Europe. American schemes for European federation were branded as anti-Soviet, and their Polish, British, and American initiators were roundly scored. The paper also took "the stand that the Soviet Union being the strongest power on the continent . . . must play the leading role in the organization of post-war Europe."[3]

Given both Cordell Hull's and the president's emphasis on the federation idea, this could not have encouraged the secretary of state in his assessment of the prospects for Russian cooperation in postwar Europe. Hull was not very optimistic about the chance for an agreement with the Russians in the first place; this merely confirmed his worst fears.

---

[1]W. Averell Harriman to Harry Hopkins with attached copy of a letter he sent to Roosevelt, July 5, 1943, Hopkins Papers, Harriman Folder, FDRL.
[2]Ibid.
[3]William Standley to Cordell Hull, July 26, 1943, DSF 861.917/37.

Equally discouraging for the Russians was President Roosevelt's disavowal of an Office of War Information broadcast attacking the king of Italy and Marshal Pietro Badoglio, who had succeeded Benito Mussolini as prime minister on July 25. The Soviet writer and journalist Ilya Ehrenburg expressed bitterness to an Associated Press correspondent, Henry Cassidy, concerning the British and American failure to consult the Soviet government on the Italian question. The Russians had not objected to their allies dealing with Vichy French Admiral Jean-François Darlan in North Africa, because they realized the possible military value of this and were not a part of that theater of war, but Italy was different. There would be no success in Italy if the Russians did not hold German soldiers on their front who might otherwise be fighting in Italy; besides, the Red Army had been actively engaged in fighting Italians in the Soviet Union.

Dealing with Badoglio was a matter of major importance, according to Ehrenburg, and he asked Cassidy if "this indicated that [the United States] would eventually be prepared to deal with Goering in Germany." Cassidy countered that President Roosevelt had made it clear that Italy still would be required to surrender unconditionally. He wanted his Soviet counterpart to explain the "Free German" movement in Moscow, which apparently aimed at overthrowing Hitler but would replace him with people who had been Nazis. Ehrenburg replied "that two could play at this game and that this was the Soviet answer in advance to any attempt to extend the 'Darlan' policy to Europe."[4]

Ambassador Standley thought that the Russians might have a legitimate complaint. Although no one had told him whether they had been informed of the plans in Italy, he recommended establishing a system to coordinate such plans with them either through the embassy or by another means acceptable to the secretary of state and the president. This might forestall Russian concerns about not being taken into American and British confidence on important matters.[5]

On August 8, General James H. Burns, the executive officer of the president's Soviet Protocol Committee, provided Harry Hopkins with an unsigned memorandum which he identified as "a very high level United States military strategic estimate of Russia." It seemed apparent to the author of the memorandum that, since Russia was the decisive factor in winning the war and would be so powerful after the war, "every effort must be made to obtain her friendship." Steps had to be taken constantly to prove to Russia that America was "genuinely anxious to be a real and sincere friend, not only in the present conflict but for many years to come." Naively, the writer suggested that the task would not be all that difficult, because the Russian people admired and were instinctively friendly to

---

[4]Standley to Hull, July 30, 1943, *FRUS: British Commonwealth, 1943*, pp. 555–56.
[5]Ibid., p. 556.

Americans and would respond to generous treatment. The memorandum added: "Of course, we should neither do nor promise anything that is not in the interests of the United States or that is not in harmony with our principles and policies."[6]

The memorandum's writer made several equally incredible "suggestions" as to how to implement improved relations with the Soviets. The U.S. representatives who did not trust Russia and who did not follow "the national policy" of the " 'good neighbor and sincere friend' to Russia" should "either be replaced or they should be required to pledge loyal support to the above policy." Ambassador Standley's criticism of the Soviet Union's reluctance to acknowledge American Lend-Lease aid and the worldwide publicity given this attack in effect branded the Russians as ingrates in the eyes of the world. This injury to Russian pride would leave a scar, and very little had been done to "correct this mistake."[7]

The writer might well have been Joe Davies. He had ignored certain realities about the Russians and about the American-Soviet relationship over the preceding decade. To expect friendship from the Russians was unrealistic, for they did not consider that there was such a thing as real friendship among nations; there were only temporary, useful allies. Furthermore, there was absolutely no prospect for a workable relationship with the Soviet Union unless the United States surrendered at least some of its long-standing principles, because the Russians were not inclined to accept the American perspectives on self-determination of peoples, abandonment of spheres of influence, and other cherished American values. They would provide only lip service to these things and expect the Americans to be satisfied.

## II

Franklin Roosevelt's policy was based on getting along with the Russians, because he needed them to win the war in Europe and the Far East, and he wanted their cooperation in making a successful peace that would last longer than the last one. But the U.S. Army and some other agencies had elements who were convinced that the Russians were determined to cease cooperation at the earliest opportunity; therefore, the United States should do nothing to aid the Russians beyond limited assistance to keep them fighting and should be prepared for eventual confrontation. These people would work to thwart FDR's policy and plans for the American-Soviet relationship if his approach conflicted with their view of the Soviet Union as a future enemy.

---

[6]Memorandum, General J. H. Burns to Hopkins, August 10, 1943, Hopkins Papers, Russia Folder, 1943, FDRL.

[7]Ibid.

Colonel Phillip Faymonville, the longtime U.S. military attaché in Moscow who was shifted to Lend-Lease director there, came under attack by the anti-Soviet element in the army. He had become so sycophantic toward Russia that he was suspected by his superiors and was under examination by the War Department as to his fitness to serve in the USSR. The case was turned over to General James H. Burns, who gave Faymonville a clean bill of health on August 14. Burns reported to Hopkins that the investigations had been initiated "secretly" by the War Department without giving Faymonville an opportunity to defend himself or even to know the charges, which included "indulgence in homosexual practices, . . . personal debauchery and responsibility for debauchery in his Lend\Lease organization . . . being blackmailed with result—is unduely [*sic*] friendly and helpful to Russia and therefore not—properly protecting the interests of the U.S. . . . Failure to cooperate properly with other American representatives in Russia." Burns admitted that the report contained much worthwhile information on Faymonville, but it also was filled with gossip and hearsay evidence, "for which General [Joseph A.] Michela seems largely responsible." Furthermore, Michela "likewise subjected to a secret one-way attack" a number of other individuals who were not sufficiently anti-Faymonville to suit him.[8]

General Burns noted that Faymonville obviously believed in giving maximum Lend-Lease aid to the Soviet Union without demanding military information as a quid pro quo, as some of his superiors thought he should; "however, this is understood to be our national policy." Michela was so determined to force Russia to provide military information that he had convinced himself, and had tried to convince others, that if it was withheld it meant that the Soviet Union was "guilty of an unfriendly act . . . or in other words, we should go to war with her."[9]

There was also no question that Faymonville enjoyed the friendship and respect of the Russians with whom he dealt, and (although Burns did not say so) this also was "national policy" at the time: to win Russian "friendship." Burns included a list of the enemies Faymonville had made: "Adm. Standley, Adm. Duncan, Gen. Michela, Col. Yeaton, Col. Boswell, Col. Gray, and Quinton Reynolds as well as some State Department officials." This enemy list was in his favor in FDR's inner circle. Burns contended that Faymonville possibly should be judged by the enemies he made. "Most of the above enemies are either definitely against or only luke warm towards Russia and to the American national concept that we should give maximum Lend/Lease aid to Russia on the theory that when one helps her one helps ourselves." Burns maintained that the attack on Faymonville was

---

[8]Memorandum, Burns to Hopkins, August 16, 1943, Hopkins Papers, President's Soviet Protocol Committee, FDRL.

[9]Ibid.

symptomatic of the attitudes prevalent among those who did not want good relations with the USSR. He recommended that, as a result of his findings, the president should "clean house" of those who were not loyally carrying out his policies. The new ambassador should be authorized to effect a purge and, "if satisfactory to [the] new Ambassador, promote Faymonville."[10] This controversy indicated the views held by the anti-Soviet element in the Roosevelt administration and in the military that there was a confrontation brewing with the USSR and that battle lines had to be drawn by branding those who disagreed with them as un-American or as traitorous to the real interests of the United States.

As had been the case in previous instances in which the president's plans for development of his Russian policy were thwarted by members of the War, Navy, or State departments, he did not "clean house." Burns's expectation was naive. The president was fully aware of the intrigue that went on in his government; he was also aware of the damage that these people could do if they turned to congressional critics. Instead of cleaning house, he placed at the top people who were loyal to him and his policies; he expected them to get around the obstructions. Soviet scholars and government functionaries cite such cases as proof of the anti-Soviet policies of the United States, probably either because they cannot understand the inner workings of the American system or because they equate the power of an American president with that of Stalin, who took care of opposition by means that few American presidents would even consider.[11] Perhaps these Soviet critics should look at the history of their own bureaucracy and its infinite ability to avoid doing what Soviet leaders have asked of it. Bureaucracies are much the same everywhere; they have a life of their own which defies alteration if at the grass roots they have elements that are determined not to accept a change in policy.[12] To root out bureaucratic

---

[10]Ibid. Phillip Faymonville was promoted to brigadier general and ultimately retired at the end of the war. Burns later recommended him for the Distinguished Service Medal. See Burns to Adjutant General, United States Army, June 20, 1946, Recommendation for Distinguished Service Medal to Colonel Phillip R. Faymonville, Ordnance Department, Hopkins Papers, Box 140, Executive Orders, F.B.I. Reports: Argentina-Faymonville Folder, FDRL. After the war Faymonville was returned to his regular rank of colonel.

[11]There is, for example, an interesting attempt to explain why the United States provided only insufficient aid to the USSR in Valentin Berezhkov's study of the diplomacy of World War II. He vacillated on the issue of American support, praising FDR for aiding Russia despite great opposition from anti-Soviet elements in both the American government and society. However, he also contended that the president made this commitment because he was embarrassed by the "capitalist" Axis states. Berezhkov, *History in the Making*, pp. 172–78.

[12]For an excellent illustration of this thesis see Howard C. Payne, *The Police State of Louis Napoleon Bonaparte, 1851–1860* (Seattle: University of Washington Press, 1966), wherein the author establishes that an entrenched bureaucracy can defy the most persistent efforts of a central administration to alter its operation by appearing to implement national policy while in fact stalling it to death.

resistance to the leadership may seem a simple solution, but it generally is not a viable course.

Struggles for control of policy were not restricted to the operation of the American mission in the USSR. In a State Department memorandum Harley Notter noted the broader context of this contest, which included competition over who would command various theaters of operation and direct the broader military spheres in which America operated. The Military Staff Committee would be the scene, "at a relatively early date," of skirmishes for position

> which will have heavy consequences upon our security situation vis-a-vis the other Great Powers. The Russians are willing to work closely with us, but a struggle for command (or at least direction) of the United Nations forces . . . will be very important and probably critical. It involves highest policy. The struggle will occur probably on the question of the size of the contribution to be made; a nation contributing the most will have the best claim to command.[13]

While Notter referred here to the divisions of air, sea, and land forces in wartime, he saw broader ramifications for postwar distributions of power and position.

In a later memorandum concerning the Moscow Declaration in October 1943, Notter called the voting formula in the future United Nations the fruit of "a carefully nurtured wartime unity of the Big Three," which made a conscious effort to avoid Woodrow Wilson's mistakes but to retain his vision. FDR and Notter were aware of the need to assure the Soviet Union about voting in the United Nations. They took into account "the Russian experience of isolation and fear of being out-voted by the capitalist West."[14]

## III

Just before the Quebec Conference, in August 1943, Hull asked his adviser on political relations, Stanley K. Hornbeck, to outline Soviet objectives in the Far East. Joseph Ballantine and Max Bishop of the Far Eastern Division of the State Department provided the estimate. They maintained that there was no difference in Soviet aims in Europe and the Far East or the Near East; the Russians had a "natural desire" to promote their national security. Ballantine and Bishop cited several examples of Russian attempts to create "well disposed and ideologically sympathetic governments in nearby areas," including Outer Mongolia and Korea. They emphasized Soviet paranoia: "[The] Soviet Government has a deep organic suspicion of any and all

---

[13]Memorandum by Harley A. Notter, 1943, Records of Harley A. Notter, 1939–1945, Miscellaneous Subject Files, Box 29, Lot 60D-224, Stettinius Book, DSF.
[14]Ibid.

non-Soviet governments," which has resulted in concerted efforts to bring all neighboring governments and peoples under Russian influence and to gain control of radical social and economic movements in these environs. They recalled the continuing Russian desire for warm-water ports, and in the Far East this required control or possession of such ports by a government subservient to the USSR.  Roosevelt would remember this concern at the Tehran Conference.

Ballantine and Bishop believed that the Russians would not do anything drastic in the Far East until after the European war had been won.  The Soviets would maintain their neutrality policy with Japan and would continue to support Chiang Kai-shek and the Guomindang in China.  However, when the European war was over, Russia's hand in the Far East would be strengthened, and then it would move wherever there were signs of social unrest and political instability. This did not mean annexation but rather encouragement of strong ties with the USSR wherever such disturbances appeared. "There will of course be a natural tendency on the part of the authorities in the areas concerned, such as China, to blame those developments on Moscow rather than on their own failure to deal effectively with social unrest."  They cautioned that the Russians still could make a separate peace with the Germans, enabling them to concentrate their power eastward and thereby improving their ability to dictate events in the Far East.[15]

This report reached Hull on August 19 during the Quebec Conference and provided him with additional incentive to get approved the Four Nations Declaration that emerged from the meeting.  This declaration bound the Soviet Union, the United States, Great Britain, and China to cooperate after the war in the establishment of an international organization that would ensure the peace, by military means if necessary, and cut off possible independent action by the Soviet Union. Hull noted the significance of the declaration: "It seemed to me that it was all-important to bring Russia in on a common determination to set up an international organization after the war.  If an agreement were reached on this point, the settlement of other problems would be easier. If Russia refused, all other problems would be magnified."[16] Hull was determined to get some commitment from the Russians concerning recognition of China as one of the Big Four participants in the postwar settlement, which would undermine any Soviet effort to take advantage of internal upheavals and would give China the opportunity to regain its traditional control of Manchuria and Inner Mongolia and possibly to restore its ties with Korea.

---

[15]*FRUS: Diplomatic Papers, Conferences at Washington and Quebec, 1943,* (Washington, DC: Government Printing Office, 1970), pp. 627–29.
[16]Hull, *Memoirs,* 2:1239.

Far Eastern affairs in every other way were peripheral to the purposes of
the Quebec Conference, from which "the most important result . . . was the
blueprint for the cross-channel attack, . . . renamed Overlord."[17] One reason
Overlord was "the most important result" was Winston Churchill's effort to
again postpone the attack on France by instead intensifying military
activities in the Mediterranean and the Balkans. George Marshall and Henry
Stimson had worked on FDR to convince him not to let the British prime
minister change the venue again.[18]

There was ample reason for their concern. In an August meeting with
the president, Secretary Stimson reported a conversation with Churchill in
which the latter was cool toward Bolero, the buildup for the invasion of the
Continent. Although Churchill assured Stimson he was not bent on
attacking the Germans through the Balkans, claiming that this was Anthony
Eden's idea, he did think that more supplies should be given to the resistance
fighters there. Roosevelt was not convinced of Churchill's sincerity:

> The President said that the British Foreign Office does not want the
> Balkans to come under Russian influence. Britain wants to get to the
> Balkans first. He said that personally he could not see the logic of this
> reasoning. He did not believe the Russians would desire to take over the
> Balkan states. Their wish is to establish kinship with the other Slav
> people. In any event, he thought it unwise to plan military strategy
> based on a gamble as to political results.[19]

In Quebec, plans were laid for a meeting of the foreign ministers at
Moscow which in turn would set up the program for Churchill, Roosevelt,
and Stalin to meet before the end of the year. Actually, the original
proposal did not call for a foreign ministers' meeting but instead for a
gathering of representatives of the various leaders, and Sumner Welles was
the intended U.S. participant. The Hull-Welles rivalry, which had simmered
for years, reached its apex before the meeting, and Welles was forced to
resign. Hull's explanation of the dismissal is only partly accurate. He
charged that the undersecretary had made end runs around him for years to the
president and to ambassadors in the field. The last straw was Welles's
attacking him and others in the department as anti-Soviet, going so far as to
release such stories to friends in the press.[20]

[17]Francis L. Loewenheim, Harold D. Langley, Manfred Jonas, eds., *Roosevelt and Churchill: Their Secret Wartime Correspondence* (New York: Saturday Review Press/E. P. Dutton, 1975), p. 366.
[18]Ibid., p. 31.
[19]Minutes of meeting held at the White House between the president and the chiefs of staff, August 10, 1943, Map Room Papers, Conferences, Box 29, Meeting of FDR with JCS 1942–1945 Folder, FDRL.
[20]Hull, *Memoirs*, 2:1230–31.

In fact, that was only the last skirmish in a long battle, and Hull did not reveal in his memoirs that he had given the president a "him or me" choice.[21]   The secretary found proof of rumors that Welles was a homosexual when he learned the results of an FBI investigation authorized by the president. William C. Bullitt and Hull joined forces to get Welles fired and, though it took more than two years, finally got their way. Bullitt's role cost him what was left of his friendship with the president, and, although Hull won, the president never forgave him.[22]

Actually, Welles was not as determinedly pro-Soviet as Bullitt and Hull believed, nor was Hull as determined to oppose accommodation with the Russians as his critics suggested. Hull's problem was his tendency to deal with the Soviet Union in swings of anger and optimism, as in his reaction to the Russians telling him that they had refused to fall for a Japanese initiative to let Japan act as a mediator for a separate peace with Germany. This raised Hull's hopes once again for fruitful relations with the Russians: "I felt that the Soviet Union's decisively adverse reaction to Japan's approach, coupled with the prompt and full information she furnished us concerning it, was a happy augury for the forthcoming [Moscow] conference."[23]

Before his departure for Moscow, Hull saw the president and, opposing FDR's plan to partition Germany, agreed with the proposal to take high moral ground by persuading Stalin to allow free elections for Poland and the Baltic States. FDR intended to inform Stalin that Britain and the United States would not fight over the Baltic States, but the best course for the sake of international opinion would be for the USSR to allow a second plebiscite there a couple of years after the war. FDR would encourage him to accept the same course for eastern Poland.  Furthermore, the Polish border should be east of the Curzon Line and should leave Lvov with Poland.[24]

Stalin wanted the representatives at the Moscow Conference to be authorized to act on military strategy, especially the Second Front. He would be the only national leader present and would assert maximum influence. He did not like the way the Italian surrender was being handled, because the Russians were being excluded. He proposed that a military-political commission be set up by the Big Three to "consider questions concerning the negotiations with the different Governments dissociating themselves from Germany." The situation of the Americans and the British acting and then informing the USSR, not always completely, had to end.[25]

[21]Standley and Ageton, *Admiral Ambassador to Russia*, p. 490.
[22]Ted Morgan, *FDR: A Biography* (New York: Simon & Schuster, 1985), pp. 677–85.
[23]Hull, *Memoirs*, 2:1263–64.
[24]Ibid., pp. 1265–66.
[25]Stalin to Churchill and Roosevelt, August 22, 1943, *FRUS: Europe, 1943*, pp. 353–54.

Stalin's suspicion of his allies was reinforced by Drew Pearson's account of Sumner Welles's departure from the administration, which gained full coverage in Russia. The Soviet journal *War and the Working Class* repeated Pearson's speculations that Welles had been driven from the State Department by Hull, and thus departed the last high-level diplomat with a benign attitude toward the USSR. The Soviet paper reported Pearson's assertion that Hull and his chief assistants, Adolf Berle, James C. Dunn, and Breckinridge Long, would like to see Russia bleed.[26]

# *IV*

Cordell Hull referred to the gathering of the foreign ministers in Moscow as the Tripartite Conference. He laid out for the president the items he wanted to have included in the agenda: a Four Nations Declaration providing for postwar consultation and cooperation among the four major powers during and after the war; preliminary discussions on the treatment of Germany, including questions of reparations, borders, and the form of government; rehabilitation of the USSR to repair the war damages; collaboration on matters relating to agriculture, transport and communications, finance and trade, and the International Labor Organization; items other governments might wish to raise; and discussion of methods of dealing with contemporary political and economic issues that might arise as the war progressed.[27]

A prescient assessment of the Russian situation was prepared for Hull by the Department of State policy planning staff in an unsigned memorandum of September 27. The writer stressed Russia's western frontier problem which, he asserted, was really six problems, each with a different political and historical footing "yet all are related by Russia's overwhelming desire for long-term security." It was important to discover which of the six was "the *key* problem" and to "put it *first*, and find a solution, [then] the remaining problems will prove more manageable."

The memorandum proposed that the key to Russia's western frontier problem lay in the future of the Baltic States. These areas had been lost while Russian power was at a low ebb, and it was as if the United States in similar circumstances had lost Arizona, New Mexico, and southern California. Just as would be the case with America, Russia wanted to have back its lost provinces. "The USSR balances the security of 170,000,000 Russians against the weakness of 5,000,000 peoples in the Baltic republics." The question was: Should the United States stand on

---

[26]Translation of an item in *War and the Working Class*, September 15, 1943, reported by Maxwell Hamilton, Box 1351C, Moscow 711 SOVIET UNION-UNITED STATES, Post Files.

[27]*FRUS: Diplomatic Papers*, vol. 1, *General, 1943* (Washington, DC: Government Printing Office, 1963), pp. 521–23.

self-determination or on expediency? "Shall we insist on sovereign equality or will we accept the facts and realism of inequality? We forced Union on the South in 1865. Is there a distinction between big and little moralities in international affairs? What is the political position of the American negotiators to be?"

The crucial question was whether the United States would be willing to go to war to restore independence to the Baltic States. If not, was the American government prepared to excommunicate Russia for violating American principles and thereby leave the USSR out of future international agreements? The author of the memorandum thought that the answers to these questions were clear: "We must work with Russia through thick and thin." The United States had no choice but to accept Russian hegemony where it was justified by reality and by historical precedents. Americans might ask for complete neutralization of the Baltic States, Bukovina, and parts of Finland, with their policies to be tied to the Soviet Union. However, he was not inclined to even suggest such a plan for Poland or Bessarabia, as the Poles had exceeded the proposed boundary at the Curzon Line of 1919 "when she had Russia down (1922). Her subsequent conquest of the Vilna region was vicious and inexcusable." The United States preferred a border east of the Curzon Line, but that was apparently negotiable. Bessarabia likewise had been stripped from Russia by Romanian opportunism and political adventure and should go back to its traditional possessors. He advised no commitments on the Straits question and noted that "*Turkey must be consulted.*"[28]

Had Secretary Hull or FDR taken this memorandum to heart, many of the later problems with the Soviet Union could have been avoided. The author of the memorandum was in the best tradition of American diplomacy; policymakers in the nineteenth century had consistently distinguished between principles and vital interests. They had refused to promulgate policy based on idealism where the nation clearly had not the means to ensure implementation of its ideals and where national security was not concerned.[29]

President Roosevelt wrote Stalin on October 4 to make sure that the Soviet leader understood that anything decided at the foreign ministers' conference could be reevaluated when they met personally. He was sure that they would "find a meeting of the minds for the important decisions which must finally be made by us." The foreign ministers could "clear the ground,"

---

[28]Unsigned memorandum to Hull, September 27, 1943, Policy Planning Staff, Box 17, Russia Folder, Hull Papers.

[29]An excellent example was Daniel Webster's refusal to recognize the independence of Hungary when the Hungarian revolutionary leader Louis Kossuth asked for American support. Webster pointed out that the United States did not have the power to ensure Hungarian independence under the nose of a powerful Austrian state. See Norman A. Graebner, *Ideas and Diplomacy* (New York: Oxford University Press, 1964), pp. 283–85.

but if difficulties emerged from that gathering "I would still have every confidence that they can be reconciled when you and Churchill and I meet."[30] This would not make Hull's task in Moscow any easier; the Russians now knew that decisions made there were challengeable. In the same message FDR backed down partway on his determination not to discuss the cross-Channel invasion: "While I do not consider this conference as one to plan or recommend military strategy, I have no objection to and would welcome the widest exchange of views of your proposal relating to an expedition directed against France." General John Deane would be a member of the mission and would "be informed fully of our plans and intentions."[31]

Meeting with Admiral William Leahy and a group from the State Department, FDR discussed what the Americans and their allies wanted to achieve at the Moscow Conference. The Russians wanted a commission to be established to deal with questions relating to enemy and liberated territories. Roosevelt and Hull wanted broader representation than the Soviet Union had in mind; for example, Brazil should be brought in when its interests were involved. They wanted China to be included as one of the primary decision makers, but they knew that this would be opposed by both the British and the Russians. Someone inserted: "Churchill does not like China." The Russians would insist that, as they were not involved in the Far Eastern war, they could not enter into any arrangements with China. This could be circumvented by making provision for China's inclusion when the Soviets entered the war. Roosevelt was adamant on this issue: "The four-power concept should be preserved, even at the cost of getting no agreement at this time. China is too important a factor, both now and in the future, both because of herself and because of her influence over British India, to be alienated."[32] On October 6, Stalin wrote Roosevelt absolutely rejecting discussion of a Four Nations Declaration at the Moscow Conference: "If I understand you correctly, at the Moscow conference will be discussed questions concerning only our three countries, and, thus, it can be considered as agreed upon that the question of the declaration of four nations is not included."[33]

President Roosevelt wanted those attending the conference to remember that he favored partition of Germany into three or more states deprived of all military activities including armaments industries. Especially East Prussia should be detached, and all "dangerous elements of the population forcibly removed." Later he said that division of Germany would be on a trial-and-error basis; maybe a customs union could be tried, and possibly the whole thing might have to be abandoned if it proved unworkable. If Hull left this

---

[30]FDR to Stalin, October 4, 1943, *FRUS: Diplomatic Papers, Conferences at Cairo and Teheran, 1943* (Washington, DC: Government Printing Office, 1961), p. 2.
[31]Ibid.
[32]*FRUS: General, 1943*, pp. 541–42.
[33]Stalin to FDR, October 6, 1943, ibid., p. 548.

meeting with any clear idea about the president's German policy, he had to
have been clairvoyant. However, the president took an emphatic stand on
the reparations question. He did not want to fall into the same trap America
had found itself in after World War I. "As regards reparation, there will be
no exaction in money, but rather in manpower and equipment." FDR told
this group that when he met with Stalin he intended to appeal to him "on
grounds of high morality" concerning the Baltic States and Poland.[34] He
reiterated his plan to ask Stalin to have another plebiscite in the Baltic
States a couple of years after the war was over in order to make the Soviet
Union look good in the eyes of the world, and the same idea might apply to
eastern Poland. In order to provide the Russians with access to the sea,
perhaps international trusteeships should be established for the Baltic
passages, the Kiel Canal, the Persian Gulf, and the Straits.

While he was thinking about trusteeships, FDR said that the British
might make a gesture of goodwill by returning Hong Kong to Chinese
sovereignty with the idea that China would respond in kind by immediately
making it a free port under international trustees. He referred to a draft
declaration proposed some time earlier as having "great possibilities" to
pressure colonial powers to move toward developing "their colonies for the
good of the dependent peoples and of the world."[35] The British had tried to
outline the areas where special interests would predominate. According to a
British aide-mémoire, the lack of a coordinated policy might lead to spheres
of interest by accident. Roosevelt suspected another motive: "He did not
think much of the proposed British draft. He further said that it smacked too
much [of] 'spheres of influence' policies, the very thing which it was
supposedly to prevent." The president's disapproval was passed along to the
British.[36]

Despite his fear of air travel, Cordell Hull looked forward to his trip,
partly because he foresaw better prospects of dealing with the Russians.
The appointment of Andrei Gromyko as the new Soviet ambassador to the
United States encouraged the secretary. Gromyko assured Hull that there was
no serious divergence of interests between their two nations and that "there
are no questions which can not be settled amicably and without serious
difficulty." Gromyko echoed and reechoed the same viewpoint, and his

---

[34]While the president and Hull leaned toward opposing permanent annexation by the
USSR of the Baltic States without another plebiscite, Walter Lippmann suggested to the
Department of State that the Baltic States had only been recognized conditionally in 1922
by the United States and that recognition had been granted "eluctantly and with the belief
that it was provisional." This was included in a memorandum by Hallett Johnson, assistant
chief of the blockade and supply division of the department, because he thought it might
be useful for the secretary as he prepared for the Moscow Conference. Johnson
memorandum, October 7, 1943, DSF 861.014/276.

[35]*FRUS: General, 1943*, pp. 542–43.

[36]Memorandum, October 8, 1943, attached to the British Aide-Mémoire of October 5,
1943, ibid., p. 544.

"remarks were encouraging compared to those of his predecessors."[37] On this high note the Americans prepared to meet at Moscow to determine the future of the American-Soviet relationship with a tentative and somewhat confused agenda in mind.

---

[37]Memorandum of conversation between Hull and the Soviet ambassador, Andrei A. Gromyko, October 6, 1943, DSF 711.61/938.

# VII

## Strategies for War and Peace

BY LATE 1943 the Allied forces had turned from retreat and defeat sufficiently to make Franklin Roosevelt feel that American-Soviet discussions could begin to turn toward victory and postwar relations. Roosevelt and Cordell Hull were convinced that much of the tension in the Allied camp resulted from a failure to talk out the issues. FDR stepped up his efforts to get the Americans, British, and Russians together to plan the end of the war and to talk about the peace. A foundation for the president's meeting with his allies was laid by the Tripartite Conference of foreign ministers in Moscow.

When Loy Henderson asked to be relieved of his assignment on the European desk, Charles Bohlen replaced him and became the first of the Soviet specialists trained in the 1920s to serve in that position.[1] Bohlen admitted to ambivalence concerning the USSR. He empathized with the Russian people but did not trust their leaders. He knew that it would be difficult to persuade anyone in the government of the difference, and he did not try: "On the contrary, I went right along with everyone else, doing everything I could to help our embattled ally. During the war, there was always this ambiguity in my attitude toward the Soviet Union."[2]

Bohlen criticized the tendency to promise too much to the Soviet Union, including commitments to the second front before it was possible to launch it and to more Lend-Lease aid than could be fulfilled. He accurately assessed the reasons for this tendency:

I always thought that the primary reason for the overcommitments to the Kremlin was the fear that the Soviet armies might collapse, that the Bolshevik regime might surrender or make a deal with Hitler. Some people in the administration felt that encouragement, even when based on false premises, would stiffen the Soviet will. If the bleak truth had been told, the discouragement might have been too great for the

---

[1]Loy Henderson was a Soviet specialist, but he did not undergo the training regimen, through which Robert Kelley put his young charges, of language, cultural, and history courses in Paris or, as was the case with George Kennan, in Berlin.
[2]Bohlen, *Witness to History*, pp. 125–26.

Russians. Part of the blame for our overoptimistic encouragement can
be placed on the Russians, with their pessimistic outlook.[3]

When Bohlen took over the European desk, he agreed with Henderson that
the government was "dealing with the Soviets on an emotional instead of a
realistic basis." He disagreed with Henderson, however, on changing
America's Soviet policy, "if only because I did not see then, and cannot see
in retrospect, what other course we could have followed given the military
facts of the war."[4] In other words, the Russians were carrying the brunt of
the war in Europe; failure to aid them as completely as possible could bring
their defeat and surrender to Germany.

While Hull was in Moscow, President Roosevelt assigned him the task
of trying to get Stalin to meet with FDR and Winston Churchill. Hull
proposed they should get together at Basra in the Iraqi desert, but he was
rebuffed. Hull tried extreme flattery to persuade Stalin to go himself rather
than send V. M. Molotov:

> Through all past history . . . more than three-fourths of the human race
> until very recently have simply had to have leadership. Real leaders
> appear in the world only every one or two centuries. You yourself have
> demonstrated that leadership both at home and abroad, and you have a
> responsibility to exercise it in this stage of gravest possible world
> crisis by immediately appearing out in the world in close conjunction
> with President Roosevelt and Churchill.[5]

This did not change Stalin's mind on the Basra meeting.

However, according to Hull, it was at this point that Stalin promised
that after the victory in Europe the USSR would immediately enter the war
against Japan: "The Marshal's statement of his decision was forthright. He
made it emphatically, it was entirely unsolicited, and he asked nothing in
return."[6] Bohlen thought that Hull's recollection of "no quid pro quos" was
naive. He contended that close scrutiny of Hull's account raised "serious
doubts about what Stalin meant." Hull did not ask what price Stalin would
demand for Soviet entry into the Asian war. That the dictator did not
mention any did not mean that conditions were not in his mind. This blind
spot was one of Cordell Hull's faults as secretary of state. As Bohlen
described it, "he did not understand and indeed, true to American tradition,
rejected the concept of power in world affairs."[7]

Plenty of differences surfaced at the Tripartite Conference. The
Russians and the British expressed concern over the idea of a Four Nations

---

[3]Ibid., p. 124.
[4]Ibid., p. 125.
[5]Hull, *Memoirs*, 2:1039.
[6]Ibid., pp. 1309–10.
[7]Bohlen, *Witness to History*, p. 128.

Declaration. The Russians were suspicious of the "separate" peace being arranged in Italy, and they were not satisfied by the American and British explanations of their dealings with the Italians.[8] The powers disagreed on Iran. The British proposed to win the Iranians' cooperation in the war and to minimize actions that might injure their economy. The British and American representatives thought that they could invite the USSR to participate with them in collaborative programs, perhaps by making the Soviet Union responsible for gathering the grain supplies in northern Iran while the British and Americans controlled access to the oil in the southern part of the country. The Russians had a rougher approach in mind, and they suspected their allies' motives.

Hull reported to FDR that one area of discord at the conference resulted from Soviet requests for some part of the Italian navy: "I am convinced that the Soviet authorities are bitterly disappointed at our reaction to their request. . . . My impression is that they desire this shipping as a token to convince their people of our recognition of the part the Soviet forces have played in the collapse of Italy and as an indication that our three countries are collaborating." Since the Americans and the British had opposed the insistent Soviet request that Turkey and Sweden be forced to enter the war, this "small gesture" had become vitally important to a continued cooperative relationship.[9]

There was considerable caviling in Moscow on the dismemberment of Germany. Hull presented a discussion paper, on which the British and Soviet foreign ministers commented. He reversed Roosevelt's emphasis without completely ignoring his instructions. Roosevelt assumed that it would be best to dismember Germany but brought up the prospect that this might not be possible. Hull began with the statement that dismemberment might be impossible, but, as opinion was divided on the subject in the United States, it might be a matter worthy of discussion if the other two powers agreed. Anthony Eden said that the British public was undecided, but it would certainly accept the decision of the German people to separate and would honor the position of the Allies. Molotov interjected that he had heard that American opinion favored dismemberment but that Hull's paper seemed to belie that view. While the USSR would favor dividing Germany into smaller states, because the Soviet people seemed to desire it, his government would be willing to discuss alternatives. The foreign ministers knew that they would not be the ones to settle the issue; it would await action by the leaders of the three powers.[10]

---

[8]Chargé in the Soviet Union, Maxwell Hamilton, to secretary of state, October 19, 1943, *FRUS: General, 1943*, p. 569.

[9]Hull to FDR, October 30, 1943, ibid., p. 672.

[10]Summary of seventh session of Tripartite Conference, October 25, 1943, drafted by Charles Bohlen, ibid., pp. 629–34.

Hull tried to ease his allies' fears that they might be abandoned by America by promising a different approach after World War II than that which had prevailed after 1918: "This time the United States was prepared to play its part in the post-war world." Molotov "warmly welcomed" these views. In the mood of the moment, Hull was enthusiastic; if they could emphasize to their people "that they are in fact allies and comrades in the common struggle . . . nothing could prevent their becoming fast friends. Mr. Molotov agreed entirely."[11]

It was fairly easy for the foreign ministers to agree on principles governing the postwar world, as their implementation would depend on who was interpreting them. For example, Eden maintained that their application in central and eastern Europe included no interference with the forms of government, federations, or associations to be based on mutual welfare, Great Power support for such combinations in the general interest of prosperity, and no separate areas of responsibility for individual Great Powers. He contended that the Russians did not object.[12] Eden's observations were too optimistic: Haggling over the final declaration of the conference reinforced suspicions that the USSR intended to gain spheres of influence, and the Russians continued to suspect Anglo-American policy in Italy and possible American leniency toward Finland.[13] A meeting of the Big Three leaders would have to deal with these concerns.

Speaking with the press on October 29, President Roosevelt lauded the accomplishments of the foreign ministers. He was particularly pleased with the spirit of the conference; for this, he gave Hull most of the credit. FDR told the newsmen that the Moscow meeting "refuted predictions of cynics who thought talks would be clouded with suspicion and would accomplish little." The correspondents tried to get the president to discuss specifics, but he refused. He contended that the agenda "concerned matters of general policy, and . . . if Mr. Hull was bound by instructions and the British and the Russian delegates likewise, no progress would have been made." Instead, they had "thrashed things out in a friendly spirit and with complete give and take." A reporter asked if the success of the meeting strengthened the president's belief in Soviet willingness to cooperate in the postwar world; FDR responded that he had always been confident of the USSR's desire to maintain peace.[14]

Charles Bohlen later evaluated the conference and concluded that there were two decisions of importance: "the setting up of the European Advisory

---

[11]Memorandum of conversation by Bohlen, October 23, 1943, participants: Hull and V. M. Molotov with their interpreters, Bohlen and Valentin Berezhkov, ibid., p. 615.

[12]Summary of sixth session of Tripartite Conference, October 24, 1943, ibid., p. 628.

[13]Summary of twelfth session of Tripartite Conference, October 30, 1943, ibid., pp. 679–83.

[14]Acting Secretary of State Edward Stettinius to W. Averell Harriman, October 30, 1943, DSF 740.0011, Moscow/122a. See also *FRUS: General, 1943*, pp. 672–73.

Council to draw up surrender terms for Germany and the other enemy states in Europe" and "the Soviet agreement in principle to the establishment of a world organization for the preservation of future peace."[15] He accurately judged Hull's attendance at the Moscow meeting as a "high point" in the secretary's career, primarily because Hull got what he wanted from the Russians and the British when they agreed to a postwar peacekeeping organization. This had become Hull's fondest hope for avoiding another world war, a hope shared by FDR. The Soviet willingness to participate in such an organization was a surprise to American Soviet experts, who were pleased by the commitment. Bohlen guessed that the Russians had their own special motives in mind: "Viewed in retrospect, it was obvious that the Bolsheviks felt that one way of watching and controlling the Allied powers and, above all, of preventing them from ganging up against the Soviet Union was to be in on all of the deliberations from their inception."[16]

Bohlen tried to fathom Hull's success at Moscow, and he decided that despite, or perhaps because of, his weaknesses the Russians liked him. They appreciated his blunt, straightforward manner of dealing with problems; for example, at the final gathering before the conference concluded, "Hull said he would like to take the Axis leaders before a drumhead court-martial and shoot them the following morning." Bohlen believed it probably was not due to any special talents of Hull that the Moscow Conference succeeded:

> The real reason for the success of the 1943 Moscow meeting was that the military situation had improved so much that the pressure was temporarily off on the thorny issues of supplies and to a lesser degree the opening of a second front. . . . As a consequence of the military gains, the Soviets, while still pushing for the opening of a second front, could afford to wait until the Roosevelt-Churchill-Stalin conference scheduled for the next month.[17]

## II

In one sense, Moscow was a test for the prospects of success at a Big Three conference. If the Tripartite Conference had resulted in bickering and discordance, the three leaders would certainly have approached their gathering at Tehran with more trepidation. President Roosevelt received a series of assessments after Moscow that augured well for his hopes to cement the alliance for victory and to ensure postwar American-Soviet cooperation. On

---

[15]Bohlen, *Witness to History*, pp. 127–28.
[16]Ibid., pp. 128–29.
[17]Ibid., p. 130.

October 31, Cordell Hull wrote to FDR announcing a new Stalin who talked and acted "one hundred percent in favor of . . . cooperation in every way which the Four Nations Declaration proclaims." He enumerated the areas in which Stalin seemed to be willing to cooperate: "political, economic, military [and] specially including postwar organization for peace, world order under law, economic benefits, etc., etc."[18]

President Roosevelt was reassured about Soviet attitudes not only from Hull but also from Averell Harriman, who described the Russians as becoming more enthusiastic about the conference as it went along: "It was interesting to watch how Molotov expanded as the days passed as he began to realize more and more that we had not come with a united front against him and were ready to expose frankly our preliminary thoughts." Harriman believed that the Soviet Union had initially not intended to permit China to be a participant in the Four Nations Declaration, but nonetheless this was achieved: "Their acceptance of China is a clear indication that they are genuinely satisfied with the way things went and are ready to make important concessions to further the new intimacy." However, this new attitude was not so well established that the United States could feel free to "take liberties with them."

Harriman cautioned that several real difficulties remained. The second front issue was still paramount to Stalin and his advisers, and there had to be action in this area soon. The Russians would be tougher in their demands for reparations from Germany than the Americans were ready to permit. They expected the Americans to accept their 1941 frontiers without serious question, and the problem of Poland "is even tougher than we believed. . . . They are determined to recognize only a Polish government that will be a whole-heartedly friendly neighbor. On the other hand, Molotov told me definitely that they were willing to have a strong independent Poland, giving expression to whatever social and political system the Polish people wanted." Harriman was suspicious of Soviet promises that they were not interested in extending their system, especially if such expansion proved to be the only way the Russians could get the kind of neighbors they wanted.[19]

*Izvestiia* heralded the tenth anniversary of the American-Soviet recognition agreement with a promise of continuing improvement in the relations of the two countries.[20] Harriman analyzed this article, which mentioned several significant events demonstrating the strengthening of the

---

[18]Hull to FDR, October 31, 1943, *FRUS: General, 1943*, pp. 690–91. Hull connected the Four Nations Declaration to the implementation of the postwar peacekeeping organization, and for this reason he was especially pleased when the Soviets changed their minds on October 30 and agreed to sign the declaration along with China whose ambassador, Foo Ping-sheung, signed for his government. See Hull, *Memoirs*, 2:1306.

[19]Harriman to FDR, November 4, 1943, *FRUS: Conferences at Cairo and Teheran, 1943*, pp. 152–55.

[20]"The Strengthening of Soviet-American Friendship," *Izvestiia*, November 16, 1943.

relationship and President Roosevelt's determination to oppose disturbers of the peace. This had led, the article noted, to "recognition of a community of interests," beginning with the talks between FDR and Maxim Litvinov in 1933 and continuing with the "quarantine" speech of 1937 and "the agreement on the principles for mutual assistance in the war against aggression signed at Washington during Molotov's visit in 1942." Harriman stressed the article's reference to continuing collaboration in the postwar world.[21]

On November 17, Harriman summarized a *Pravda* story giving "greater emphasis to the obstacles and hostility which the President was obliged to overcome in establishing diplomatic relations . . . and in developing a policy of friendship and cooperation." Referring to policies of the Hearst, McCormick, and Patterson newspapers, *Pravda* quoted Harold Ickes's comment that the Russians could take some consolation from the fact that these people "also hate their own country." They were not to be feared, because there was a "steadily growing understanding of the masses of the American people of the importance of strengthening Soviet-American relations." Harriman identified an important common theme in the *Izvestiia* and *Pravda* articles: They gave credit to the Americans for highly valued assistance to the USSR in the war against the aggressors.[22] This item was of interest, because Americans had complained about the paucity of public acknowledgment of Allied aid to the Red Army.

Roosevelt wanted desperately to arrange a meeting of the Big Four, but Stalin would not meet with the Chinese because of the neutrality pact with Japan. Thus, FDR and Churchill met Chiang Kai-shek at Cairo during November 22–26, where Chiang received assurances from Roosevelt that Japan would be forced to surrender Formosa, Manchuria, and all Pacific possessions. In return China would agree to Russian acquisition of all of Sakhalin and the Kurile Islands as well as to Dairen becoming a free port.[23]

As Franklin Roosevelt prepared to leave Cairo for his talks with Stalin and Churchill, he felt optimistic about the meeting and its potential results. His secretary of state, his ambassador to the Soviet Union, and the Russians themselves spoke in generous terms about the preparatory conference at Moscow, the developing "new" relationship, and happy expectations of collaboration in the postwar world. These various reports did not neglect areas of disagreement that might get in the way of cooperation, but disagreement was to some extent downplayed in favor of a rosier view.

On his way to Tehran aboard the USS *Iowa*, President Roosevelt met with his Joint Chiefs of Staff in the comfortable setting of the admiral's cabin. They discussed important matters that might be considered at the

---

[21]Harriman to Hull, November 16, 1943, DSF 711.61/951.
[22]Harriman to Hull, November 17, 1943, DSF 711.61/952.
[23]Lester H. Brune, ed., *Chronological History of United States Foreign Relations, 1776 to January 20, 1981*, 2 vols. (New York: Garland, 1985), 2:815.

forthcoming meeting, and paramount was the question of what to do about Germany and the rest of Europe at the end of the war. They took up a memorandum, prepared by Admiral William D. Leahy, which asked for "guidance" concerning "spheres of influence." Previously the president and Hull had refused to discuss such divisions, and in fact they opposed the use of the term because of its bad connotation from World War I. Ironically, the Department of State, which became responsible for position papers on diplomatic matters after the war, did not bring up the issue of spheres; it was introduced by representatives of the War and Navy departments. Leahy's memorandum observed that the USSR would offer no objection to breaking up Germany after the war, as though this division were a settled matter. The most acceptable division apparently was to group the southern "Catholic" states into one country, the northwestern or "Protestant" region into another, and the northeastern states into a section where the religion was "Prussianism."

One item of concern was who should supervise which area during reconstruction. Leahy warned that the British would like to see the United States take the southern region and include part of France in its occupation. Roosevelt "did not like that arrangement. We do not want to be concerned with reconstituting France. France is a British 'baby.' " Instead, the British should be assigned France, along with Luxembourg, Belgium, Baden, Bavaria, and Württemberg, while "the United States should take northwestern Germany . . . and we should go as far as Berlin. The Soviets could then take the territory to the east thereof."[24]

On his arrival at Tehran, FDR stayed at the Soviet legation after being persuaded by the Secret Service and Ambassador Harriman that Nazi agents abounded in the city and that there might be assassination attempts if there were too much travel to and from the various legations. Roosevelt and Stalin first met alone with their interpreters, to get acquainted. Marshal Stalin raised the question of the future of France, describing "in considerable length the reasons why, in his opinion, France deserved no considerate treatment from the Allies and, above all, had no right to retain her former empire." He charged that the French ruling class was "rotten to the core," had surrendered ignominiously to the German invaders, and had provided aid to the enemy. "He therefore felt that it would be not only unjust but dangerous to leave in French hands any important strategic points after the war." Given FDR's own views of the French, this tirade was unlikely to upset him. He told Stalin that "it was necessary to eliminate in the future government of France anybody over forty years old and particularly anybody who had formed part of the French Government." He thought that Dakar and New Caledonia represented a threat to New Zealand and Australia and

---

[24]Minutes of president's meeting with the Joint Chiefs of Staff, November 19, 1943, admiral's cabin, USS *Iowa, FRUS: Conferences at Cairo and Teheran, 1943*, p. 253.

should be under a UN trusteeship. Further, he spoke for twenty-one American republics "when he said that Dakar in unsure hands was a direct threat to the Americas."[25]

When Churchill met with FDR and Stalin, he disavowed any intent to expand British territorial possessions as a result of the war. Nonetheless, Churchill noted that, since the United States, Great Britain, the USSR, and China would be "responsible for the future peace of the world, it was obviously necessary that certain strategic points throughout the world should be under [their] control."[26] Considering Great Britain's previous opposition to including China as a Great Power, this was a startling departure. Stalin continued to focus on France, pressing for a specific agreement that it would be excluded from Great Power status.

Roosevelt changed the subject by bringing up the treatment of Germany. He wanted the word *Reich* to be stricken from the German language. Stalin argued that this was not enough; Germany itself had to be "rendered impotent ever again to plunge the world into war. . . . Unless the victorious Allies retained in their hands the strategic positions necessary to prevent any recrudescence of German militarism, they would have failed in their duty." Thereafter in the conversation Stalin "took the lead," hammering away at his arguments that to control Germany and to prevent German rearmament was not enough; stronger measures were required.[27] He illustrated the impossibility of reforming the Germans with a story about his experience in Leipzig in 1907, "when 200 German workers failed to appear at an important mass meeting because there was no controller at the station platform to punch their tickets which would permit them to leave the station." Stalin believed "that this mentality of discipline and obedience could not be changed." He then questioned the unconditional surrender doctrine; he argued that it merely served to unite the German people. To specify exactly what they could expect, "no matter how harsh," would "hasten the day of German capitulation."[28]

When President Roosevelt brought up the questions of free navigation of the Baltic Sea and possibly some form of trusteeship or international state in the vicinity of the Kiel Canal to ensure access from both directions, the Russian translator misinterpreted the remark as referring to the Baltic

---

[25]Memorandum of Roosevelt-Stalin conversation, November 28, 1943, PSF, Teheran Trip File, FDRL.

[26]Memorandum of Marshal Stalin's views as expressed during the evening, November 28, 1943, Map Room Papers, Sextant Conferences, Box 28, 3f Folder, FDRL. A Copy of this memorandum reprinted in *FRUS: Conferences at Cairo and Teheran, 1943*, pp. 513–14, states that this was a supplemental memorandum prepared by Bohlen.

[27]Ibid.

[28]Ibid. Stalin's story about the German workers was apparently one he remembered vividly, as he used it again when he touched on the Germans at his meeting with the Yugoslavian Communist Milovan Djilas. See Milovan Djilas, *Conversations with Stalin* (New York: Harcourt, Brace, 1962), p. 79.

States. Stalin responded that the question had been settled by the plebiscite and was not open for discussion. Obviously, the Russians expected Roosevelt to plead for independence of the Baltic States. When Roosevelt's statement was clarified, Stalin agreed.

In a discussion of "certain outlying possessions," FDR expressed his interest "in the possibility of a sovereignty fashioned in a collective body such as the United Nations; a concept which had never been developed in past history." This oblique introduction to the issue of UN trusteeships was typical of Roosevelt. He knew that it was the wrong time to discuss his scheme, but, because it was a part of his overall plan for postwar security and for the elimination of colonialism, he wanted to make sure the concept was implanted in the minds of his two colleagues. Roosevelt planted the seed and awaited the chance to nurture it.

Stalin was no less adept at cultivating ideas for future reference. He tried to get FDR and Churchill to discuss at dinner their positions on the postwar fate of Germany and France. He asked them to express their "exact views" on these matters "without, however, stating clearly what solutions he himself proposed." He especially wanted to know "exactly what form of security organization would be developed after the war and how far the United States and British governments were prepared to go in implementing the police power of such an organization."[29] It is likely that Stalin did this to give FDR a chance to expand on the Four Policemen concept that he had expressed to Molotov during the commissar's 1942 visit to Washington, but the president did not oblige. He waited until the next day to bring up the policing power.

After dinner the president retired, whereupon Churchill and Stalin returned to the German question. Stalin became more forthright on the need to treat Germany harshly. Churchill proposed several measures: There should be no aviation industry, the general staff system should be abolished, industry should be constantly supervised, "and territorial dismemberment of the Reich" should be mandatory. Stalin wondered if this would be enough to keep Germany down. Any factory could make fuses for shells. As the Germans were a very talented and able people, they could easily revive within fifteen to twenty years "and again become a threat to the world." Churchill professed to be able to see only fifty years into the future, and the responsibility to ensure that Germany did not again threaten the world during that time rested on the three powers gathered at Tehran. Concentrated education of the German people over a generation could reverse the indoctrination they had undergone at the hands of their leaders over the preceding several decades. In other words, leadership was the key. Stalin was dissatisfied with Churchill's program for Germany.

---

[29]Memorandum of Marshal Stalin's views as expressed during the evening, November 28, 1943, *FRUS: Conferences at Cairo and Teheran, 1943*, pp. 513–14.

Churchill reminded Stalin that Great Britain had gone to war to defend Poland from disintegration; a strong independent Poland was "a necessary instrument in the European orchestra." He guaranteed Stalin that, personally, he had "no attachment to any specific frontier between Poland and the Soviet Union; [and] that he felt that the consideration of Soviet security on their western frontiers was a governing factor." Anthony Eden interrupted to ask Stalin if he had understood him correctly at dinner when he said that the Soviet Union favored a Polish western border on the Oder River. Stalin emphatically supported such a frontier and promised that the Soviet Union would help the Poles to achieve it. Churchill used three matchsticks, representing the Soviet Union, Poland, and Germany, to illustrate how Poland could be moved westward, "as soldiers . . . execute the drill 'left close.' " Stalin was willing to reach an understanding, but he desired to examine it further.[30]

## III

Churchill, Roosevelt, and Stalin made general suggestions and tested one another on how their ideas would be received in the first few sessions of their meeting; thereafter, they got down to the issues that had brought them together. On November 29, FDR tried to answer Stalin's question about the postwar security organization. He guessed that there would be some thirty-five nations involved, meeting periodically at different places for discussion and to make recommendations to a smaller body. Stalin wanted to know if the organization would be European or worldwide; FDR answered that it would be worldwide. The executive committee would consist of the USSR, the United States, Great Britain, and China, along with two additional European countries, one South American, one Near Eastern, one Far Eastern, and one British Dominion. He joked that Churchill did not like his proposal because the British would only have two votes. This committee would deal with nonmilitary questions. Stalin wondered if its decisions were binding on all nations, and FDR responded: yes and no. He would hope that nations with disputes on nonmilitary matters would accept its guidance, but he was sure that the Congress of the United States would not accept as binding the decision of such an entity. Here, of course, he had in mind Woodrow Wilson's difficulties in selling the League Covenant to Congress, which had rejected Articles 10 and 15 because they would commit the United States to the decisions of a "foreign body."[31]

---

[30]Memorandum of conversation, dinner meeting, November 28, 1943, including the president, Mr. Hopkins, Ambassador Harriman, Mr. Bohlen; Mr. Churchill, Mr. Eden, Sir Archibald Clark Kerr, Colonel Birse; Marshal Stalin, Mr. Molotov, Mr. Pavlov, in Map Room Papers, Sextant Conferences, Box 28, 3f Folder, FDRL.

[31]Proceedings of the conference, November 29, 1943, *FRUS: Conferences at Cairo and Teheran*, pp. 529–33.

President Roosevelt then turned to his Four Policemen concept, saying that the signatories of the Four Nations Declaration would have the power to deal immediately with any threat to the peace. Stalin did not believe that the smaller nations of Europe would be very happy with the Four Policemen idea, and Stalin himself would certainly object to China having a voice in Europe's affairs. Stalin proposed one committee for Europe, another for the Far East, and another for other areas. This was similar to Churchill's proposal for regional organizations, but FDR "doubted if the United States Congress would agree to the United States' participation in an exclusively European Committee which might be able to force the dispatch of American troops to Europe." Why he thought that Congress might agree to send troops worldwide, which was implied in his own plan, was unclear at this point. Stalin caught him up on this, proclaiming "that the world organization . . . might also require the sending of American troops to Europe." Roosevelt envisioned committing only U.S. air and naval forces, with the British and Russians providing the ground troops.[32]

Stalin changed the subject. Did Churchill really believe in Operation Overlord, or were the British only agreeing to pacify the Russians? Churchill hedged and proposed that the British and American staffs should meet the next morning to work out a joint point of view to present to the conference.[33] To Stalin's question of who would command Overlord, Churchill and Roosevelt had to admit that this had not been decided yet. Roosevelt added that all commanders except for the supreme commander had been selected. Harry Hopkins found Stalin's pressure much to his satisfaction; later, he told Lord Moran, of Churchill's staff, that "there was no God-damn alternative left."[34]

Churchill avowed that he was committed to Overlord, but the Mediterranean theater should not be "ruthlessly cast aside as valueless merely on the question of a month's delay in Overlord." Stalin was persuaded to accept the Mediterranean operations as important, but he still insisted that they were diversions. FDR countered that it was unwise for the British forces to be idle for six months awaiting Overlord, that they should continue to pressure Germany from the south. Stalin did not wish the British to remain inactive, but he opposed transfers to the south, which would interfere with an early launching of the cross-Channel attack.[35]

At dinner that same evening Stalin began to goad Winston Churchill. Bohlen recorded that the atmosphere was tense: "Marshal Stalin lost no opportunity to get in a dig at Mr. Churchill. Almost every remark . . . had a

---

[32]Ibid.

[33]Second plenary meeting, November 29, 1943, ibid., p. 539.

[34]Charles M. Wilson, Lord Moran, *Churchill: Taken from the Diaries of Lord Moran: The Struggle for Survival, 1940–1945* (Boston: Houghton Mifflin, 1966), p. 149.

[35]Combined chiefs of staff minutes, November 29, 1943, *FRUS: Conferences at Cairo and Teheran, 1943*, pp. 541–48.

sharp edge. . . . He apparently desired to put and keep the Prime Minister on the defensive."[36] Bohlen thought that this was largely due to Stalin's anger over the British reluctance on Overlord. Stalin implied that Churchill nursed a secret affection for Germany and wanted a soft peace. He specifically asserted that 50,000 to 100,000 of the German commanding staff should be liquidated. The president jokingly interjected that the figure should be 49,000 or more. Churchill took strong exception to the idea of executing soldiers who had fought for their country.[37]

Stalin also referred to Roosevelt's comments earlier about taking control of strategic locations, such as Dakar, and supported his idea of trusteeship. Churchill took this as a threat aimed against the British Empire, as he knew the anticolonial posture of both of his allies. He disavowed any desire to acquire new territory but indicated that he was prepared to fight a war to hold on to what Britain had, specifically mentioning Singapore and Hong Kong. He admitted that the British might eventually relinquish portions of the empire, but it would be entirely their own decision. Stalin backed off a bit. He commended the British soldiers who had fought well, and he even said that he favored an extension of the British Empire, especially around Gibraltar.[38]

Churchill shifted to the Soviet Union's territorial ambitions. Stalin would not discuss this: "There is no need to speak at the present time about any Soviet desires, but when the time comes, we will speak."[39] This should have alerted the Americans that their dreams of peace without annexations were not going to be fulfilled. Stalin had clearly identified his desire for territory; he simply chose not to mention specifics yet. Perhaps Stalin remembered the American refusal to permit the British and the Russians to discuss such things when they signed their treaty of alliance, and he was satisfied to meet the American demand for postponement of the question until the end of the war.

Either under instructions from Roosevelt or of his own accord, Harry Hopkins went to see Churchill after the Russian dinner and told the prime minister that the British had nothing to gain from continuing to oppose Overlord. Both Roosevelt and Stalin were "adamant" that the invasion should take place, so perhaps he should "yield with grace." The following morning Churchill capitulated and promised full British support for an attack in May. Stalin expressed "his great satisfaction with this decision."[40]

In a luncheon conversation on the Far East, Churchill brought up the communiqué from the Cairo Conference. Because the USSR was not at war with Japan, Stalin could make no commitments, but he thoroughly

---

[36]Tripartite dinner meeting, November 29, 1943, ibid., p. 553.
[37]Ibid., pp. 553–54.
[38]Ibid., p. 554.
[39]Ibid., pp. 554–55.
[40]Bohlen, *Witness to History*, p. 148.

approved of the statements. It was right that Korea should be independent and that Manchuria, Formosa, and the Pescadores Islands should be returned to China. However, the Chinese should be made to fight, which they had not yet done. The prime minister and the president agreed.

Churchill then surprised Stalin by suggesting that such a large country as Russia should have access to warm-water ports. Given Britain's opposition to this for more than a century, it was an incredible departure. Churchill added that such a settlement would probably be a part of the general peace agreement and could no doubt be determined as among friends. Stalin took advantage of Churchill's comment to bring up the neutralization of the Dardanelles, which the prime minister did not want to discuss because the Allies were trying to get Turkey to enter the war on their side. Churchill welcomed the USSR's naval and merchant fleets to the oceans of the world. Stalin reminded Churchill that Lord Curzon had had other ideas, but the prime minister allowed that that had been a different time, and Stalin agreed. Churchill then focused on warm-water ports in the Far East. Stalin wished to defer this until after the USSR entered the war against Japan, but he did mention that Russia had no ice-free ports there. When Roosevelt suggested that Dairen might be made a free port, Stalin said that he did not think the Chinese would like this. The president failed to mention that he had already gained Chinese acquiescence, provided that the powers guaranteed the security of the port.

Churchill tried to convince Roosevelt and Stalin that if they could settle territorial adjustments at Tehran the world could remain at peace. He reminded them that hungry and ambitious nations were dangerous and that "he would like to see the leading nations of the world in the position of rich, happy men." They set part of the afternoon agenda aside to discuss "political matters," with special reference "to Poland, Finland, and Sweden."[41]

Hopkins, Eden, and Molotov also met at lunch that day. The commissar began the conversation by asserting that France was not a country merely overpowered by Germany but one collaborating with the German strategies. In a roundabout fashion, Molotov suggested that strategic areas could be entrusted only to the Great Powers, and France would not be among them. Hopkins interjected that FDR believed that the control of strategic places would have to be worked out among the nations represented at Tehran "in a manner which will not start each of the three powers arming against the others." This danger could be avoided if they decided "the basic questions regarding strong points and who will control these." Poland was next on their agenda. Eden referred to the "indiscreet conversation" that had occurred earlier between Churchill and Stalin about

---

[41]Roosevelt, Churchill, Stalin luncheon meeting, November 30, 1943, Bohlen minutes, *FRUS: Conferences at Cairo and Teheran, 1943*, pp. 565–68.

the Poles. The British did not want Poland to be a subject of friction between their countries. However, "if the question of two steps to the left was to be considered for Poland," Eden wanted to know "how large these steps would be."[42]

Hopkins claimed that Roosevelt had spoken frankly with Stalin about Poland during their meeting on November 30. Charles Bohlen did not agree; he was convinced that FDR had dodged a full discussion. He recalled FDR's famous remark to Stalin about the six million Polish voters in America as a reason why he did not want to discuss the Polish question that Stalin and Churchill were going to bring up on the afternoon of December 1. Since Roosevelt had decided, reluctantly, that he might have to run for a third term, because the war was not over, he did not want to lose the votes of the Polish-Americans. "Therefore, while he personally agreed with Stalin's general view that Poland's frontiers should be moved to the west, he hoped that Stalin would understand why he could not take part in any such arrangements." Although Stalin pretended to understand Roosevelt's reluctance, Bohlen doubted that Stalin comprehended any aspect of internal American politics. Nonetheless, he was sure that the Soviet dictator was relieved not to have to argue over Poland at Tehran.[43]

## *IV*

When the Big Three returned to their discussion of the United Nations, Roosevelt drew a sketch of his idea for the organization. In a circle on the left he placed the forty united nations, with a line descending to the International Labor Organization, Health, Agriculture, and Food, indicating that all the members would participate in dealing with general issues relating to labor, health, hunger, and food distribution. In the middle he circled an executive committee, and on the right a third circle encompassed the Four Policemen. This scheme, which would later be altered, would provide the general format of the organization intended to keep the peace.[44]

That same evening Roosevelt, Churchill, and Stalin dined with thirty members of their delegations and celebrated the prime minister's sixty-ninth birthday. According to Bohlen's notes of the gathering, Churchill sat with FDR on his right and Stalin on his left, and "all speeches took the form of toasts, following the Russian custom and the policy established at the Stalin dinner." Churchill flattered both his American and his Russian colleagues. He praised President Roosevelt's devotion to the great principles underlying democratic civilization as well as his defense of the weak and

---

[42]Hopkins, Eden, Molotov luncheon meeting, November 30, 1943, ibid., pp. 568–75.

[43]Bohlen, *Witness to History*, p. 151.

[44]Sketch by Roosevelt dated November 30, 1943, to illustrate his concept of the United Nations Organization, Hopkins Papers, Teheran Miscellaneous File, FDRL.

helpless. He also saluted Stalin, who "was worthy to stand with the great figures of Russian history and merited the title of 'Stalin the Great.' "[45]

Stalin's response to Churchill's toast may have been one of the reasons for a later comment by Charles Bohlen that at Tehran "there were a number of disquieting indications of how Stalin's mind was working at that time."[46] The Russian leader contended that the honors attributed to him belonged to the people. "He said that even persons of medium courage and even cowards became heroes in Russia. Those who didn't, he said, were killed." While demurely deflecting the compliment, Stalin let his comrades know that the weak and helpless were not a matter of concern in the USSR; those who hesitated in the tough give-and-take of politics and war perished. Churchill observed that President Roosevelt, through "courage and foresighted action in 1933, had . . . prevented a revolution in the United States." Perhaps "the Russian people" killed the fainthearted, but in America the leader molded the stronghearted. Roosevelt had guided his country through the "tumultuous stream of party friction and internal politics amidst the violent freedoms of democracy."[47] This was as close as Churchill would come to saying that one could deal with crises in a democratic system effectively and that Stalin might as well know that he was facing a leader who had come through his own crucible.

When Roosevelt toasted Sir Alan Brooke, the British army's chief of staff, Stalin stood with the others but did not drink. He commented, "with a twinkle in his eye," that he regretted Sir Alan's "grim and distrustful attitude" toward the USSR. He then drank to Brooke's health, wishing that he "would come to know us better and would find that we are not so bad after all."[48] Bohlen described the atmosphere at that moment among the British delegation as "fearful," because the general's Irish temper was well known. Brooke waited for some time, presumably to let his temper cool, then rose to his feet and talked about British cover plans of using dummy tanks and planes to deceive the Germans. Turning to Stalin, Sir Alan said that possibly he had misjudged the Russians because of what he termed the excellent "Soviet cover plan" in the early part of the war of associating with Germany.

Stalin could have turned the evening to disaster by taking special umbrage at this reference to the Nazi-Soviet pact; he chose not to. Stalin interjected: "That is possible," and everyone laughed in relief. Sir Alan proffered a real desire for closer collaboration with the Russians. Stalin

---

[45]Dinner, British legation, November 30, 1943, Map Room Papers, Sextant Conferences, Box 28, Documents concerning the Transfer of Presidential Papers to the Department of State, February 4, 1946, FDRL.

[46]Bohlen, *Witness to History*, p. 151.

[47]Dinner, British legation, November 30, 1943, Map Room Papers, Box 28, FDRL.

[48]Ibid.

responded, "That is possible, . . . even probable."[49] Brooke had the last thrust, however. Bohlen commented that everyone thought the general would then toast Marshal Klementi Voroshilov, "but instead he broke away completely from his vein and abruptly proposed the health of Admiral Leahy."[50] General Brooke was undoubtedly familiar with the less than trustful attitude of the admiral toward the Russians, and he chose to single out for a toast his American colleague, a kindred spirit.

Churchill tried to smooth over the awkward moment by suggesting that changing political complexions were abroad in the world, and he could definitely say that in Great Britain "complexions are becoming a trifle pinker." Stalin quickly responded: "That is a sign of good health." Just before the dinner ended, Stalin surprised his colleagues by toasting the enormous productive capacity of the United States, which had doubled the combined aircraft production of Great Britain and the Soviet Union. Without this production from the United States, the war would have been lost. He expressed his gratitude and that of the Russian people for this contribution under President Roosevelt's leadership and warmly toasted the president. Roosevelt picked up on Churchill's theme concerning political complexions: "I like to think of this in terms of the rainbow. In our country the rainbow is a symbol of good fortune and of hope. It has many varying colors, each individualistic, but blending into one glorious whole." The meeting at Tehran had proved that "our nations can come together in a harmonious whole, moving unitedly for the common good of ourselves and of the world. So as we leave this historic gathering, we can see in the sky, for the first time, that traditional symbol of hope, the rainbow."[51]

The president, as the conference concluded, elevated the career prospects of the interpreter, notetaker, and general handyman of the meetings, Charles E. Bohlen. FDR congratulated him for the great help he had provided "in the difficult process of interchanging thoughts through the medium of two widely divergent languages." He praised Bohlen's precise knowledge of the "meaning of the Russian language" and his "understanding of the Russian mentality [which] have made a real contribution to my important talks in Teheran." He was thankful, because Stalin had understood every nuance of what he had said.[52] Although Bohlen, a professional diplomat, was supposed to take such things in stride, this may have contributed to his exhilaration about the Tehran Conference. He mentioned that he was "impressed by the confidence and optimism of the

[49]Bohlen, *Witness to History*, pp. 149–50.

[50]Dinner, British legation, November 30, 1943, Map Room Papers, Box 28, FDRL.

[51]Ibid.

[52]FDR to Bohlen, November 30, 1943, PPF 8593, copy in OF 220, FDRL. This was not simply due to Bohlen's excellent translating ability. Stalin understood English far better than he let on. See Elliott Roosevelt, "Why Stalin 'Never Forgave' Eleanor Roosevelt," *Parade Magazine*, February 9, 1986.

three leaders—a justified confidence in view of the fact that the military decisions made at Teheran led to the defeat and surrender of Germany. A realist on Soviet policy always has his doubts, but there are times when he is hopeful."[53]

According to T. Michael Ruddy, Bohlen, like many Soviet experts in the Department of State, was not as enamored of prospects for real cooperation with the Soviet Union as the Roosevelt White House appeared to be. Although his skepticism continued, he began to gain a different view from his association with Hopkins and Roosevelt. Hopkins and Bohlen had not hit it off at their first meeting in 1942, but Hopkins changed his mind when he was impressed by Bohlen's performance at Cairo and Tehran. Ambassador Harriman wanted Bohlen in Moscow when George Kennan, who was supposed to go there, was preempted by John G. Winant to serve on the European Advisory Commission. Hopkins was determined to get Bohlen assigned to Washington, and with Department of State pressure he "was reassigned to Washington in January 1944 as Chief of the Division of Eastern European Affairs."[54]

After President Roosevelt left Tehran, he sent a message to Stalin in which he called the Tehran Conference "historic," as it proved their ability not only to wage war together "but to work in utmost harmony for the peace to come." FDR had waited a long time to meet Stalin and to prove to him that he was not dealing with either reactionaries or enemies in America. Roosevelt told Stalin how much he had enjoyed meeting him "face to face" and that he hoped they would meet again. In the meantime he wished the Red Army "the greatest success."[55]

President Roosevelt and Secretary Hull believed that their frankness at Moscow and Tehran would shortly bring forth Soviet acceptance of the new relationship. Then they could get on with winning the war and determining the framework for the postwar world. Stalin, for his part, thought that he had cleared the way for Soviet security.

---

[53]Bohlen, *Witness to History*, p. 154.
[54]T. Michael Ruddy, *The Cautious Diplomat: Charles E. Bohlen and the Soviet Union, 1929–1969* (Kent, OH: Kent State University Press), pp. 21–22.
[55]FDR to Stalin, December 3, 1943, *FRUS: Conferences at Cairo and Teheran*, p. 785.

# VIII

## Assessing the Russians on the Road to Victory

THE PRESIDENT OF THE USSR, Mikhail Kalinin, reviewed 1943 in his New Year's message by touting the military successes of the Red Army and the Allied unity resulting from the meetings at Moscow and Tehran. He acknowledged that, parallel with the Red Army's advances, the Allies had driven the Nazis from North Africa, Sicily, Sardinia, and Corsica and were advancing on Rome. At the same time, the Allied bombers had systematically destroyed German industrial capacity with devastating air raids and had forced the collapse of Hitler's strongest fascist ally in Europe, which allowed the Italian people to be brought into the struggle against Germany.

According to President Kalinin, the Moscow Conference "assured the further Rapprochement of the Allies in their affairs and paved the way for the meeting of the leaders of the Allied countries" at the Tehran Conference, which was "in reality the greatest event of our times, a historical landmark in the struggle with the German aggressor. All of the efforts of the Germans to separate the freedom loving nations failed." This conference was historic because "the leaders of the three great powers reached full agreement on questions of war and peace."[1]

If Kalinin could present this optimistic picture of the developing relationship between the Allies, it is no wonder that the Americans also expected a smoother course in their dealings with the Russians after Tehran. Certainly, Franklin Roosevelt believed this. He wrote Sumner Welles that he thought the meetings at Cairo and Tehran had gone well and "that as a roving Ambassador for the first time I did not 'pull any boners.' "[2]

In a press commentary covering FDR's address to Congress on the Tehran Conference, the Russians told their readers of Roosevelt's

---

[1]W. Averell Harriman to Cordell Hull, January 3, 1944, *FRUS: Diplomatic Papers*, vol. 4, *Europe, 1944* (Washington, DC: Government Printing Office, 1966), pp. 801–2.
[2]Roosevelt to Sumner Welles, January 4, 1944, PPF 2961, Sumner Welles Folder, FDRL.

determination not to repeat the mistakes of the 1920s, wherein isolationism and unpreparedness produced disaster. The Soviet writer stressed FDR's emphasis that the purpose of the United Nations was to ensure physical, economic, social, and moral security. The president had also scored those who attacked the Tehran proceedings and warned against a postwar lapse into reaction, quoting Benjamin Franklin's assertion that those who did not hang together would hang separately.[3] The secretary of state and the president must have been encouraged to see that the Russians stressed the points in his speech concerning postwar cooperation.

Maxwell Hamilton, who served in Moscow as minister counselor, assessed Soviet-American relations for 1943, and his dispatch revealed mixed emotions about Soviet policies. The Russians had gone on the offensive not only in the military campaigns of the past year but also in diplomacy. He acknowledged the "marked forward steps toward international cooperation" made by the two major conferences at the end of the year. He very astutely perceived that the Russians had decided that they could no longer postpone decisions on matters relating to the end of the war and the postwar era, thus their willingness to meet Allied leaders at Moscow and Tehran. There were positive signs for cooperation in the communiqué issued at the end of the gathering of the Big Three leaders: "The foundations for collaboration both during and after the war had been laid. The tremendous problems of the peace and of the political, economic and social reconstruction of Europe had not been solved, but there had been removed the chief obstacles that lay in the way of a joint approach to them by the three great powers that would carry the main burden of their solution."[4] However, as the Red Army approached the old borders of Russia and faced liberating the nations formerly in the Soviet or Russian sphere, acute problems for Soviet diplomacy would arise. The government would have "to reveal to an increasing extent the objectives of its foreign policy and this in turn will largely determine the character of Soviet relations with the United States and Great Britain."[5] What Hamilton ignored was that American interpretations of Soviet policy also would have a major bearing on the future of American-Soviet relations, and vice versa.

It did not take long for the high expectations for the new relationship to turn to doubts in some quarters. On January 9, Averell Harriman wrote to Cordell Hull and FDR telling them that V. M. Molotov and others, despite their inclination to be friendly with members of the American military mission, showed little willingness to cooperate with them. Harriman tried to fathom this and decided that it was not due to ill will, but rather to "the bottlenecking of all decisions in the Kremlin" and because the "spirit of

[3]Harriman to Hull, January 13, 1944, Box 1360 C Moscow, 800.1, Post Files.
[4]Maxwell Hamilton to Hull, "Review of Soviet Relations during 1943," February 8, 1944, DSF 861.00/12055.
[5]Ibid.

Teheran has not percolated to lower echelons."[6]   Later, Harriman partly attributed this change in attitude to "elements in the Party and Government which are inherently suspicious of foreign influence, including the NKVD and certain isolationist circles," who were upset by the popular support for cooperation after the meetings of the Allied powers.[7]

An event of the spring of 1944 illustrated that a group of Russians did indeed suspect that postwar relations with the Americans would not rest on cooperation. Captain Victor Kravchenko, who defected from the Soviet military mission when it was in New York, revealed that his assignment was to spy for the USSR on the United States.  In an effort to maintain smooth relations with the Russians, Joe Davies tried to get Hull to agree to turn Kravchenko over to Ambassador Andrei Gromyko, but Hull told him "he was not impressed with the Russian Government's request, and was going to recommend that it not be granted."  Davies went to Edwin "Pa" Watson, one of Roosevelt's aides, to try to reverse Hull's decision on the grounds that the secretary was being "poisoned by some of the State Department 'underlings' against Russia."[8]

Davies admitted that his only concern was to ensure that the "fine understanding" between Russia and the United States not be alienated.  He knew what Kravchenko's fate would be, so he came up with a tricky plan to serve American-Soviet relations and to save the Russian at the same time. FDR should grant extradition in principle but postpone the date, "he hoped, indefinitely."  The Russians contended throughout that the captain was an unworthy officer, not a member of any mission, and that to preserve friendly relations he should be returned.[9]  Gromyko obviously tried to get the Americans to believe that they were dealing with a villain of no real consequence, because he knew what Kravchenko could tell them, and it did not bode well for a continuing trustful and friendly relationship. Kravchenko, in fact, did reveal the Soviet suspicions concerning the durability of the alliance.[10]

Differences arose concerning Soviet objections to the unconditional surrender doctrine.  Roosevelt had used the term to assure the Russians that there would be no separate peace and to make clear to the enemy powers that they could not simply change governments and create the illusion that their military leaders had not lost the war.  The Soviet Union no longer feared that Britain and the United States might sign a separate peace, but it was

---

[6]Harriman to Hull and FDR, January 9, 1944, DSF 711.61/968. See also *FRUS: Europe, 1944*, pp. 802–3.
    [7]Harriman to Hull, February 4, 1944, Box 1363 B Moscow, 891-891, REVIEWS OF TRENDS OF SOVIET PRESS-1944, Post Files.
    [8]Memorandum, Edwin M. Watson to the president, May 18, 1944, PSF, Russia Folder, FDRL.
    [9]Ibid.
    [10]Victor Kravchenko, *I Chose Freedom* (New York: Garden City Publishing, 1946), pp. 4, 443–45.

convinced that unconditional surrender was being used to persuade the German people to fight to the end. Later in the year the Soviets tried to prove Roosevelt's error by publishing an interview with a captured German general, Edmund Offmeister, who claimed that Hitler and Propaganda Minister Joseph Goebbels employed the doctrine to stiffen resistance and to overcome the "glittering phrases" of the Atlantic Charter, which appealed to the German people.[11]

Roosevelt did not want to specify conditions for the surrender. The Allies should convince the German people that their destruction was not intended; if they renounced the philosophy of conquest, there would be an opportunity for generations without war. The Germans and the Russians should be given the example of Appomattox. (Robert E. Lee had wanted conditions, but Ulysses S. Grant had said that he would have to trust him and then proved his fairness.) A few such illustrations would have more effect than "a lot of conversations" among the Allies trying to define terms of surrender. "Whatever words we might agree on would probably have to be modified or changed the first time some nation wanted to surrender."[12] The president ignored the fact that part of the Soviet concern stemmed from the British-American surrender agreement with Italy. The Russians wanted the terms to be specified in advance so that not only the Germans would know what to expect, but also the Russians.

Some of the Germans were attempting to induce the British and the Russians to arrange a separate peace and thus get around unconditional surrender. The American minister to Sweden, Herschel V. Johnson, reported a Soviet news agency dispatch revealing the conversations between Joachim von Ribbentrop and two Englishmen wherein the German sought a separate peace.[13] Shortly after this, Ambassador Gromyko informed Hull that the Berlin government was prepared to send a high official "to start peace negotiations between the U.S.S.R. and Germany," but the Soviets had refused.[14] The effort of elements in Germany to establish such contacts resulted partly from their convictions of the inevitability of defeat and partly from desires to split the Allies.

Averell Harriman tried to explain to Secretary Hull what could substantively alter the tentative agreements on the postwar world made at Tehran. If Russia recovered quickly from the war, and various "satellite countries" because of war exhaustion and possible indemnities were prostrate, the satellites might look to union with the Russians for quick

---

[11]Memorandum, John Franklin Carter to Edward Stettinius, August 31, 1944, DSF 740.0011 EW/8-3144.

[12]FDR to Hull, January 17, 1944, PSF, State Department, Hull Folder, FDRL. See also *FRUS: Diplomatic Papers*, vol. 1, *General, 1944* (Washington, DC: Government Printing Office, 1966), p. 494.

[13]Johnson to Hull, January 18, 1944, ibid., pp. 494–95.

[14]Andrei Gromyko to Hull, February 3, 1944, ibid., pp. 498–99.

relief of intolerable economic conditions. "Thus without perhaps its now being the intention of the Soviet Government to expand the Union, pressure may come from the outside for expansion." Although Stalin and his principal advisers aimed to consolidate what they had, there were still those in the Communist Party possessed of the revolutionary spirit who might welcome an aggressive course. With this in mind, it was time to talk to Molotov about eastern Europe in order to "ascertain what the Soviet general attitude is." He posed a very pertinent question: "Has the US sufficient interest in the development of sound economic conditions under a democratic form of government within those countries to justify a program being developed now through which it might be hoped that politically stable conditions might result?"[15] Several people in the Department of State were thinking about that very problem, but they were not prepared to propose a solution at the time. Like FDR, they awaited events to see what changes would really be necessary in American policy toward eastern Europe.

The government's approach to Russia rested partly on how U.S. citizens and the media viewed the Russians. According to a memorandum from the Department of State's Division of Public Liaison, popular faith in postwar cooperation with the USSR declined from 51 percent after Tehran to 42 percent in late February. The *New York Times, Washington Star*, and *Providence Journal* questioned whether Russia really intended to pursue the collaboration envisaged at Moscow and Tehran. Most commentators suggested that Russia intended to build up its own security zone in eastern Europe, but they were not particularly concerned about this. Most of the nation's press refused to take sides on the Polish boundary question and regarded favorably "the Soviet claims to Eastern Poland." The writer was amazed that the largest group favoring the Soviet demand came from small city newspapers, which based their evaluation on the "justice" of Russian historic and ethnic claims to the territory, admiration for the Red Army's achievements, and the assumption that the USSR's dominance in eastern Europe was "inevitable."[16] Most American editors and newswriters were less concerned about self-determination than some observers have indicated. If President Roosevelt and the State Department based policy on public opinion and the media, they relied more on elite opinion and special interest groups than on a substantial popular opposition to Soviet objectives.

---

[15]Harriman to Hull, February 20, 1944, DSF 861.01/2314.

[16]Division of Public Liaison, Department of State, Office of Public Information, *PUBLIC ATTITUDES ON FOREIGN POLICY*, Report No. 13, February 29, 1944, *PUBLIC ATTITUDES TOWARD RUSSIA*, January 15-February 15, DSF 711.61/986.

## *II*

As Soviet plans for the peace and disagreement within the administration on how to approach the Russians became clearer, Roosevelt knew that he had to remain the controlling force in American military and diplomatic strategy. During his bid for reelection in 1944, he ordered his campaign people to stress an editorial by Walter Lippmann emphasizing the difference between strategy and tactics and that FDR's role was to be a strategist.[17] The president recognized that he was responsible for the broader conduct of the war and the preparation for the peace. His determination not to let this role pass to anyone else accounts for his frequent signing of wartime messages to the Joint Chiefs of Staff and others as "Commander in Chief."[18]

President Roosevelt became very upset when the Combined Chiefs of Staff decided to refuse to authorize Soviet representation on the Allied Control Commission unless the Russians acknowledged the right of French participation. FDR sent an angry memorandum to Cordell Hull informing him that this decision had exceeded the authority of the Joint Chiefs of Staff, as the president had approved Soviet participation and had not yet made up his mind about the French. The president ordered that "the Soviet representation should go through at once. You might tell the Soviet Ambassador that I have directed that the Soviet representation be carried out. I cannot understand this action on the part of the Combined Staffs."[19] FDR probably could understand the refusal, because he had dealt with military obstruction of his plans to work with the Soviet Union for some time.

Roosevelt was again reminded of the opposition to his plans for reconstruction in Europe by a memorandum he received from William Leahy. The admiral tried to get Roosevelt to agree with a Joint Chiefs of Staff position on restoring Germany quickly to act as a balancing force in Europe and on eliminating the old system in that country by legal fiat. Roosevelt adamantly refused to alter either the unconditional surrender principle or his plans to divide Germany lest there be another world war, which he was determined to avoid.[20] On August 25, Henry Morgenthau

---

[17]Memorandum, FDR to Paul Porter, July 17, 1944, OF 220, Russia, 1941–1945, Box 2, Folder 1944, FDRL.

[18]Eric Larrabee in his study *Commander in Chief: Franklin Delano Roosevelt, His Lieutenants and Their War* (New York: Harper & Row, 1987) literally devotes 647 pages to developing the thesis that Roosevelt was indeed consciously the strategist and he arranged and implemented the larger plans for the conduct of the war. FDR kept in mind throughout the conflict the necessity for political connection of the war and the peace in the interest of ensuring that the forces of evil, the Axis powers, should not prevail. Given the complexity of the larger issues of the war, plans for the peace often took a back seat, but they were never completely out of mind.

[19]Memorandum, FDR to Hull with copy to Admiral Leahy, January 12, 1944, PSF, Departmental, State Department, Cordell Hull, 1944, Box 94, FDRL.

[20]FDR to the Joint Chiefs of Staff, April 1, 1944, *FRUS: General, 1944*, pp. 501–2.

tried to convince FDR that he dealt with two kinds of people: "one like Eden who believes we must cooperate with Russia and that we must trust Russia for the peace of the world, and there is the other school, which is illustrated by the remark of Mr. Churchill who said, 'What are we going to have between the white snows of Russia and the white cliffs of Dover?' " He conjectured that Churchill was implying that England needed a strong Germany to balance Russia. Roosevelt said that he belonged "to the same school as Eden."[21]

President Roosevelt's apparent belief that he could persuade Stalin to cooperate with the United States bothered the Department of State's Policy Planning Staff. Despite apparent breakthroughs in allaying hostility and suspicion, the Soviet Union still seemed bound to some degree by its old antagonism to capitalist nations. As proof of this, members of the staff noted continuing references in the USSR to the "irreconcilable chasm" between socialism and capitalism and to the belief that "any temporary association in a common interest was an association of expediency." They did not want the administration to place too much trust in Soviet willingness to get along after the war simply because they were willing to get along while they faced a common enemy.[22]

On April 4, Cordell Hull sent a worried note to FDR asking if the president really wanted to adhere rigidly to the unconditional surrender doctrine in the face of Anglo-Soviet opposition. The British had asked for an exemption to the principle for satellite Axis states in Europe, and they were supported in this by the Russians. Hull was afraid that Roosevelt's flat refusal would anger the Russians, who would not understand the American position, especially when they had laid down conditions for surrender to the Finns without objection from the United States. Why, then, would the Americans not accept the same for Romania and Hungary in light of the military advantage that might be gained? "We might find ourselves in the position of being accused of having rendered more difficult the Soviet military task."[23] Roosevelt again ignored the pressure to change his position.

Although Hull was willing to give in to the Soviet Union on unconditional surrender and FDR was not, in other areas of Soviet-American relations the State Department was less conciliatory than was the president. Some of FDR's advisers hoped that economic aid would bend the Russians to American principles, due to the weakened condition of the USSR. Averell Harriman foresaw the prospect for successful economic pressure and worried about the Fourth and Fifth Protocols for Soviet aid. Harriman did

---

[21]Morgenthau Diaries, August 25, 1944, pp. 1389–92, Morgenthau Papers, FDRL.

[22]Memorandum from the Policy Planning Staff by Charles Bohlen, March 24, 1944, Policy Planning Staff, OF, 220 Russia, 1941–45, Box 17, Russia Folder, FDRL.

[23]Hull to FDR, April 4, 1944, PSF, Departmental, State Department, 1944 January–September, Box 91, Hull Folder, FDRL.

not want the Russians to build a reserve for peacetime reconstruction out of the wartime requirements for victory: These two areas should be separated and the protocols strictly supervised lest the Soviets use war materiél for purposes other than defeating the Axis powers. The Russians seemed to be anticipating the end of the war and were placing Lend-Lease orders for items that had nothing to do with ensuring victory. Perhaps it was time "to know more about the real need for some of the Soviet requests . . . and unless they can be reasonably justified for the war, they should not be granted under lend-lease terms but against credits for reconstruction."[24] Harriman wanted no misunderstanding of what he thought the pressures on the Soviet Union should be. He wrote Harry Hopkins on February 13 that if aid to the Soviet Union for reconstruction were to be of real value to the United States, it should be made clear to the Russians that assistance depended on their playing "the international game with us in accordance with our standards."[25]

Roosevelt refused to hedge on the supply issue, and he made his point forcefully to Hull. He reminded his secretary of state that Russia continued to be a major factor in achieving the defeat of Germany. The State Department had requested that the Russians identify specific needs in the Fourth Protocol. The president did not like this, and he ordered Hull to go back to the more general formula, to make the new protocol "in accordance with the procedure and formula utilized in the Third Protocol."[26]

The State Department's concern about pressuring the Soviet Union rested partly on trends that the department noted in the USSR's approach to eastern Europe. On April 20 the American embassy in Moscow, assessing the prospects for getting along with the Soviets, identified a disturbing drift in their policy. While the Russians gave no indication that they did not value the alliance with the Americans and the British, they were increasingly emphasizing their security demands. It did not appear that they would insist on Communist governments everywhere, but they would not tolerate unfriendly governments on their border.[27]

On June 6, 1944, the Soviets finally got their second front. After the Allied forces had moved off the beaches of Normandy and had engaged the Germans inland, the Russians felt more sure of their position. Ambassador Harriman perceived some ominous signs of the new Soviet confidence. On June 19 the ambassador reported a speech by Vice Commissar of Foreign Affairs Andrei Vyshinsky, which he termed "a more aggressive presentation of Stalinist ideology than any that has recently come to the attention of the

---

[24]Harriman to Hull, January 9, 1944, *FRUS: Europe, 1944*, pp. 1035–36.

[25]Harriman to Harry Hopkins, February 13, 1944, ibid., pp. 1052–53.

[26]Memorandum, Roosevelt to Hull, February 14, 1944, ibid., p. 1053.

[27]Paraphrase of telegram received from American embassy in Moscow to secretary of state, April 20, 1944, No. 1369, CCS 350.05 USSR (5-6-44), Box 707, Record Group 218 (U.S. Joint Chiefs of Staff Files), Geographical File, 1942–1945, National Archives and Federal Records Center, Suitland, Maryland.

Embassy." Vyshinsky's speech was stridently nationalistic. Victorious Soviet troops would march into Berlin, the heart of Germany, which meant that "the future belongs to us." He acknowledged the power of the Anglo-Soviet-American coalition, but he bragged that it had been created by Soviet efforts, which "showed the realization of other governments that cooperation with the Soviet Union was necessary."[28]

## III

Despite suspicions that the Soviet Union might be planning to double-cross its allies, the Americans would not give it the justification for saying it was self-defense. The Office of War Information knew what the position of the commander in chief was on such matters, so it refused a proposal from the Political Warfare Division (PWD) to act on its belief that there would be a conflict of interest between Great Britain and the United States on one side and the Russians on the other in Germany at the end of the war. PWD worked with its British counterpart and urged that the Russians should be kept out of Germany and that the Germans should be propagandized to join the West in an anti-Soviet bloc. British representatives intended to build up Germany to "offset the Russian menace."[29] Edward Stettinius branded the PWD scheme as "entirely contrary to [the] policy of the Department. The American Government is committed to the principle of mutual consultation and cooperation and cannot approve of any project which excludes the Soviet Union."[30]

The Americans grew more frustrated with Soviet intransigence on the United Nations structure at the Dumbarton Oaks Conference, which began in Washington on August 21 and lasted until October 7.[31] The alarmed Norwegian representative in Moscow called on Harriman to relate a conversation he had had with Maxim Litvinov, who had stated that the Norwegians would have to realize that "the day of the glory of the small nations was over, implying that the large nations would be the dominating factor in world affairs." Harriman tried to soothe the Norwegian envoy by telling him that Secretary Hull had asserted that any plans emerging from the Dumbarton Oaks Conference would eventually be submitted to all members of the United Nations.[32] Had the Norwegian seen the memorandum prepared by Stettinius for the president on the British, American, and Soviet areas of agreement and disagreement at Dumbarton Oaks, he would not have been reassured. The Americans wanted an

---

[28]Harriman to Hull, June 29, 1944, DSF 861.00/6-2944.

[29]James C. Dunn to William Phillips, August 10, 1944, DSF 740.0011 EW/8-1044.

[30]Stettinius to Phillips, August 11, 1944, DSF 740.0011 EW/8-1044.

[31]For details of the discussion at Dumbarton Oaks and the various disputes that were hashed out there see Hull, *Memoirs*, 2:1671-1711.

[32]Harriman to Hull, August 23, 1944, DSF 500.CC/8-2344.

organization to deal with security and with economic and social cooperation, and in this they were supported by the British. The Soviet Union wanted the UN Security Council to be separate from an organization for economic and social cooperation. In other words, a security council dominated by the Big Four would have the final say on who was violating the principles of the United Nations and would have a police force available to enforce its decisions. If this plan were approved, Norway's fears for its position in the world would be justified; the small nations would be subservient to the Great Powers.[33]

Roosevelt was disturbed by some of the Soviet plans for the postwar organization discussed at Dumbarton Oaks, and he expressed his concern to Stalin. He objected to the Soviet request that each of the sixteen republics of the USSR should have an individual membership in the United Nations. If this request were to continue, there would be no such organization. Dropping the matter for now would not, Roosevelt assured Stalin, preclude discussing such membership after the organization was formed, "and the Assembly would have full authority to deal with the question at that time."[34] Roosevelt wanted the United States and the USSR to be committed to a collective security organization first, and then membership rules could be refined.

Cordell Hull spoke to Ambassador Gromyko concerning Soviet insistence at Dumbarton Oaks that members of the council should be able to vote on matters that came before them relating to their own interests. Hull attempted, unsuccessfully, to persuade Gromyko to abandon this position.[35]

Either the president changed his mind from an earlier suggestion made to the Russians, or he was not fully informed about the American positions at Dumbarton Oaks. The Soviet Union proposed precisely what Roosevelt had suggested to it previously concerning taking care of Soviet security needs by permitting the leasing of bases or the transfer of base rights in neighboring areas. When the Russians mentioned this as an alternative for nations with armies too small to contribute to the UN security forces, they met strong opposition from the American delegation.[36]

Roosevelt tried to convince the Russians at Dumbarton Oaks to moderate their positions by approaching both Stalin and Ambassador Gromyko. Stalin reaffirmed the Soviet insistence on being permitted to vote on matters affecting Russia in the Security Council, stressing the need for unanimity of the four powers on such questions as might be discussed there.

---

[33]Memorandum, Stettinius to FDR, August 23, 1944, PSF, Dumbarton Oaks, Box 145, FDRL.

[34]FDR to Stalin, August 31, 1944, *FRUS: General, 1944*, p. 760.

[35]Memorandum of conversation with Andrei Gromyko, August 31, 1944, ibid.

[36]Stettinius Diaries, September 5, 1944, p. 6, Records of Harley Notter, 1939–1945, Dumbarton Oaks, Box no. 190, Lot 60D-224, Volume I, August 20, 1944-September 7, 1944, National Archives, Washington, DC. Concerning leasing bases, FDR had proposed at Tehran that the Russians might lease Port Arthur.

He made the reason for this insistence clear: "As to the Soviet Union, it cannot also ignore the presence of certain absurd prejudices which OFTEN hinder an actually objective attitude toward the U.S.S.R. And the other nations also should weigh the consequences which the lack of unanimity among the leading powers may bring about."[37]

Stettinius was given the task of testing Gromyko on a possible change of heart on the voting issue. Gromyko boldly responded that "the Russian position on voting in the Council would never be departed from—a month from now or three months from now." Stettinius asserted that this might destroy any chance for a United Nations Organization. Gromyko said that then there could be no such organization, because it could not exist without Soviet support. Stettinius wanted the president to know "the firmness with which Gromyko had talked."[38] Hull thought that the president might wish to contact Churchill and Stalin, which he already had done, apparently without Hull knowing about it.

Hull was being gradually bypassed in the decision-making process, probably from below as well as by the president. Eleanor Roosevelt had heard that there was too much power in the hands of some of the conservatives in the Department of State and that things were going badly at the conference because it was being handled by Leo Pasvolsky, James C. Dunn, and Breckinridge Long. When she spoke to her husband about this, he responded angrily: "I don't know who your informer is but he just doesn't know what he is talking about because Stettinius comes to my office every afternoon . . . with a list of questions, and I decide what they should do the next day at Dumbarton Oaks."[39] Apparently the agenda was discussed between FDR and Stettinius, without Hull.

During September the State Department inundated FDR with information on the issues he would need to decide from that point through the making of peace. He received a memorandum of September 6 stressing the need to convince the Russians that the United States and Great Britain would not tolerate violation of certain basic principles. "This would require greater willingness on our part to risk Soviet displeasure and franker and more realistic discussions with the Soviet Union in regard to its policies in Europe." Roosevelt must have blanched at the memorandum's recommendation on Germany, for it directly contradicted his position at Tehran. The department suggested that "this Government should oppose a

---

[37]Stalin to FDR, September 14, 1944, *FRUS: General, 1944*, pp. 806–7. The Soviets were still reluctant to include China, but the British were the ones most opposed; the United States ignored this opposition and included China. Although the Soviets were willing to allow the Chinese to sit in on deliberations on the Far East, they wanted them excluded from discussions pertaining to Europe.

[38]Cover memorandum to Hopkins from Stettinius asking him to bring it to the president's attention, September 18, 1944, PSF, Departmental, State Department, 1944, Box 94, FDRL.

[39]Morgenthau Diaries, September 2, 1944, p. 1428, Morgenthau Papers, FDRL.

forcible partition of Germany into two or more separate states." Far-reaching security measures for control of Germany were needed, but the United States should not render that country incapable of playing a role in the economic stability of Europe. Perhaps a federal system guaranteeing the breakup of Prussia would be acceptable. "Acceptable to whom?" must have been Roosevelt's question, for it certainly would not have been acceptable to him or to the Soviet Union. Another contradiction of the president's stated preferences was the department's proposal to immediately rearm the French so that they might resume their necessary role in the European balance of power. The United States should supply the French with arms, which would preclude them from going elsewhere and accepting political conditions in return for weapons.[40]

Although FDR did not comment on this memorandum, it must have irritated him. The fears expressed to him by Morgenthau and others concerning Department of State policy being contrary to his own must have seemed well founded. The problem was that he had not stated to the department his preferences on Germany, French rearmament, or some other issues touched upon in the memorandum. The language of the communiqué indicated either that the State Department did not know the president's inclinations on several of the matters treated therein or that it had heard of them and were trying to head them off.

It became more and more obvious to Roosevelt during September that the issues separating the Allies were going to have to be resolved by himself, Churchill, and Stalin. This conviction was reinforced in a conversation with Stettinius on September 27. The Russians had accepted American amendments on human rights at the Dumbarton Oaks Conference, which had surprised the president. But Stettinius listed other issues that the heads of state would have to settle among themselves: voting in the Security Council, a statute on the International Court of Justice, initial membership in the United Nations, the question of trusteeships, and liquidation of the League of Nations. FDR dismissed the voting question with the assurance that a formula could be discovered. He thought that the conference participants would have discussed trusteeships, and Stettinius said that they had not done so at the specific request of the Joint Chiefs of Staff. The undersecretary of state baldly told Roosevelt that his naval people were not sympathetic to his point of view on trusteeships and that he would have to deal with them on the matter.[41]

Secretary Hull requested that FDR feel out the British and the Russians on the treatment of German industry. Such exploration, in Roosevelt's view, was ill timed. He was more concerned with preventing uncontrolled

---

[40]Memorandum, T. C. A. in the Department of State to FDR. September 6, 1944, DSF 740.0011/9-644.

[41]Stettinius Diaries, September 27, 1944, Dumbarton Oaks, vol. 2, pp. 9–10, Records of Harley A. Notter.

German access to the resources and basic industries of the Ruhr and Saar basins, which could be converted into armaments production, and he wanted to deal directly with Stalin and the prime minister on this subject. FDR denied that he intended to make "Germany a wholly agricultural nation again, and yet somebody down the line has handed this out to the press. I wish we could catch and chastise him."[42] He need not have searched any further than the treasury secretary.

FDR had a far better grasp of certain realities of American-Soviet relations than did most in the government. While it was true that the Americans did not know what the Russians had in mind, Roosevelt understood that they would do what they wished in the occupied territories. Furthermore, it was unwise to "merely record protests . . . unless there is some chance of the protests being heeded"; such complaints would be counterproductive.[43] The president's knowledge of history made him worry about the Balkans, where no less than three European wars had been spawned. He confided to Ambassador Harriman that who had what sort of influence was of less concern than was another matter: "My active interest at the present time in the Balkan area is that such steps as are practicable should be taken to insure against the Balkans getting us into a future international war."[44]

## *IV*

Harriman became so concerned about apparent changes in Soviet policy that he asked to see the president at the earliest possible moment. He perceived arrogance in a statement by Molotov in response to criticism of the Soviet attitude toward the Warsaw uprising. The Russians had refused to aid the Poles and had denied assistance to the Americans and British who wished to drop supplies to the Polish forces and then land in Russia. "The indifference of the Soviets to world opinion regarding their ruthless attitude toward the uprising in Warsaw and their unyielding policy toward Poland are best described by the statement of Molotov that the Soviets would judge their friends by those who accept the Soviet position."[45]

Harriman attributed this petulant and unfriendly attitude to Stalin's advisers, who were gaining the upper hand in American-Russian relations, which boded ill for postwar collaboration. "The policy appears to be crystalizing [*sic*] to force the British and us to accept all Soviet policies

---

[42]FDR to Hull, September 29, 1944, PSF, Departmental, State Department, Cordell Hull Folder, 1944, Box 94, FDRL.

[43]Ibid.

[44]FDR to Harriman, October 11, 1944, *FRUS: Europe, 1944*, p. 1009.

[45]Harriman to Hopkins, September 11, 1944, Map Room Papers, Box 13, Hopkins Messages, 1944 Folder, FDRL. There was a notation on the memorandum that a copy was given to Churchill at Quebec at FDR's suggestion.

which the Army backs by its strength and prestige." All of this rested on the Soviet thesis that they had won the war with little assistance, and in payment they demanded acceptance of whatever they wanted. Perhaps the threat of withholding reconstruction aid if the Russians continued to be a "world bully" might be effective. The Soviet Union seemed bent on expanding its control to the Pacific and China when circumstances permitted. The Americans had to convince Stalin that the advice of his colleagues was "leading him into difficulties and to strengthen the hand of those around Stalin who want to play the game along our lines." Instead of "drastic action" the United States should take "a firm but friendly quid pro quo attitude."[46]

Several points in this dispatch worried Hull, who requested a clarification of the Soviet position. Harriman assured him that Stalin and the Kremlin had not definitely determined to reverse the policy of cooperation that had developed at Moscow and Tehran. Part of the problem related to delays in registering American protests to the USSR about stated or implied policies; Molotov told Harriman that the Russians assumed that when the Americans made no comment on a suggested policy, this meant approval. The Americans sometimes failed to understand Soviet language; for example, when the Russians said that they wanted "friendly governments" on their borders, they really wanted subservience.[47]

Language was not the only problem; the Russians did not understand the American governmental system. George Kennan, who had become counselor of the U.S. embassy in Moscow earlier in the year, relayed a conversation held on a flight from Moscow to Tehran on December 7, 1944, between Red Army officers and Frederick Barghoorn, one of the lower-echelon diplomats from the embassy. The Soviet pilot wanted to know if Roosevelt were president for life, and he "appeared surprised and disappointed" when told that this was not the case. Barghoorn's attempt to explain the American election system left the pilot apparently so confused that Barghoorn gave it up. The pilot maintained that FDR enjoyed "great sympathy among the Russians." Two of the officers praised the American contribution to the war effort and said that during the desperate days of Stalingrad the arrival of American bombers had been very cheering. A colonel speculated that the "Hitlerites had miscalculated in thinking that they could crush the Soviet Union before American industry could be put on a war basis."[48] Obviously, some Russians understood the importance of American aid. But this sort of respect and admiration bothered Stalin and many of his associates, so the Russians were reluctant to advertise Lend-Lease aid too broadly.

---

[46]Ibid.

[47]Harriman to Hull, September 20, 1944, DSF 500.CC/9-2044.

[48]Memorandum, George Kennan to Stettinius, December 7, 1944, DSF 123 Barghoorn, Frederick A., January 27, 1945.

Confusion was not restricted to the Russians. The American public was increasingly perplexed and disillusioned by British and Russian attempts to create spheres of influence, according to Stettinius. They reacted strongly to armed conflict between British and Greek forces and to the rumored British refusal to use the consultation machinery of the Allied Control Commission concerning policy in Italy. Americans also opposed unilateral Soviet seizure of Polish territory because it appeared to them that the British and Russians were deciding the issue without consulting Poland. Stettinius supposed "that American opinion would be satisfied should . . . a meeting [of the Big Three] be able to develop an agreement on boundary issues."[49] Whereas in June the public attitude had been less sympathetic to Poland and more ready to accept Soviet annexation of Polish territory, a December poll reflected the public reaction to the Russian refusal to help the Polish underground forces during the Warsaw uprising. To teach the Poles a lesson and simultaneously allow German troops to eliminate indigenous Polish leadership, which then cleared the way for Stalin to insert his own Moscow-trained Poles into leadership positions at a later date, he lost points with American public opinion and, more importantly, upset U.S. officials as well. The Warsaw uprising more than anything else was what caused Ambassador Harriman to become disenchanted with the Russians.

Poland was not the only source of concern for American policymakers. Although they were unwilling to speak directly to the Soviet Union about postwar boundaries, they followed with interest Russian conversations with other east Europeans concerning their boundaries. After Eduard Beneš, representing the Czech government-in-exile, met with Stalin, he was interviewed by the U.S. representative in Algiers on January 3, 1944. Beneš told the American that he had "settled everything between Czechoslovakia and Russia." Neither the Czechs nor the Russians would interfere with the other's affairs, and Russia would stay east of the Carpathian Mountains. The Czechs, no doubt with some recollection of Poland's decision to take Czech territory when it was offered by Germany after Munich, decided that Poland's problems with the Soviet Union were none of their affair. Although the Poles had suffered at German hands also, they had to make their own peace with the USSR and reconcile themselves to losing eastern Poland in return for East Prussia. Beneš judged his own people as realistic and the Poles as "romantic" in what they expected from the Russians. Soviet power in eastern Europe was a guarantee against a resurgent Germany.[50]

Roosevelt instructed Ambassador Harriman to discuss Finland with Molotov to discover if any action could be taken to ease Soviet demands on

---

[49]Memorandum, Stettinius to FDR, December 30, 1944, PSF, Department of State, Stettinius Folder, FDRL.

[50]Edwin C. Wilson to Hull, January 3, 1944, Box 1375B Moscow 711-711, 1944, 711-Czechoslovakia, Post Files.

the Finns.[51]  He reported ominous signs on September 14, 1944. Colonel General A. A. Zhdanov, who reputedly had engineered the border incident that had started the Russo-Finnish War and who was one of the signers of the treaty ending that struggle, was named to deal with Finnish affairs. He had also overseen Soviet absorption of Estonia, and Harriman described him as a "ruthless character."[52]

Harriman's dispatches during this period reflected his alarm over Soviet behavior throughout eastern Europe, the Balkans, and Turkey. The Soviet Union apparently was trying to isolate Turkey by preventing its entry into the war on the Allied side. If the Russians could arrange this, Turkey would fall into the category of unfriendly neutrals and possibly would be prevented from entering the United Nations Organization at the end of the war. Part of the Russian case against Turkey was the continued closure of the Dardanelles to Allied ships carrying war materials to the USSR. Harriman believed that in Turkey's own interest it should enter the war immediately and present the Soviet Union with a fait accompli by opening the Dardanelles. "This action would also . . . tend to lessen possible future difficulties between the Soviet Union and the British over Turkey and her interests."[53]

On September 19 corroboration of Soviet pressure on Turkey reached the Department of State through the U.S. naval attaché at Beyoglu. The Spanish minister to Ankara told Lt. Commander George Earle that the Soviets were demanding withdrawal of Turkish troops within fifty kilometers of the Caucasian and Thracian borders, replacement of all Anglo-Saxon technicians with Russians, and abrogation of the Montreux Convention guaranteeing Turkish control of the Dardanelles so long as they were open to all countries. They also insisted on an international commission to control the Straits, with a Russian as chairman, plus to grant to the USSR a naval and air base in Anatolia to protect the Straits.[54]

Long-standing suspicions about Soviet ambitions to violate the Atlantic Charter in eastern Europe seemed to be substantiated on September 17.[55]  Chargé in Moscow Alexander Kirk sent word to the department that the Russians were displacing the government of Romania, which had thrown out the Nazis, and were demobilizing its army. It appeared that the

---

[51]Harriman memorandum, May 23, 1944, DSF 123-Harriman, W. Averall [*sic*].

[52]Harriman to Hull, September 14, 1944, *FRUS: Diplomatic Papers*, vol. 3, *British Commonwealth and Europe, 1944* (Washington, DC: Government Printing Office, 1965), pp. 620–21.

[53]Harriman to Hull, September 13, 1944, DSF 740.0011 E.W./9-1344.

[54]Memorandum, C. S. Colclough, Office of the Chief of Naval Operations, to Gordon P. Merriam at the Department of State, September 19, 1944, DSF 740.0011 E.W./9-1944.

[55]Cordell Hull had warned FDR in 1942 that the Russians would attempt to seize Bessarabia and other parts of Romania in violation of the principles set forth in the Atlantic Charter. See memorandum, Hull to FDR, February 5, 1942, with enclosures, Box 304, Footnote Folder, Hopkins Papers, FDRL.

Red Army was behaving very badly toward the Romanians and had even shot some of the Russian officers who had tried to restrain excesses, although they had not bothered American and British military personnel.[56]

# V

In October 1944, after Stalin had again refused to leave Russia to meet Churchill and FDR, Churchill insisted that he should go to Moscow. Especially disturbing to the prime minister were the Soviet "attempts to edge out the British and the Americans from their share in the satellite States," combined with "their cynical attitude toward the Polish revolt in Warsaw."[57]

Roosevelt, who could not leave the country during the election campaign, was not happy about Churchill and Stalin getting together without him. Although he did not oppose the meeting outright, he made sure that Stalin knew that he could not make any commitments binding on the Americans without the president being present. Roosevelt tried to be subtle in his admonition, but not too subtle: "You, naturally, understand that in this global war there is literally no question, political or military, in which the United States is not interested. I am firmly convinced that the three of us, and only the three of us, can find the solution to the still unresolved questions."[58] He also made it clear that having Harriman attend the conference between the Soviet and British leaders with the intent that the ambassador truly represent the Americans was not an acceptable alternative. Harriman could attend, but only as an observer; he could commit the United States to nothing.

In a message to Churchill, FDR specifically disapproved a suggestion from the prime minister that he might take up the UN voting question with Stalin. He told Churchill that there would be plenty of time to consider this when they all met.[59] The British believed that the Americans were unaware of the danger of delaying a settlement with Stalin on the Balkans, Iran, Poland, and Hungary. Churchill thought the need to deal quickly was urgent because he expected a German collapse by the end of the year.[60]

Churchill journeyed in October to Moscow, where he proposed to Stalin "that the Russians might have 90 per cent predominance in Roumania and Great Britain a 90 per cent predominance in Greece, while

---

[56]Alexander Kirk to Hull, September 17, 1944, DSF 740.0011 E.W./9-1744 with cover memorandum by Charles Bohlen of September 29.

[57]Sir Llewellyn Woodward, *British Foreign Policy in the Second World War*, 5 vols. (London: Her Majesty's Stationery Office, 1971), 3:146.

[58]Roosevelt to Harriman with a message for Stalin, October 4, 1944, and Roosevelt to Churchill, October 4, 1944, *FRUS: Diplomatic Papers, Conferences at Malta and Yalta, 1945* (Washington, DC: Government Printing Office, 1955), pp. 6–8.

[59]Ibid.

[60]Woodward, *British Foreign Policy in the Second World War*, 3: 146–50.

Yugoslavia was shared on a 'fifty-fifty basis.' " Churchill wrote it all down and added: "Hungary 50-50, Bulgaria—Russia 75 per cent." Stalin took a blue pencil, made a tick on the paper, and "the matter was thus agreed." Churchill had second thoughts and wrote Stalin on October 11, stating that these numbers were merely to see if they were in approximate agreement. The percentages would appear to others to be "crude and even callous, if they were exposed to the scrutiny of the foreign offices and diplomats all over the world."[61] This was certainly the way they would appear to the Americans.

Harriman told Roosevelt what the British were up to: Churchill had used the "unpopular term," spheres of influence, but Eden tried to tell Harriman that this was not what Churchill meant. Rather, the prime minister's objective was "to work out a practical agreement on how the problems of each country are going to be dealt with and the relative responsibility of the Russians [and] the British." Why Eden thought the Americans would not see what the British proposed as spheres of influence is unclear, for that is exactly what the British had suggested. They wanted the Russians to abstain from independent action in Yugoslavia until the three powers could mediate differences there. They caused Stalin's agreement to exert pressure on the Communists in Greece to be a constructive influence in a new government. They asked for American support in working on a settlement, lest there be "political turmoil."[62] Churchill appealed to FDR: "It is absolutely necessary we should try to get a common mind about the Balkans, so that we may prevent civil war breaking out in several countries when probably you and I would be in sympathy with one side and U.J. [Uncle Joe] with the other."[63]

While the British pleaded for a quick decision on the Balkans, the Department of State's Policy Planning Staff completely misread what was going on. It viewed the situation in eastern Europe as a squabble between the British and the Russians. A subcommittee, headed by Adolf Berle, recommended that the Americans should stand by their established principles of self-determination of peoples, equality of opportunity in trade, and other matters such as freedom of information and free speech. It enumerated the countries where these principles should be applied—Hungary, Romania, Bulgaria, Yugoslavia, Albania, Greece, and Turkey—and added that the United States should guide economic development and stability in Albania.[64]

---

[61]Ibid., 150–51.

[62]Harriman to FDR, October 11, 1944, *FRUS: Europe, 1944*, pp. 1009–10.

[63]Churchill to Roosevelt, October 11, 1944, ibid., pp. 1010–11.

[64]Report to the policy committee regarding United States interests and policy in Eastern and Southeastern Europe and the Near East from the subcommittee composed of Mr. Berle and the directors of the four area offices, October 25, 1944, Department of State, Records of the Office of European Affairs, Policy Planning Staff, Reference Subject Files, 1940–1947, Yugoslavia, Box 17, Policy Committee Folder, POLICY COMMITTEE PC-8 (Revised), National Archives, Washington, DC. Like the British, the U.S. Department of State representatives considered Turkey as integrally involved in Balkan affairs.

This document foretold a conflict in policy between the president's advisers who wished to encourage accommodating both the British and the Russians in eastern Europe and a small group in the Department of State led by Berle and James C. Dunn. They saw no need to change any of the traditional American foreign policy principles where eastern Europe was concerned and certainly did not trust what the British and Russians desired in the way of settlements in that region.

On November 11, Stettinius forwarded the final document to the president with a cover memorandum explaining that the department had spent several months giving "the most serious thought to the conditions prevailing in Eastern and Southeastern Europe and the Near East." They had concluded that there was a "possibility that these countries might become the object of rivalry between Britain and Russia to a degree which might endanger not only their own independence but the stability of the post-war settlements."[65] The department recommended that the United States should not take any view of affairs in the region different from policy and principles applicable elsewhere, as though there were no difference between Mexico and Poland. It sustained the right of the regional powers to conduct their own foreign affairs and to maintain their independence and right of self-determination without external interference so long as they did not threaten the security of other powers, and it insisted that the United States should not abandon its "position that territorial settlements should be left until the end of the war."[66] Winston Churchill's conjecture that the Americans were naive about eastern Europe may have been very much on target. The prime minister sought a deal while he could get it, but the Americans "seemed, as before, unaware of the gravity of the danger." Instead, they "seemed more inclined to suspect British motives . . . than to face the possibility of a new Russian imperialism."[67]

Concern over the Near East was addressed by George Kennan in a dispatch to Hull of November 7. He thought that Soviet pressure in northern Iran was a desire not so much to secure oil reserves as to prevent potential foreign penetration of the area adjacent to Soviet borders. Northern Iran's proximity to the Caucasus oil fields, which the USSR had nearly lost to the Germans, made the Russians skittish about others being in a position to move across their border from Iran. Therefore, the dispatch surmised, the Kremlin "probably sees no other way to assure this than by seeking greater political and economic control for itself and finds this aim consistent with

---

[65]Cover memorandum, Stettinius to FDR, November 11, 1944, accompanying a position paper from the Policy Planning Staff, "United States Interests and Policy in Eastern and Southeastern Europe and the Near East," November 8, 1944, PSF, Departmental, State Department Folder, 1944, Box 91, FDRL.

[66]Policy Planning Staff position paper was reprinted in *FRUS: Europe, 1944*, pp. 1025–26, but did not include the Stettinius cover memorandum.

[67]Woodward, *British Foreign Policy in the Second World War*, 3:147.

contemporary Soviet conceptions of prestige." The method of penetration might seem unimaginative and old fashioned, but the department should bear in mind "that there is extensive preoccupation in Moscow today with the methods as well as the aims of Tsarist diplomacy."[68]

Kennan's assessment of Soviet behavior in Iran apparently hit the bull's-eye. The Soviet pressure on Iran had been precipitated by the negotiations between the Tehran government and American and British oil companies for concessions in southern Iran. These negotiations seemed about to reach a satisfactory conclusion when suddenly a Soviet delegation showed up demanding an exclusive oil and minerals concession in the five northern provinces. The Iranians announced that all negotiations were terminated for the duration of the war.[69] On December 8, President Roosevelt decided that Harriman should take up the matter with Stalin personally, that it should not be put off until the next Big Three meeting. FDR remembered that the Tehran agreement was "pretty definite and my contribution was to suggest to Stalin and Churchill that three or four Trustees build a new port in Iran at the head of the Persian Gulf (free port), take over the whole railroad from there into Russia, and run the thing for the good of all. Stalin's comment was merely that it was an interesting idea and he offered no objection."[70]

Perhaps the Russian maneuvers were getting under FDR's skin, and possibly pressure from the Department of State and the British made him believe that he had to do something. Probably he was not yet concerned about the solidity of the alliance. But there were some loose threads that might unravel its fabric, and he wanted them to be neatly tucked in before they got out of hand. Soviet experts in the Department of State, like their compatriot Kennan, were less sanguine.

## *VI*

President Roosevelt and the Department of State did not forget that Poland was a key to Stalin's trustworthiness for postwar cooperation. However, the Poles presented problems by trying to secure for themselves major power status, which the Americans and British feared would turn the Russians surly. Averell Harriman wrote Secretary of State Hull on January 11, 1944, that Molotov had summoned him to the Kremlin shortly after midnight to present him with a paper stating the Soviet position on Poland. He complained that, as everyone else seemed to be talking about Poland, Russia could not remain silent. Molotov insisted that his statement "would be

[68]Kennan to Hull, November 7, 1944, DSF 891.6363/11-744.
[69]Memorandum, Wallace Murray to Stettinius, November 20, 1944, DSF 891.6363/11-2044.
[70]FDR to Stettinius, December 8, 1944, PSF, Diplomatic, Russia, 1944, Box 68, FDRL.

found to conform to the spirit of the conversations at Teheran with President Roosevelt and Prime Minister Churchill." Harriman surmised that apparently the Russians were ready to deal with the Polish government-in-exile, provided it eliminated its extreme anti-Soviet elements and adjusted its position on the location of the Polish-Soviet border. The Poles should recognize that they could "make a better deal now than if they wait, living, as they appear to be, in the hope that we and the British will eventually pull their chestnuts out of the fire."[71]

Harriman's daughter, Kathleen, had visited the site of the Katyn Forest massacre. Based on limited evidence and controlled interviews with witnesses, she found some support for the claim of the Russians that the villains of the massacre were German. It appeared that most of the soldiers had not been officers; each man had been executed, as was the style of the Gestapo, with one shot; and the dates of papers found on the corpses seemed to indicate that the Germans had shot those whom they captured when the Russians retreated, thereby leaving behind the Poles. The evidence, in other words, apparently contradicted German claims that the Russians had killed the Poles in 1940, before the Germans overran the area in 1941.[72] *Pravda* and *Izvestiia* charged that the Polish government-in-exile "took an active part in the anti-Soviet campaign regarding the 'murders in Katyn,' " and this accounted for the Soviet government breaking relations with the London Poles.[73]

Winston Churchill tried to get the London Poles to take a more realistic view of their position. He told them that the British government understood the Soviet Union's security demands concerning borders. Twice within a generation Germany had overrun Russia, and the British did not wish the USSR to be endangered by that prospect again. He acknowledged that Britain had gone to war for the sake of the Poles, but they should not forget the Russian role in defeating Germany. Russia and her allies had a right to ask that Poland should accept revised frontiers. The Russians were willing to give East Prussia to Poland in compensation, and this should be accepted. The prime minister intended to convey the essence of this discussion to Stalin.[74] Roosevelt admonished Churchill that perhaps "Uncle Joe" should be advised that, if he accepted clear definitions of Polish boundaries and resolved other questions at issue, the Poles might of their own accord get rid of the persons in their government whom the Russians found objectionable.

---

[71]Harriman to Hull, January 11, and response from Hull, January 15, 1944, Box 1358B, Moscow, 711-711, 1944, 711 Poland, Post Files.

[72]Harriman to Hull, January 25, 1944, Box 1360A, Moscow, 711.4-711.9, 1944, 711.6 Katyn Forest Affair, Post Files.

[73]Harriman to Hull, January 26, 1944, ibid.

[74]Churchill to Roosevelt, January 28, 1944, *FRUS: British Commonwealth and Europe, 1944*, pp. 1240–43.

He hoped in this fashion to avoid any disruption of the accords reached at Moscow and Tehran.[75]

While Harriman was home on leave he met with President Roosevelt, who instructed him to tell Stalin that he still hoped that the Russians could find a satisfactory solution to the Polish problem and "to express the hope the Soviets would give the Poles a 'break.' "[76] In early June, Harriman told Molotov that the president still stood by the agreements guaranteeing genuine independence for Poland and that he assumed the Russians did too. Harriman emphasized the need to keep Poland fighting the real enemy, Germany.[77] He finally was permitted to see Stalin to deliver the president's thoughts on Poland, and he reported that it was the first friendly talk they had had on the subject. Harriman "got the feeling that he saw a solution in the making which would be acceptable all around." He should have taken more notice of Stalin's reluctance to admit any credence for the London Poles. Stalin pumped up his Lublin Poles and ran down the Polish government-in-exile.[78]

If the Americans did not see what the Russians were driving at, they were not paying attention. The Russians wanted the obstreperous London Poles to be dumped in favor of their own subservient group, nurtured in Russia, and they were in a position, or soon would be, to insert them without Allied assistance. Perhaps Stalin's intent was clear enough to make the Americans and the British believe that they could only try for a coalition government and hope for the best. Meanwhile, the Russians set about making sure that there was no military force left in Poland to be empathetic to the London government by sitting out the Warsaw uprising against the Germans and opposing efforts by the Americans and British to assist the beleaguered Warsaw fighters. Cordell Hull wanted to tell the Kremlin that, even though the Russians would not help, the Americans and British would "furnish such aid on the grounds of our clear obligation to aid any forces of the United Nations which are engaged in fighting the Germans."[79]

The Soviet contention that the Warsaw uprising was a surprise instigated by the London Poles in order to make political capital out of the liberation of the city received a coup de grace when a radio message from the Polish group in Moscow was translated in London. The message clearly

---

[75]FDR to Churchill, February 8, 1944, ibid., pp. 1245–46.

[76]Stettinius memorandum of Harriman's discussion with the president, May 23, 1944, DSF 123 Harriman, W. Averell/74.

[77]Harriman to FDR and Hull, June 7, 1944, PSF, Diplomatic, Russia, 1944, Box 68, FDRL.

[78]Harriman to Hull, June 12, 1944, *FRUS: British Commonwealth and Europe, 1944*, pp. 1282–83. The Lublin Poles were Communists who spent most of the war in the USSR and who were inserted as a provisional government in Lublin when eastern Poland was captured by Soviet forces.

[79]Memorandum, Hull to FDR, August 17, 1944, PSF, Diplomatic, Russia, 1944, Box 68, FDRL.

indicated that on July 30 an appeal for the uprising came from Poles inside Russia, promising that Soviet armies were on their way to help in the liberation.[80] Ambassador John G. Winant conjectured from London that the Russians had prevented full-scale aid for the Warsaw Poles in order to let the Poles know to whom they owed blind obedience in the future if they were to get along in the world of Great Powers.[81] He might also have noted that this presented an object lesson to the London Poles concerning their pretensions to postwar Great Power status.

Winston Churchill made another attempt to straighten out the Polish imbroglio. Stalin agreed to meet with Stanislaw Mikolajczyk at Churchill's urging, and according to the prime minister they met for over an hour in a "very friendly talk." Stalin also agreed to help the leader of the London Poles, who in turn promised him to "form and conduct a government thoroughly friendly to the Russians. He explained his plan but Stalin made it clear that the Lublin Poles must have the majority." Churchill told Stalin later that any government must be split fifty-fifty between London and Lublin and must include Mikolajczyk, lest the Western world not believe that an independent Poland had been established. Stalin at first agreed and then backed off on the fifty-fifty proposal, but Churchill and Mikolajczyk thought that the Russians would come around. The Polish leader would urge his London colleagues to accept the Curzon Line as the border of Poland, with Lwow going to Russia.[82]

A series of articles in *Pravda* and *Izvestiia* made obvious Stalin's plans to oust the London Poles and install a pro-Soviet government.[83] When Stalin rejected a request to delay recognition of the Lublin government, Roosevelt expressed his disappointment. The United States definitely would not transfer recognition from the London to the Lublin Poles and would await the determination of the Polish people as to what government should be recognized.[84]

# *VII*

One of the persistent doubters of the efficacy of policies aimed at American-Soviet cooperation removed himself from direct contact with the question. On September 29, 1944, Cordell Hull visited FDR and told him that he planned to resign as secretary of state due to ill health resulting in part from

---

[80]Ambassador Winant in London to Hull, September 8, 1944, DSF 740.0011 E.W./9-844.

[81]Winant to Hull, September 10, 1944, DSF 740.0011 E.W./9-1044.

[82]Churchill to FDR, October 22, 1944, *FRUS: Europe, 1944*, pp. 1023–24.

[83]Kennan to Hull, October 24, 1944, DSF 861.9111/10-2444.

[84]FDR to Stalin, December 30, 1944, *FRUS: British Commonwealth and Europe, 1944*, pp. 1444-45.

exhaustion. Roosevelt apparently did not believe that Hull would quit; however, on November 21 the secretary asked for acceptance of his resignation. Roosevelt tried to persuade him to stay on until the official end of his third administration, January 20. Hull declined, and the president named Edward R. Stettinius, Jr., to succeed him.[85]

Henry Morgenthau took credit for suggesting Stettinius. According to his recollection, he called on Eleanor Roosevelt and told her that in light of Hull's resignation he wanted to say that "between Wallace, Byrnes, and Stettinius, I think the President would be most comfortable with Stettinius." His reason was that so long as FDR wished to be his own secretary of state this would be a good appointment, because what he wanted was "merely a good clerk." He opposed Henry Wallace as being "too unstable to be Secretary of State." He thought that no one would be comfortable with James Byrnes, and he probably would resign within a few months rather than put up with the sort of things Byrnes pulled. Eleanor promised Morgenthau that she would speak to FDR right away.[86] Getting to the president early may have been important, because Harriman and Hopkins intended to support Byrnes.[87]

Perhaps Hull wore himself out trying to fight off British-Soviet attacks on his view of the postwar world. Late in the spring of 1944 he learned of Soviet-British arrangements on percentages of influence in eastern Europe. Although both parties tried to deny that they were discussing spheres of influence by using the euphemism "taking the lead," Hull and the State Department failed to see any difference. The department agreed with a Joint Chiefs of Staff recommendation to avoid the danger of a future war derived from a return to struggles over territorial position. If the British and the Russians were permitted to return to the old balance-of-power system, the natural tendency of the Americans to side with Britain would draw them into the quarrel.[88]

Although the Americans wanted to delay discussion of territorial splits in Europe, they wanted to know specifically what the Soviet Union would require in the way of compensation for its participation in the Pacific war. Harriman took this up with Stalin. With a map in front of him, Stalin pointed to the Kurile Islands and Lower Sakhalin Island and proposed that these areas should be returned to Russia because they controlled the approaches to Vladivostok. He then drew a line around the southern Liaotung Peninsula, including Port Arthur and Dairen, "saying that the Russians wished again to lease these ports and the surrounding area."

[85]Hull, *Memoirs*, 2:715–19.

[86]Morgenthau Diaries, November 27, 1944, p. 1467, Morgenthau Papers, FDRL.

[87]Harriman and Abel, *Special Envoy*, p. 372.

[88]Undated, unsigned memorandum, State Department to FDR, "American Policy toward Spheres of Influence," Hopkins Papers, Special Assistant to the President, 1941–1945, Container 170, Europe Section, FDRL.

Harriman recalled that President Roosevelt had discussed this question at Tehran and had acknowledged the need for Russian access to a warm-water port on the Pacific. But the president had referred to free ports rather than to leaseholds, which would give the Russians what they needed but would be more in line "with present day concepts of how international questions of this kind could be dealt with." Stalin agreed to discuss this later. Then the Soviet leader mentioned his desire to lease the Chinese-Eastern Railway in Manchuria and thus to connect Vladivostok by rail to Manchuli, Harbin, and Dairen.[89]

Harriman wondered what the Russians planned concerning the sovereignty of Manchuria, and Stalin denied any intent to wrest it away from China. Harriman reminded Roosevelt, however, that "with control of the railroad operations and with the probability of Russian troops to protect the railroad Soviet influence will be great." Stalin said that he had failed to mention at Tehran the recognition of the status quo in Outer Mongolia as an independent republic, but that was important. Harriman was not surprised at Stalin's position; the ambassador had been convinced "for many months that this would be the Soviet attitude because of their desire for protection for their long Southern Siberian boundary." Harriman made no comments to Stalin about any of this, but he thought that the president should have this information before he met with the Soviet leader.[90]

On December 16, Harriman urged the president to make some clear-cut decisions on the Far East before Soviet entry into the Pacific war lest the Russians make their own decisions separately. "I believe that it must be assumed that if no arrangement is made before the Russians attack the Japanese the Soviets will back the Communists in the north and turn over to them the administration of the Chinese territory the Red Army liberates. The situation then will be increasingly difficult for the Generalissimo [Chiang Kai-shek]."[91]

Thus, President Roosevelt was carefully apprised during the last six months of 1944 of several pressing issues in the American-Soviet relationship which would need serious discussion. Most of these matters were postponed until the next meeting between Roosevelt, Stalin, and Churchill.

---

[89]Harriman to FDR, December 15, 1944, Map Room Papers, Harriman dispatches, Box 11, July 1-December 31, 1944, FDRL.
[90]Ibid.
[91]Harriman to FDR, December 16, 1944, ibid.

# *IX*

## *Preparing for Peace in War: The Conference at Yalta*

AS PRESIDENT ROOSEVELT became more concerned over the postwar relationship with the USSR, he began to press for another meeting with Winston Churchill and Stalin. Stalin was agreeable, but he was in no hurry. He commented that, although such a meeting would be useful, he needed to be close to the battle zone. Roosevelt tried to persuade the Soviet leader by putting him in an uncomfortable situation. Stalin had often stressed Roosevelt's crucial role and how important it was to have him as the American leader during such a critical period. With this no doubt in mind, FDR urged that a Big Three meeting would have a favorable effect on his chances to win the fall election for president.[1] Over the next six months Roosevelt continued to instruct Harriman to keep after Stalin for a meeting in the near future. FDR and Churchill finally capitulated to Stalin's insistence that any meeting would have to be within easy traveling distance of Moscow. Stalin selected the Black Sea resort of Yalta in the Crimea.[2]

In preparation for the Yalta Conference, the Department of State outlined the issues with which the president would have to deal. The desiderata that the department urged on Roosevelt included prodding the Russians and the British to compromise on the voting procedure for the UN Security Council along lines acceptable to the United States. The president also should push for agreement on an Emergency European High Commission, comprised of the United States, Great Britain, the USSR, and France, which would work out a common Allied political program for liberated Europe. It also wanted acquiescence to an American plan for the short-term and long-term political and economic treatment of Germany. FDR was to persuade the Soviet Union to allow U.S. representation on the Allied Control Commissions in the countries liberated by the Red Army.

---

[1]Stalin to Roosevelt, July 22, 1944, and Roosevelt to Stalin, July 27, 1944, *FRUS: Conferences at Malta and Yalta*, pp. 4–5.
[2]See messages of October 8, 1944, through January 1, 1945, ibid., pp. 8–27.

Completely disregarding the known Soviet position on Poland, the department urged the president to persuade the Russians to ensure "the emergence of a free, independent, and democratic Poland" as well as immediate "establishment of an interim government which would be broadly representative of the Polish people and acceptable to all the major allies."[3]

The department expressed concern over Soviet policy in Iran and wanted the Russians to live up to the Declaration on Iran of December 1, 1943. In regard to China, FDR was to encourage Stalin to use his influence to get the Communists to agree to a coalition government similar to that which had been proposed by the new U.S. ambassador to China, General Patrick Hurley. And, finally, the president should attempt to establish a common Big Three policy "in regard to the question of the rearming of the Western European democracies in the postwar period."[4] This contradicted FDR's plan to have only the Big Four retain their arms immediately after the war.

How the Russians might be persuaded to agree to these American desiderata was revealed in a memorandum from W. Averell Harriman sent to FDR by Edward R. Stettinius, Jr. Russia had asked for $6 billion in postwar credits to be repaid over thirty years at 2.5 percent interest. Harriman suggested, with no contradiction from Stettinius, that the president should keep in mind that it was in America's interest to assist in the development of the Soviet economy, but with quid pro quos attached. The Russians had to understand that the American credits were contingent on "their behavior in international matters, and . . . the discussion of these . . . credits should be wholly divorced from the current lend-lease negotiations."[5]

The State Department knew what the Soviets would demand. John D. Hickerson set forth the Soviet plans as he saw them in a memorandum of January 8. The department already knew what the terms were for Finland and the Baltic States, and these were accomplished facts. Personally, he did not like this; but there it was, and nothing short of war would change it. Eastern Poland was going to be Russian, and the Poles would have to accept East Prussia in compensation. There would be adjustments in Romania as well. He proposed that there should be no opposition to incorporation of the Baltic States, transfer of East Prussia, and use of the Curzon Line as a frontier between Poland and Russia. These concessions would be worthwhile if they made it possible to win the war and organize the peace with Soviet cooperation. Hickerson believed that, if his suggestions were taken, an immediate effort should be made to prepare public opinion for these territorial alterations, including off-the-record conversations with

---

[3]"United States Political Desiderata in Regard to the Forthcoming Meeting," undated, Hopkins Papers, Sherwood Collection, Book 10: Yalta Conference Folder, FDRL.

[4]Ibid.

[5]Memorandum, Edward Stettinius to FDR, January 8, 1945, PSF, Departmental, State Department, 1945, Box 91, FDRL.

Congress, outstanding newspaper editors, writers, columnists, and radio commentators.[6]

Roosevelt took Hickerson's advice up to a point. FDR met with seven U.S. senators in January and admitted to them that spheres of influence were going to exist and that little could be done about it because occupying forces could control the circumstances. He mentioned eastern Europe and implied that the alternative there to spheres was a break with Russia that the United States could not afford. He told the senators that he hoped that this could eventually be changed as the United Nations made collective security a reality and worked toward world stability.[7]

Several times during 1944 the president indicated that he might agree to certain Soviet demands, but scarcely anyone of influence in the United States seemed to encourage this approach. Certainly only a few in the State Department did. This may have been the tragedy of the pre-Yalta period; Americans knew what Russia demanded, knew that the United States could not effectively resist Soviet objectives without war, and still insisted that the Russians surrender their claims. Hickerson put the matter succinctly when he allowed that Americans might not like it, but what could they do about it? Roosevelt decided that at Yalta he would have to persuade Stalin that the United Nations could replace spheres of influence in guaranteeing Soviet security.

## *II*

On January 22, 1945, two days after his fourth inauguration, FDR left for the Norfolk, Virginia, navy yards to board the cruiser *Quincy* for his trip to the Crimea. He tried to prepare for every problem he might confront by taking an assortment of political, diplomatic, and military people with him.[8] It is questionable whether FDR actually looked at the Black Book (prepared by Hickerson as a briefing document) aboard ship, where he spent his time resting and discussing his plans with those he chose to meet in his cabin. However, the Department of State had made sure that FDR saw the Black Book before he left.

Had the president seen a message from George Kennan to his interpreter, Charles Bohlen, he might have further suspected the wisdom of the Soviet experts in the department who agreed with Kennan's view. Kennan maintained that the United States had its head in the clouds if it expected anything other than a harsh postwar division into spheres of

---

[6]John D. Hickerson memorandum, January 8, 1945, *FRUS: Conferences at Malta and Yalta*, pp. 93–96.

[7]Dallek, *Franklin D. Roosevelt and American Foreign Policy*, pp. 507–8.

[8]Morgan, *FDR: A Biography*, p. 744.

influence based on power politics. He thought that the quest for a new League of Nations was quixotic and Wilsonian.

What really shocked Bohlen, who believed in the U.S. role for eastern Europe, was Kennan's admonition that the Americans should abandon having anything to do with the immediate future of eastern and southeastern Europe "unless we are willing to go the whole hog and oppose with all the physical and diplomatic resources at our disposal the domination of the area by any other single power. Lacking the will to do this, we should write these territories off."[9] Kennan did not despair of a reasonable relationship with the USSR, if the United States would be realistic and give up the dreams engendered at Dumbarton Oaks that the Russians would accept collective security guarantees resting on the United Nations Organization. Instead, the Americans should agree frankly to divide Europe into spheres of influence.[10] Kennan understood Europe's traditional balance-of-power political structure. He did not believe that Russia or Great Britain would abandon it. Soviet power would ensure continuance of the old system, because the Russians would be in physical possession of the territories they wished to annex or control.

Bohlen had been around Roosevelt and his advisers long enough to know that they would be very unlikely to accept such a blatant division of Europe, if for no other reason than that the public probably would not forgive any administration that did not at least try to get the Soviet Union to join in ensuring the peace by means other than power politics. In addition, the determination to create a United Nations Organization and to become a charter member were extremely important, not because it would be capable of averting war among the Great Powers, but because it would prevent the American people from slipping back into isolationism.[11]

Ambassador Harriman, like Kennan, was convinced that the Russians were bent on domination in eastern and central Europe, but he thought that something could be done about it. On January 10, he described to Stettinius the Soviets' technique of takeover: They eschewed direct annexation in favor of using occupation troops, secret police, local Communist parties, sponsored cultural societies, labor unions, sympathetic leftist organizations, and economic pressure "to assure the establishment of regimes which, while maintaining an outward appearance of independence and of broad popular support, actually depend for their existence on groups responsive to all suggestions emanating from the Kremlin." Soviet conceptions of security ignored the "similar needs or rights of other countries." Russia should not have the benefits of the United Nations Organization without recognizing

---

[9]As quoted in Hugh De Santis, *The Diplomacy of Silence: The American Foreign Service, the Soviet Union, and the Cold War, 1933–1947* (Chicago: University of Chicago Press, 1980), p. 131.

[10]Ibid.

[11]Bohlen, *Witness to History*, pp. 175–77.

the rights of other members.[12]  Several times he proposed that U.S. economic pressure might change the Soviet approach.

British and American officials met at Malta, presumably to prepare an agenda on military matters for the Yalta Conference, but political issues were discussed as well.  Stettinius opposed any plans to abandon the principles of self-determination or to allow Soviet expansion beyond limits already grudgingly accepted by the department. He suspected at Malta that the British were preparing to depart from these American principles in eastern Europe.  He told Anthony Eden and Sir Alexander Cadogan that it was impossible for the United States to recognize the Lublin Poles; public reaction could prejudice the question of American participation in the United Nations after the war.[13]  Cadogan tried to present a compromise in the form of an interim government for Poland comprised of a presidential council, which would avoid a fusion of the Lublin and London Poles.  The American and British representatives agreed to present this to Churchill and Roosevelt with the warning that American public opinion would probably not accept anything less.

Eden was concerned about the American inclination to resist Soviet requests for concessions in both Europe and the Far East. He suggested that the Russians should at least be offered a warm-water port to encourage them to enter the Far Eastern war.  Someone raised the desirability of cooperation between the Guomindang and the Communists in China.  When Stettinius interjected that President Roosevelt understood that the British were opposed to a coalition, Eden denied it; the British were most anxious to promote such unity.[14]

Obviously, the secretary of state intended to restrict the influence Churchill might bring to bear on FDR by getting agreement to basic positions from the Foreign Office representatives at the Malta Conference before Churchill and Roosevelt reached the Crimea.  Equally important, having the British lined up behind acceptable positions would forestall President Roosevelt taking a British plan and rearranging it.  State Department personnel knew what they wanted from Yalta, and they seemed determined not to let FDR go far astray from the proposals they had been selling him over the previous several months.

[12]W. Averell Harriman to Stettinius, January 10, 1945, *FRUS: Conferences at Malta and Yalta*, pp. 450–55.
[13]Meeting of the foreign ministers, Malta, February 1, 1945, ibid., p. 499.
[14]Ibid., pp. 499–502.

## *III*

When President Roosevelt arrived at the Crimean resort of Yalta, he was ensconced by the Russians in Tsar Nicholas II's Livadia Palace.[15] It had to be sprayed for lice and other vermin several times, and it was a rambling structure of more than fifty rooms overlooking the Black Sea with only one fully functioning bathroom.[16]  Before the conference began, Stettinius attempted to ensure that Roosevelt knew the agenda he was to pursue and how it should be approached.  The delegates should seek adoption of the American proposal for a voting formula in the United Nations and immediate announcement of a UN conference.  He advised against making a definitive agreement concerning German boundaries unless it was absolutely necessary.  The minorities question required that FDR oppose "so far as possible" indiscriminate mass transfers of populations; instead, transfers should be gradual and should be done under UN supervision.  The Curzon Line was to be adhered to in the north and center; in the south, the eastern line of Lwow province was to be the Polish border.  German territory transferred to Poland should include East Prussia, with the exception of Koenigsberg, which was to go to Russia along with a small coastal salient of Pomerania and Upper Silesia.[17]

Stettinius tried to get FDR to accept the Anglo-American plans from Malta.  The secretary urged the president to promote an interim representative government in Poland until free elections could be held and to insist that the government be comprised of elements from the London Poles (including Stanislaw Mikolajczyk, whose Peasant party was the most important in Poland), along with other moderate Poles abroad.  The president was to solicit Soviet and British support for American efforts to bring about a Guomindang-Communist agreement.  Cooperation between the two Chinese factions would expedite conclusion of the Pacific war and prevent internal conflict and foreign intervention in China.[18]  How well the president stuck to his secretary of state's proposals is questionable.  However, that he adhered to them in some areas where he might better have abandoned them is unquestionable.

Stettinius stressed the "seven major topics" for FDR to pursue with Churchill and Stalin: Germany, Poland, eastern Europe, the United Nations, the Far East, postwar economic problems, and the conclusion of the war in Europe.  Regarding the United Nations, the secretary of state wanted FDR first to take up when and where the organizing conference should be held.

---

[15]This is the spelling used in the *FRUS* volume on the conference, and it will be used here, although Livadiia and Livadiya are better transliterations of the name.

[16]Diane Shaver Clemens, *Yalta* (New York: Oxford University Press, 1970), pp. 113–17.

[17]Memorandum of suggested items for the president from Stettinius, Malta, February 2, 1945, *FRUS: Conferences at Malta and Yalta*, pp. 567–68.

[18]Ibid., pp. 568–69.

Ambassador Harriman said that Stalin would want quid pro quos in return for Soviet entry into the Pacific war: the southern half of Sakhalin and the Kuriles, the status quo in Outer Mongolia, and control over the railroad to Dairen. FDR wanted to know Chiang Kai-shek's views before proceeding on Mongolia.[19]

Before the general opening of the meetings, Roosevelt met with Stalin and V. M. Molotov with only their interpreters, Bohlen and V. N. Pavlov, present. Stalin played to Roosevelt's known likes and prejudices, and vice versa. FDR began by declaring that after seeing the devastation the Germans had perpetrated in the Crimea he was even "more bloodthirsty" toward them than before, and he hoped that Stalin would again propose a toast to the execution of fifty thousand German officers. Stalin charged that the Germans were "savages and seemed to hate with a sadistic hatred the creative work of human beings." Then, knowing FDR's contempt for Charles de Gaulle, Stalin belittled the French general even though he had recently signed a treaty of alliance with France and had called the general an able negotiator. FDR's response to a question regarding a zone of occupation for France in Germany was that the French could have one, but only out of kindness, not because they deserved it. Stalin was not enthusiastic and wanted this to be considered further.[20]

Stalin and Roosevelt then went together into the grand ballroom of the palace where the regular sessions were to take place. FDR proposed that they have informal sessions and speak frankly and freely, "since he had discovered through experience that the best way to conduct business expeditiously" was through this form of discourse.[21] Bohlen considered the approach chaotic and was amazed "that any agreement could emerge from such confusion." He realized, however, that there were some advantages. The constant switching from topic to topic kept tempers from flaring, and, therefore, "despite the difficulties and disappointments, the atmosphere remained pleasant throughout the conference."[22]

Flare-ups between the Anglo-American group and the Russians were expected; ironically, this was not the locus of the first disagreement. Stalin was willing to join the United States and Great Britain in protecting the rights of small nations, but he denied their right to question the actions of the major powers. Churchill approved Stalin's reservation: "The eagle should permit the small birds to sing and care not whereof they sang." In other words, the small nations could talk all they wanted, but the Big Three would retain the power to act. Churchill expanded on this idea to Anthony

---

[19]Meeting of the president with his advisers, February 4, 1945, ibid., pp. 566–67.

[20]Roosevelt-Stalin meeting, February 4, 1945, 4 P.M., Livadia Palace, ibid., pp. 571–73.

[21]First plenary meeting, February 4, 1945, 5 P.M., Livadia Palace, Bohlen minutes, ibid., p. 574.

[22]Bohlen, *Witness to History*, p. 179.

Eden as they walked out after dinner; anything which preserved unity among
the Big Three had his vote, even if it meant excluding small powers from
matters before the Security Council. Eden countered that this would
guarantee that the small powers would reject the United Nations, and it
would not be acceptable to British public opinion. The prime minister was
peeved and retorted sharply that "he did not agree in the slightest with Mr.
Eden because he was thinking of the realities of the international
situation."[23]

During the discussions that evening, as Churchill and Stalin attempted
to get around the American voting formula for the UN Security Council,
they could not comprehend why the Americans were so circumspect. After
all, FDR had talked frankly to the British and the Russians about the need
for the Big Three to make up the controlling force in keeping the peace.
Stalin did not understand Roosevelt's fear that the American public would
reject membership in the United Nations if the president failed to get some
representation on the Security Council for the smaller nations as well as a
voting formula that appealed to the public. Even the prime minister was
somewhat hazy about why the Americans acted as they did. Churchill tried
to understand the voting formula for the Security Council, and Bohlen, who
understood quite clearly why the Americans had proposed a compromise
giving the appearance of small-power participation without the substance,
tried to explain it to the prime minister. He related a story about a Southern
plantation owner who had given a black man a present of a bottle of
whiskey. When asked how he liked it, the black man proclaimed that it was
perfect. Pressed to describe why this was so, he answered: "If it had been
any better it would not have been given to me, and if it had been any worse
I could not have drunk it." Churchill left the room still arguing with
Eden.[24]

*IV*

One of the first items considered at Yalta was how to finally defeat the Third
Reich so as to ensure against a revived German threat. President Roosevelt
opened the session of February 5 by declaring that he understood that they
would take up the question of Germany beginning with zones of occupation.
Although this had been discussed and presumably settled by the European
Advisory Commission, there was still the question of whether or not France
would have a zone. Stalin preferred to discuss dismemberment first, which
he gathered they all still favored. He recounted the two plans presented to
him by his colleagues: Roosevelt's division of Germany into five parts and

[23]Tripartite dinner meeting, February 4, 1945, 8:30 P.M., Livadia Palace, *FRUS:
Conferences at Malta and Yalta*, pp. 589–90.
[24]Ibid., pp. 590–91.

Churchill's two-part division. Stalin went on record favoring the president's proposal. Churchill interjected that the few days they had had in these meetings were not sufficient to determine the exact divisions. This determination should be made later by a subcommittee with technical experts who could assess questions of economic and demographic distributions, whether Prussia should be subdivided, and what to do about the Ruhr and Saar industrial regions. FDR tried to settle the issue by proposing that they agree to dismemberment, charge a commission of the foreign ministers with working out the details, and add to the surrender terms a clause that Germany would be broken up into smaller states. The Germans should not be able to say that they were betrayed by later additions to the surrender document; they should know in advance and should have to accept dismemberment without specifics.[25]

The Big Three agreed in principle to divide Germany and then took up French participation. Here Roosevelt played middleman. Stalin contested France's right to a zone of occupation on the ground that this might encourage other states to ask for participation. Churchill insisted that it was important that France play a leading role in Europe to help keep Germany under control, as it was not known how long the United States would agree to remain on the Continent. FDR cautioned that two years was probably the extent of the American commitment to stay in Europe; therefore, they should honor the French request for a zone. Churchill wanted France as a block not only against a revived Germany but also against Soviet expansion in Europe.

The former ambassador to Great Britain, Ivan Maisky, who was at this point deputy commissar of foreign affairs, brought up the Soviet proposal for reparations. This plan envisioned removing from the national wealth of Germany industrial plants, machine tools, railroad rolling stock, and similar industrial items within two years from the end of the war, with additional annual payments in kind to continue for ten years. He contended that reducing German heavy industry by 80 percent would help to prevent a resurgence of aggression. This would all add up to the equivalent of $10 billion. Churchill reminded them of the results after World War I and concluded "that if you wished a horse to pull a wagon that you would have to give it fodder." Roosevelt again tried to mediate. He supported the Soviet claims, "since he felt that the German standard of living should not be higher than that of the Soviet Union." But the Germans should be allowed to live in such a way as to not become a burden on the world. Maisky countered that the Soviet demand was equal to only about 10 percent of the current U.S. budget and equal to about six months of the expenditures of the British government on the war. Since the Germans would have no military expenditures, there was no reason why they would not be able to give a

---

[25]Bohlen minutes, treatment of Germany, ibid., pp. 611–15.

modest but still decent standard of living to their people. Maisky also presented a total figure for reparations due to all of the Allies: $20 billion, with half to go to the USSR.[26]

Differences of opinion on reparations emerged from the Soviet insistence on presenting an exact figure owed by Germany. Churchill objected, and Roosevelt was not enthusiastic, either. Harry Hopkins broke the deadlock by suggesting to FDR that, since the Russians had given in on a number of issues important to the Americans, why not let them state an amount they thought just. Then, "simply say it is all referred to the Reparations Commission with the minutes to show the British disagree about any mention of the 10 billion."[27] Roosevelt accepted Hopkins's idea, and so did his colleagues; the final statement proposed that the Reparations Commission should use $20 billion as a basis for discussion, with half to go to the Soviet Union.[28]

When the foreign secretaries took up the issue of Germany, on February 6, Stettinius followed his instructions from FDR only to a point. He added dismemberment to the surrender document but sided with the British in proposing that the task of working out the details be given to the European Advisory Commission. Eden wanted the term to be more precisely defined than did Molotov. Stettinius had submitted two drafts for the statement, one appealing to the British representative and the other to the Russian. They agreed to send both versions back to their bosses.[29] Surprisingly, when the subject was brought up in the afternoon before Churchill, Stalin, and Roosevelt, Molotov withdrew his objection and accepted the draft Eden preferred. Stettinius stated his preference for referring reparations and the question of the French zone to the Allied Control Commission without eliciting any objection.[30]

General George Marshall and his British colleague, Sir Alan Brooke, wanted an all-out Soviet offensive to give them cover as they crossed the Rhine, probably in April. General Alexei Antonov promised that the Red Army would keep the pressure on the Germans, weather permitting. The Russians, for their part, wanted the British and Americans to concentrate on keeping German troops from transferring from Italy to the eastern front. They argued over how many divisions each faced, but in general they agreed to help one another in the last thrust at German forces.[31]

Some Soviet and Western military leaders and historians have claimed that Stalin could have taken Berlin during the Crimean Conference, thereby

---

[26]Ibid., pp. 617–22.

[27]Robert Sherwood, *Roosevelt and Hopkins: An Intimate History* (New York: Harper, 1948), p. 860.

[28]Harriman and Abel, *Special Envoy*, p. 404.

[29]Meeting of the foreign ministers, February 6, 1945, *FRUS: Conferences at Malta and Yalta*, pp. 655–57.

[30]Fourth plenary meeting, February 7, 1945, Bohlen minutes, ibid., pp. 709–12.

[31]Clemens, *Yalta*, pp. 132–36.

strengthening his bargaining position with Roosevelt and Churchill. Why did he not do this, if he had the opportunity? Diane Shaver Clemens in her pioneer study of Yalta agreed that the opportunity was there, but Stalin did not attack because it would have been costly in manpower, the attack might have failed, his supply lines were stretched to a dangerous point, and such a move would have alarmed Roosevelt and Churchill, from whom he wanted cooperation on other matters that were more important to Russia than was control of Germany.[32] Two Red Army generals have debated whether Berlin could have been taken without great risk in February. General Vasily I. Chuikov has contended that Berlin was available for the taking, but Stalin ordered a diversion to the north at the last minute.[33] Marshal Georgy K. Zhukov has disagreed; it would have been "the purest adventurism" to attack Berlin in February.[34] The Americans, who expected to be bogged down on the western border of Germany long enough for the Russians to easily beat them to the Reich capital, were perplexed by Stalin's failure to advance.[35] The British, meanwhile, wanted to make a dash for Berlin without major forces to back them up and before a significant number of troops had crossed the Rhine River; General Dwight Eisenhower told Field Marshal Bernard L. Montgomery that his scheme was "nuts," and it probably was.[36]

Agreement on the occupation zones for Germany resulted from the encouragement of Roosevelt's foreign policy advisers, who reacted to the rapidity of the Soviet thrust into Germany. It appeared that the Russians would be much further into the territory of the Reich at the end of the war than the British and Americans would be: The Red Army was only forty miles from Berlin, while the other Allies staggered under the German counteroffensive in the Ardennes Forest. As Warren Kimball pointed out in his important collection of the Roosevelt-Churchill correspondence, the Red Army offensive, "which had begun only three weeks earlier from positions south of Warsaw, had swept 250 miles westward." Roosevelt's advisers did not realize

> that Soviet armies had reached the limit of their lines of communication and supply (they did not begin their assault on Berlin until mid-April), [therefore] a number of American diplomats nervously recommended that the President quickly ratify the occupation zones for

---

[32]Ibid., pp. 85–95.

[33]Ibid., p. 86.

[34]As quoted in Seweryn Bialer, ed., *Stalin and His Generals: Soviet Military Memoirs of World War II* (New York: Pegasus Books, 1969), p. 510.

[35]Mosley, *Marshall: Hero for Our Times*, p. 308. In his two-volume study of the Red Army General Staff, General of the Army S. M. Shtemenko mentioned the thrust of January against the Wehrmacht by Russian forces and acknowledged that it was intended to aid the Allies who were facing resistance in the Ardennes, but he failed to say anything about why it stopped. See S. M. Shtemenko, *The Soviet General Staff at War, 1941–1945*, 2 vols. (Moscow: Progress Publishers, 1986), 2:410–11.

[36]Mosley, *Marshall: Hero for Our Times*, p. 308.

Germany worked out by the European Advisory Commission lest Stalin
claim no agreement existed and permit his armies to occupy portions of
western Germany.[37]

Like a number of other agreements made at Yalta, this one rested on an
evaluation of circumstances that appeared to be realistic at the time but have
since been judged hasty or ill-advised. Averell Harriman did a précis of the
circumstances surrounding the Yalta decisions for the U.S. Senate Armed
Services and Foreign Relations committees in 1951. He stressed the
context at Yalta: Everyone believed that Russia was essential to the winning
of the war. He noted the fear of some of the Department of State people at
the end of 1944 and early in 1945 that if the Russians were not tied to
specific agreements over Germany they might occupy and control nearly all
of the country.[38]

# V

Roosevelt and his Department of State advisers were eager to gain Anglo-
Soviet agreement on the UN Security Council voting question. On
February 6, the Big Three discussed this, assuming the establishment of the
United Nations itself without question. Stalin read FDR's message to
himself and Churchill of December 5, 1944, which asserted that each
member would have one vote and that decisions on procedural matters would
require seven votes. Other matters also would require an affirmative vote of
the seven members, but this would have to include the five permanent ones.
If the dispute involved a permanent member, it would refrain from voting.
Stalin reiterated the American rationale for the formula: To preserve the
peace there should be unanimity among the major powers, and the American
people would require a provision for a fair hearing for all member nations,
large and small. Churchill interjected that the future security of the world
depended on the friendship and cooperation of the Big Three, but there had to
be a provision for presentation of grievances by small states lest it appear
that the major powers were trying to rule the world, which was not their
intent. This was somewhat removed from his comment that the Big Three
should let the little birds sing without concern for the cause of their singing.

Stalin took umbrage and wanted to know to which power the prime
minister was referring. He was sure that Churchill did not have in mind the
United States or Great Britain, leaving only the Soviet Union. Churchill

[37]Warren F. Kimball, ed., *Churchill and Roosevelt: The Complete Correspondence*,
vol. 3, *Alliance Declining, February 1944–April 1945* (Princeton: Princeton University
Press, 1984), p. 524.

[38]Statement of W. Averell Harriman, special assistant to the president, regarding our
wartime relations with the Soviet Union, particularly as they concern the agreements
reached at Yalta, July 13, 1951, with cover letter from George M. Elsey to Herman Kahn,
August 20, 1951, PPF 6207, FDRL.

explained that he meant the impression that the other states would have of all three of them. "Marshal Stalin then said ironically that it looks as though two Great Powers have already accepted a document which would avoid any such accusation but that the third has not yet signified its assent."[39] Taking Churchill's line about securing the peace for fifty years, he avowed that this was the kind of organization they had to create. As long as the three leaders in the room lived, none would be aggressors; but ten years later, who would be the leaders? A new generation might not understand the horrors of war they had experienced. Possibly the Soviet Union would stand alone in a dispute against Great Britain, the United States, and others tied to them; this could precipitate a crisis they all wished to avoid.

Churchill and Stalin exchanged examples. The prime minister could appreciate Stalin's concern, but the world organization would not replace diplomacy in disputes among the powers. Stalin and his colleagues in the Kremlin could not forget that during the Finnish War, at the instigation of England and France, the League of Nations had expelled the Soviet Union and mobilized world opinion against it, "even going so far as to speak of a crusade." Churchill reminded Stalin that they had been very angry at the Soviet Union at the time (without specifically mentioning the Nazi-Soviet pact), but under the provisions of Dumbarton Oaks no one could be expelled. Stalin said that he was thinking not of expulsion but of mobilizing public opinion, that is, votes.[40]

Poland was next on Roosevelt's agenda. He contended that he could present a detached perspective, because the United States had no real interest in Poland except a fair settlement. Americans were ready to agree to the Curzon Line, as he had intimated at Tehran, but world opinion might be more satisfied if the Soviet Union were to grant concessions to Poland in the oil-bearing region around Lwow, although FDR would not insist on this. Churchill also accepted the Curzon Line and the incorporation of Lwow, but he reminded everyone that England had gone to war for Poland at risk of the life of the British nation. As a matter of honor, his government could not agree to a settlement that did not leave Poland a free and independent state.

Stalin claimed to understand the British position, but he asserted that, for the USSR, Poland concerned both honor and security. When Churchill proposed that they create a Polish government at Yalta, Stalin retorted that he was called a dictator, but he had enough democratic feelings not to act without consulting the Poles. As a military man, he demanded that the country liberated by the Red Army not harass it from the rear by civil war,

---

[39]Third plenary meeting, February 6, 1945, *FRUS: Conferences at Malta and Yalta*, pp. 660–64.
[40]Ibid., pp. 664–67.

and he would support a government that would guarantee this in Poland. Churchill agreed that anyone who attacked the Red Army should be punished, but he still could not accept the Lublin Poles as the governers of the country. Stalin pointed out the nature of the security problem for the USSR: Poland had been used too many times as a corridor to attack Russia.[41] At this juncture, it should have been apparent that the only government that Stalin would permit in Poland was one that he could control. The Soviet Union might permit participation of a few London Poles, but any intransigence on their part would find them excluded from the new government altogether. The British, and to a lesser extent the Americans, tried to pass this message on to the London Poles, with only limited success.

All of this sparring proved how unlikely it was that American ideals would emerge triumphant over Soviet military control and security demands on Poland. Roosevelt had determined before he left for Yalta that he would try to secure the acceptance of American principles on eastern Europe, including Poland. Nonetheless, he was not prepared to confront the Soviet Union if it meant an antagonistic relationship, and he made this clear both before he left for Yalta and during the discussions on Poland and the rest of eastern Europe. The Department of State had suggested leaving the European questions to a "High Commission for Europe" for a variety of reasons. John Hickerson thought that this would reassure public opinion that Allied cooperation in the solution of Europe's postwar problems would continue while the United Nations was being established. Charles Bohlen believed that such a commission would compel the Soviet Union to share responsibility for eastern Europe. Leo Pasvolsky, special assistant on international organization affairs, argued that such an arrangement would prepare the way for public acceptance of the United Nations. Stettinius apparently accepted this; he told the British that such a commission would reassure Americans of the value of an organization for international cooperation in solving Europe's problems.[42]

Roosevelt, however, was not happy with the idea of a high commission, and he was supported in his opposition by James Byrnes, who thought that such a committee would be rejected by the American people and by Congress; it might require U.S. troops to stay in Europe and would thus injure the chances for acceptance of the United Nations. However, the president did not abandon the ideas behind the State Department's commission proposal. Instead, he

> seized upon the draft declaration for Allied goals for liberated Europe attached to the commission proposal. Vaguely worded, this declaration

---

[41]Ibid., pp. 667–79.

[42]Lynn Etheridge Davis, *The Cold War Begins: Soviet-American Conflict over East Europe* (Princeton: Princeton University Press, 1974), pp. 173–74.

reaffirmed Allied faith in the principles of the Atlantic Charter and expressed the intention of the Allies to see established in liberated Europe representative governments through the holding of free elections. . . . The declaration was acceptable to Roosevelt since it represented a reiteration of the United States commitment to the Atlantic Charter principles and required no specific American involvement in the affairs of the individual European countries.[43]

Diane Shaver Clemens has contended, correctly, that Roosevelt and Churchill were aware of the indefensibility of their stand on Poland. According to Clemens, "one reflection of the weakness of their bargaining stance was that Churchill and Roosevelt had to raise the issue of Poland themselves." Stalin, secure in his position, was prepared either not to mention it or merely to respond to the initiatives of his Western colleagues.[44]

After several days of wrangling, Molotov focused on the American draft for a proposed settlement in Poland and objected to a British version that would have guaranteed a new government rather than a reorganization of the existing Lublin or Warsaw government. Molotov's version asserted that "the Provisional Government which is now functioning in Poland should therefore be reorganized on a broader democratic basis with the inclusion of democratic leaders from Poland itself and from Poles abroad."[45] The Soviet Union would supervise the elections, which would expand the Soviet puppet regime rather than form a new government or a coalition based on the existing London government.

As Clemens has pointed out, the final draft on Poland illustrated the days of work that went into the agreement and stemmed from "the American proposal (which paralleled the original Soviet proposal), amended by Molotov, redrafted by the British, and then further amended by Molotov. It also showed the revisions of two foreign ministers' meetings, and of Churchill's private talks with Stalin." Because of British opposition to the Oder-Neisse Line, as well as Roosevelt's desire to avoid saying anything about boundaries that might give him trouble at home, they compromised on the final statement. Since "Roosevelt remained wary of any commitment by the United States to frontiers before a peace treaty," the language was irresolute. "Heads of the Three Governments" felt rather than recognized "that there should be consideration of the Curzon Line and compensation in the west for Poland."[46] Roosevelt had earlier acknowledged that the Oder-Neisse Line was acceptable, but Hopkins's note that Churchill

---

[43]Ibid., pp. 174–75.

[44]Clemens, *Yalta*, pp. 177–78.

[45]Draft presented by foreign ministers to the plenary session, February 10, 1945, *FRUS: Conferences at Malta and Yalta*, p. 898.

[46]Clemens, *Yalta*, pp. 212–13.

was in trouble with his cabinet and FDR's long-standing desire to postpone such decisions probably determined his course.[47]

President Roosevelt ultimately tried to get his way on the Polish question by persuading the Russians to subscribe wholeheartedly to the Declaration on Liberated Europe, which emerged at the end of the Yalta Conference. The statement averred that the three assembled powers agreed to meet during the period of chaos after the war to assist "the peoples liberated from the domination of Nazi Germany and the peoples of the former Axis satellite states of Europe to solve by democratic means their pressing political and economic problems." The phrase "by democratic means" was key to FDR's plan to hold the Russians, or at least persuade Americans that the Russians were held, to American principles concerning self-determination of peoples, free elections, and the other guarantees specified or implied in the Atlantic Charter. In fact, a specific pledge to uphold the principles of the charter was included in the declaration.[48] FDR had to know, or at least suspect, that the Russians viewed democracy differently, since their perspective had been pointed out to him by his Soviet experts and ambassadors to the Kremlin over and over again. However, as Averell Harriman contended, Roosevelt was not bothered by different interpretations so long as he could make his own.[49]

In keeping with FDR's proclivity to permit words to have different meanings depending upon who read them, he did not object when Molotov changed the draft of the declaration from "[the signatories] will immediately establish appropriate machinery for the carrying out of the joint responsibilities set forth in this declaration" to "they will immediately take measures for the carrying out of mutual consultation."[50] State Department representatives at the conference prodded Roosevelt to support the British in defining what would be the shared obligations in eastern Europe, but the president paid no attention to these importunings. This was another illustration of FDR's penchant for handling the broad issues of principle himself and leaving the details to be ironed out by subordinates, as he had done on the debt question in the recognition agreement with the Soviet Union in 1933. The results had soured American-Soviet relations, and there was a sense of déjà vu when the criticisms of Yalta poured forth in succeeding years. Harriman touched on this in his defense of Yalta, focusing on the wording of the Declaration on Liberated Europe: "Roosevelt and Churchill obtained the pledge of Stalin for joint action to secure the

---

[47]Ibid., p. 213. Clemens referred to Hopkins's note but did not mention Roosevelt's earlier agreement about the boundaries.

[48]Declaration on Liberated Europe, *FRUS: Conferences at Malta and Yalta*, pp. 971–72.

[49]Harriman and Abel, *Special Envoy*, p. 399.

[50]Meeting of the foreign ministers, February 10, 1945, *FRUS: Conferences at Malta and Yalta*, p. 873.

fundamental freedoms for the people in territories overrun by the Red Army."[51]  He neglected to mention the Soviet definitions that emerged at Yalta.

# VI

Roosevelt was willing to accept the transfer of Far Eastern territory to Stalin partly because he was convinced that the USSR had to be assured that Siberia would be protected from a revived Japan.  Also, he knew that Sakhalin, the Kuriles, Dairen, and Port Arthur had been either Russian or under Russian influence before the Russo-Japanese War,[52] and he wanted the Soviet leader to believe that recognition of the USSR's security interests was primary in any settlement.  General George Marshall presented another cogent reason for being nice to Stalin: The Americans needed him.  Marshall wanted FDR to press for a date for Soviet entry into the Pacific war.  The U.S. Army chief of staff sent a memorandum to the president arguing that two basic military questions had to be settled at the conference.  First, the United States had to obtain guarantees that the Russians would enter the Far Eastern war.  Second, when they did so, it was essential to keep open a supply line across the Pacific to Siberia.  Thus, the Soviet Union had to be persuaded to permit bases for American air forces in the Komsomolsk-Nikolaevsk area.  The Russian military staff had disapproved a request for such bases, and only Stalin could countermand this decision.[53]

Getting Stalin's cooperation for an Asian agenda was the subject of private discussions between Roosevelt and Stalin on February 8.  The president presented a plan for postwar Asia excluding French and British colonial authority from Indochina and Hong Kong, respectively; the latter would become an international port, while Indochina would become independent.  FDR invited Stalin to expand Soviet influence in northern Asia, while the United States would take responsibility for other Asian areas, including shared oversight of Korea between themselves and China. As this scenario developed, Stalin responded affirmatively to the American request for air bases at Komsomolsk or Nikolaevsk.

Stalin introduced his requirements for his country to enter the war against Japan.  The Soviet quid pro quos were those predicted to FDR by Harriman on February 4.  FDR agreed that the Russians could have the

---

[51]Harriman statement to the Committees on Armed Services and Foreign Relations of the Senate, July 13, 1951, p. 8, PPF 6207, FDRL.

[52]The Kuriles had actually been transferred to Japan in an agreement of 1875. In the Treaty of St. Petersburg, Japan ceded all of Sakhalin Island to Russia in return for which the Russians recognized Japanese sovereignty in the Kurile Islands. See Michael T. Florinsky, *Russia: A History and an Interpretation in Two Volumes* (New York: Macmillan, 1958), 2:979.

[53]Meeting of the Joint Chiefs of Staff, February 5, 1945, *FRUS: Conferences at Malta and Yalta*, p. 594.

Kuriles and Southern Sakhalin, but he resisted agreement on Port Arthur and Dairen and on control of the Manchurian railways because he could not commit to this without Chiang Kai-shek's approval. He returned to his idea that perhaps the Russians could lease Port Arthur and that Dairen should be under international control. Joint Soviet-Chinese control over the railroads was acceptable to Roosevelt if Chiang agreed. Stalin also wanted Roosevelt to understand Soviet interests in Outer Mongolia, which would be discussed with the Chinese. Stalin supported Chiang's leadership, but he proposed that there should be a reorganization of the Guomindang to bring to the fore some of the better people who seemed not to have much influence. Roosevelt assured him that the new U.S. representatives in China, General Albert Wedemeyer and Ambassador Patrick Hurley, were making progress on this.[54] Stalin's objective in these discussions was expressed clearly by the diplomat Valentin Berezhkov, who revealed that Stalin had asserted that the Soviet people had no other reason to enter the Far Eastern war than to advance their national interests:

> [The Soviet people] well understood the reason for the war against Germany, which had threatened the very existence of their country, but they would not see why the USSR needed to attack Japan. If, however, [Stalin's] political conditions were met, it would be much easier to explain things both to the people and to the Supreme Soviet of the USSR, since then it would be a question of the country's national interests.[55]

This was an unusual admission for a Soviet diplomat, as he abandoned the usual contention that all his government's actions in the war rested on either self-defense or altruism.

In the last two days of the conference, the Americans and the Russians settled their differences over the political considerations that would dictate Soviet participation in the war against Japan. On February 10, Harriman went to the Soviet residence in the Villa Koriez to arrange with Molotov the final agreement to be presented to the Big Three the next day for their signatures. The president wanted some alterations in the Soviet proposal: He would make both Dairen and Port Arthur free ports instead of leaseholds, the Manchurian Railroad should be a joint Chinese-Soviet enterprise rather than a Russian lease, and the Chinese should be consulted before these things were put into effect. Stalin balked. The final document, signed the next day, included Port Arthur as a leasehold to Russia and called for recognition of the People's Republic of Mongolia, both without consulting

---

[54]Roosevelt-Stalin meeting, February 8, 1945, Bohlen minutes, ibid., pp. 766–72.
[55]Berezhkov, *History in the Making*, pp. 408–9.

Chiang. In all other respects it remained the same as the agreement worked out by Roosevelt and Stalin and confirmed by Harriman and Molotov.[56]

Harriman did not like the insertion of the phrase "the pre-eminent interests of the Soviet Union shall be safeguarded." Roosevelt dismissed this objection. After all, the Russians had a larger interest in the area than either the British or the Americans, and, since this was true, why not say it? Harriman presumed that this was part of Roosevelt's effort to get Stalin's cooperation on subjects of more interest to the president: "He was trying like the dickens to get Stalin to be more cooperative in other areas that he cared about, the United Nations and Poland. . . . It was my impression that as long as he could put his own interpretation on the language, he didn't much care what interpretation other people put on it."[57]

Roosevelt has been criticized for secretly surrendering Chinese territory at Yalta. Harriman explained the reasons for this decision, and they were sensible. The president did not trust his State Department or the Chongqing government to prevent leaks of information. It was important that the USSR's agreement to enter the war against Japan, within two to three months after hostilities in Europe ceased, not be broadcast to the Japanese, who might take advantage of the thin Soviet defenses to improve their own position by an invasion of Siberia.[58] It is true that FDR and Stalin discussed the arrangements on China without informing Churchill or Chiang before signing the final document, but the implication that Roosevelt kept it secret from Stettinius and his other advisers simply is not true. Harriman persuaded Roosevelt of the need to surrender territory to the Soviet Union in the Far East, not the other way around, and Stettinius raised no objection.[59]

# VII

Returning home aboard the *Quincy*, FDR was in a terrible mood. Hopkins decided to leave the ship because he needed to get back to the United States for medical treatment. Charles Bohlen also decided to leave, and no one told him that the president wanted him to stay to help with the speech he was preparing to deliver to Congress.[60] Samuel Rosenman, a longtime Roosevelt speech writer, boarded the ship at Algiers, and Bohlen helped him

---

[56]Ibid., pp. 409–10.
[57]Harriman and Abel, *Special Envoy*, p. 399.
[58]Ibid., pp. 399–400.
[59]Lowenheim, Langley, and Jonas, *Roosevelt and Churchill: Their Secret Wartime Correspondence*, p. 517. The authors asserted that the surrender of Port Arthur and Southern Sakhalin to the Russians in return for promises to enter the Far Eastern war in two or three months after the German surrender "was worked out in the strictest secrecy between Roosevelt and Stalin, and not even Secretary of State Stettinius was informed about it."
[60]Bohlen, *Witness to History*, pp. 205–6; Jim Bishop, *FDR's Last Year: April 1944–April 1945* (New York: William Morrow, 1974), pp. 450–53.

with the address for a short time. It was finished off by Rosenman and the president after Bohlen and Hopkins left.[61]

Before both men departed, General de Gaulle, who had agreed to meet the president in Algiers, abruptly changed his mind. This prompted an angry note from Roosevelt, which Bohlen persuaded him to tone down. FDR's longtime assistant and factotum, General Edwin "Pa" Watson, became seriously ill at Yalta, faded during the voyage, and died on February 20. The president's own health began to fail as well. There has been much speculation that Roosevelt was too ill at Yalta to conduct affairs of state effectively. In fact, he apparently drew on his reserve of energy to carry off the Yalta negotiations successfully, only beginning to fade noticeably on the way home. According to Bohlen, the president even recovered some of his spark during the trip.[62]

Roosevelt gave a press conference to three reporters who boarded his ship at Algiers: Robert Nixon of International News Service, Douglas Cornell of Associated Press, and Merriman Smith of United Press. He began with some comments on the United Nations and where it should be located. He recalled that Churchill had asked him, when the president had first mentioned the idea three years earlier, where it should be situated, and he had answered that it should not be at Geneva due to bad associations with the League of Nations. A recordkeeping building should have a permanent location, while the association should meet half of the time in the Azores and the rest of the time somewhere else. He commented on the great climate and location of the Azores.

When one of the newsmen asked how Roosevelt felt about Russia, the president responded that he liked it very much and then described what the Germans had done to Yalta. Questioned about reparations from the Germans, FDR judged that the Russians would get all that they could. He implied that he would accept an unusual kind of reparations when asked if the Germans would have any means of payment: "Yes, I think so. Got a lot of German prisoners." In other words, he was willing to permit the use of prisoners to help rebuild the damage caused to the Soviet Union by the Germans; he considered this a form of reparations payment. Still, another reporter inquired if Roosevelt believed that now that the conference was over, he could give any real assurance to the American people and the rest of the world; Roosevelt answered affirmatively.[63]

Shortly after this exchange, "Pa" Watson died, and the president was listless and introspective for several days. Then on February 23 he suddenly began to work again. He summoned the press, brought up Yalta, and called it "a great achievement." He praised the American newsmen for their

[61]Bohlen, *Witness to History*, pp. 205–6.
[62]Ibid., pp. 204–7.
[63]Bishop, *FDR's Last Year*, pp. 454–56.

coverage of the conference.[64]  There should have been good coverage, because he sent James Byrnes home early to prepare the congressmen and the press for the good news about the Crimean Conference.  Byrnes kept shorthand notes of the meetings he attended, but he missed the last days, when the deals were struck on the Far East.  Of course, he could not know everything that was discussed in private gatherings or in the sessions of the foreign ministers.  Nonetheless, within the limits of his knowledge about the conference, he loyally carried out his assigned task.[65]

During the press conference FDR ranged through a host of topics relating to the Yalta Conference and attendant matters.  He opposed rearmament of Japan and Germany, wanted the Allied powers to reduce armaments, and hoped that some day the Axis nations could belong to the United Nations.  He dodged questions about the division of Germany and zones of occupation.  Off the record, Roosevelt launched into his anticolonial campaign, using French Indochina as the springboard.  France had done nothing for the people there in one hundred years of occupation, and he wanted a trusteeship to educate them for independence.  Churchill had opposed this because he feared that it would be a precedent for British colonies.  He accused Churchill of being "mid-Victorian on all things like that."[66]

Winston Churchill was facing an election and had to address the House of Commons before Roosevelt could speak to Congress.  Churchill put the best face that he could on the Yalta Conference.  He avoided speaking directly about the division of Germany, but he laid out the plans for de-Nazification, disarmament, dismantling of Germany's ability to use its industrial capacity to rearm, punishment of war criminals, and compensation in kind for damages to all Allied nations.  The powers had roughly determined Poland's eastern and western borders and had agreed to the establishment of a strong, independent, homogeneous Polish state.  He inserted a subtle warning that success depended on the Soviet attitude.  His comments were directed in part to any London Poles who might read the speech, as he cautioned that the viability of Polish independence depended on the Poles honestly following a policy that would be friendly toward Russia.[67]

President Roosevelt hurried to give his address, first scheduling it for March 2 and then moving it forward a day to the first.  Like Churchill, he spoke of the forthcoming defeat of Germany, but FDR described the Allied armies going rapidly through Germany to meet the gallant Red Army.  He

---

[64]Ibid., p. 459.

[65]Lloyd C. Gardner, *Architects of Illusion: Men and Ideas in American Foreign Policy, 1941–1949* (Chicago: Quadrangle Books, 1970), p. 85. Later Byrnes presented President Harry Truman with his view of the Yalta agreements. Because of the limitations of his notes, Truman had a distorted view of what went on and who promised what to whom.

[66]Bishop, *FDR's Last Year*, pp. 459–62.

[67]Ibid., pp. 464–65.

explained that the United Nations was a peacekeeping organization, and he lauded the great strides made in that direction at Yalta. FDR assured his listeners that he and his colleagues had "argued frankly and freely across the table," but in the end they had achieved unanimous agreement on every point. The words were less important than the unity they had achieved. Here there was prolonged applause. Also like Churchill, he spoke of Hitler's forlorn hope that the Allied coalition would founder and assured his audience that Yalta had proved otherwise. The Big Three were melded together in both war and peace aims.

He mentioned the voting procedure for the UN Security Council as the result of a lengthy and complicated debate. Details of the end product he would not yet release, but he was confident that Americans would consider it a fair solution founded in justice and intended to ensure international cooperation for maintaining the peace. This could not help but alarm skeptics about the United Nations; why did he not say what the formula was, if it had been so fairly hammered out? He tried to disarm critics by saying that the structure would be bipartisanly determined at San Francisco by an equal number of Democrats and Republicans from both houses of Congress. He obviously remembered Woodrow Wilson's mistakes of partisanship.

President Roosevelt promised that the peace would rest solidly on the foundation of the principles of the Atlantic Charter, specifically mentioning freedom of religious worship. Then he backed off a bit, announcing that these things would have to be based on give-and-take compromise. He warned that the United States could not always have its way, 100 percent. He mentioned the cost of helping to reconstruct the devastated regions that the United Nations would have to bear, carefully avoiding mention of the United States' share of the cost.

Roosevelt hesitated briefly before calling the settlement on Poland an outstanding example of joint action by the Big Three. They had searched for a common ground and had found it; they agreed to create a strong, independent, and prosperous nation. He mentioned the two contending governments and said that the existing one would be reorganized on a broad democratic basis, drawing on Poles in Poland and abroad. They would recognize this temporary government until free elections could be held. He brought up the compromise on boundaries. He explained that the Russo-Polish border would be the Curzon Line and that most of the people to be incorporated into the USSR were White Russians and Ukrainians, not Poles. Poland would get in return East Prussia, with its coastline and better and richer land than the Poles lost. The Danzig question would be settled: It would be Polish. He did not agree with this settlement entirely, but he emphasized that Russia had not gotten all that it had asked for, either.

When Roosevelt mentioned the Far Eastern war, he gave the impression that the discussions about it had been held at Malta and had been military in nature. He could not very well explain his consultations with the Russians about entering the Pacific war while the Russo-Japanese neutrality pact was still in force. He focused instead on the long road to Tokyo, mentioning that, although the struggle would be difficult, the outcome was not in doubt. Roosevelt did not bamboozle, but he did obfuscate, mostly because he could not be specific about topics that had been only generally agreed to or were still secret in nature.

"No plan is perfect," Roosevelt told Congress. Even the San Francisco Conference would not present an immutable organization, and he reminded them of the changes in the U.S. Constitution that had been required over the years. Peace would last only as long as humanity demanded it, worked for it, and sacrificed for it. Statesmen had failed the fighting men of the last war; they could not afford to do so again and expect the world to survive. "And that, my friends, is the only message I can give you. I feel it very deeply as I know that all of you are feeling it today and are going to feel it in the future." Franklin Roosevelt had given his last address to the Congress of the United States and the American people.

Listening to the recording of that speech and comparing it to others, for example to his address to Congress after the Japanese attack, it is obvious that this was not one of Roosevelt's best efforts. His voice faltered, he was hoarse, he hesitated or lost his place fourteen times,[68] and, according to Samuel Rosenman, he departed from the text forty-nine times, not always with the best results.[69] Despite this, it may have been his greatest speech because to make it at all required effort beyond what he really had left: To him, it was the most important address of his career, for so much of his hope for America and the world rested on how it was received. Although Roosevelt was greeted with thunderous applause and the initial press reaction to his speech was positive, doubts about the Soviets' willingness to cooperate already had begun to surface among the American public.

At Yalta, the agendas had dealt with the issues outlined to FDR by Stettinius. The Department of State had wanted the American voting formula for the United Nations to be accepted and had got it, but in return they had to give the USSR three seats in the General Assembly. The British and the Russians offered three seats to the United States, which FDR chose to decline. The U.S. delegation had secured Soviet agreement to participate in the new international organization, which they all foresaw as

---

[68]The author has drawn on the recording of this address rather than a printed copy in order to have the flavor as well as the content. Henry Steele Commager, ed., with an introduction by Eleanor Roosevelt, "F.D.R. Speaks: Authorized Edition of Speeches, 1933–1945" (Washington, DC: Washington Records, 1960), side 12.

[69]Bishop, *FDR's Last Year*, p. 481. Bishop also includes most of the text of the address, pp. 473–80.

both a peacekeeping body and an instrument to keep the American people from sinking back into isolationism. They had wanted an agreement on the division of Germany and, under British pressure, had agreed to ask for a zone of occupation for France and for French participation in the Allied Control Commission. They got these things through compromises which gave France part of the British and American zones. The Americans had sought and achieved Soviet acceptance of the Declaration on Liberated Europe. They had insisted on defining the conditions under which a new Polish government would be formed and had reached an agreement at Yalta, although it was to be interpreted variously by the signatory powers. Finally, they had been desperate to obtain Soviet entry into the Pacific war in order to contain American casualties, and they gained Stalin's agreement to attack Japan immediately on the conclusion of the fighting in Germany.

Critics of the Yalta agreements have based their assessments either on misreadings of the actual arrangements or on hindsight evaluations of the results of Soviet policy in eastern Europe, the Middle East, and Asia after World War II, not on the realities the American and British negotiators faced at the Crimean Conference. The president and his aides thought that they were dealing with faits accomplis concerning possession of territory, the need for Soviet assistance in the Pacific theater, guarantees against a resurgent Germany or Japan, and the creation of a peacekeeping organization to prevent repeating the terrors that their people had just experienced. The end of the war in either Europe or Asia was not as clearly seen as the dates it ended might imply. That is, the president and his advisers did not know that Germany would collapse so quickly, or that Soviet participation in the Far East would not be necessary due to the success of the atomic bomb in breaking Japan's resistance. The need for the Soviets' continued participation in the war and their collaboration in the postwar world impressed not only Roosevelt but also Stettinius, Harriman, Bohlen, Hopkins, Churchill, and Eden, among others; they saw the prospect for cooperation with the Soviet Union as a distinct possibility, despite danger signs to the contrary.[70]

---

[70]Averell Harriman's statement to the Senate committees reiterates the sense of history that permeated the expectations of the attendants at the Yalta Conference and their limited vision of future events that would change the American-Soviet relationship. Harriman stressed the apparent needs that dictated decisions there and scored those who criticized Yalta with hindsight. Statement of Harriman to the Committees on Armed Services and Foreign Relations of the Senate, July 13, 1951, PPF 6207, FDRL.

# X

## *Dawn of a New Day: Clouds on the Horizon*

DESPITE SOME DOUBTS about the Yalta decisions, FDR had to believe that his meetings with Stalin were successful because his vision of the future depended on an amicable American-Soviet relationship. Reaction to the Crimean Conference from friends, well-wishers, and even some foreign policy observers gave him courage to trust that his hopes for the postwar world might be justified. The president was encouraged that the number of Americans "satisfied with Allied cooperation" had increased "from 46 to 64 per cent and that American participation in a world body with power to assure the peace now found acceptance with over 80 per cent of the public."[1] Harry Hopkins was one of those who viewed Yalta as a success, and his optimism was tempered by only slight reservations. On February 26 he wrote Lieutenant General Joseph T. McNarney that "you probably know by now that the military end of the Crimean Conference went extremely well and I feel we got much farther on the political side than we anticipated."[2] Overall, the presidential assistant felt that they had achieved much because they had gotten through to Stalin, who, in Hopkins's opinion, provided the key to all relations with the Soviet Union. Hopkins told his friend and future biographer Robert Sherwood:

> We really believed in our hearts that this was the dawn of the new day we had all been praying for and talking about for so many years. . . . The Russians had proved that they could be reasonable and farseeing and there wasn't any doubt in the minds of the President or any of us that we could live with them and get along with them peacefully for as far into the future as any of us could imagine. But I have to make one amendment to that—I think we all had in our minds the reservation that

---

[1]Dallek, *Franklin D. Roosevelt and American Foreign Policy*, p. 522.
[2]Harry Hopkins to Joseph T. McNarney, February 26, 1945, Hopkins Papers, Sherwood Collection, Book 10, Yalta Conference Folder, FDRL.

we could not foretell what the results would be if anything should happen to Stalin.[3]

Hopkins did not take up with Sherwood the question of what would happen if Roosevelt were not around to deal with the Soviet leader. When Hopkins expressed his hope for cooperation with the Russians to his son Robert, he attached another condition. Robert Hopkins said that his father "certainly worked on the hope that Stalin would honor his commitments."[4]

Revisionists on the right have contended that Roosevelt and Hopkins were taken in by Stalin at Yalta; they argue that he carefully laid plans for the Cold War after the hot war.[5] Adam Ulam has contested this view. In his study of Stalin, he argued that at Yalta it "would be wrong to see Stalin—at this in many ways most triumphant moment of his career—as entirely cynical. He had a sense of great historical occasions." Ulam assumed that Stalin knew the final victory would be in some respects anticlimactic and would be followed by inevitable discordance in the alliance. But, like Roosevelt and Hopkins,

> for the moment, he enjoyed the glow of camaraderie with two men whose greatness he clearly appreciated, for all his ruthless exploitation of their vulnerabilities, and whose attentions to him he valued. There was also a note of wistfulness, of something which looks suspiciously close to sentimentality in his avowal that he was an old man, in his assertion (for a brief moment he was sincere) that they must work together to spare the world the horrors of another war. Perhaps in his meetings with Roosevelt and Churchill, Stalin felt that he was taking a vacation from his job as tyrant and his mellowness was not entirely spurious.[6]

In keeping with FDR's fervent hope that the Russians were taking a new view of the world, he would have been pleased with part of a dispatch from George Kennan but upset by his concluding remarks. Patriarch Alexei of the Russian Orthodox church had praised the Crimean Conference and all of its works, speaking of the Christian responsibility for world peace.[7] Kennan analyzed Alexei's enthusiasm in this and a number of other dispatches. The Russian Orthodox church was willingly serving the foreign

---

[3]Sherwood, *Roosevelt and Hopkins*, p. 870.

[4]As quoted in Tuttle, *Harry L. Hopkins*   267.

[5]For example, see the various representations of this view in Harry Elmer Barnes, ed., *Perpetual War for Perpetual Peace* (Caldwell, ID: Caxton Printers, 1953).

[6]Adam B. Ulam, *Stalin: The Man and His Era* (New York: Viking Press, 1973), pp. 608–9.

[7]George Kennan to Edward Stettinius, February 17, 1945, DSF 740.0011/2-1745. Roosevelt would have been upset because Kennan advised that the rapprochement was intended to use the church for nationalistic purposes and the church was willing to cooperate in this endeavor.

policy objectives of the state, and there was a definite change occurring in the attitude of the state toward the church. Kennan foresaw the regime's taking advantage of a patriotic surge connecting the Russian past with the Soviet present, bringing the art forms of the church into favorable consideration as part of the Russian heritage, showing that the state had no reason to fear the church, and proving that it was living up to the pledges made in the Soviet constitution of 1936.[8]

Secretary of State Edward Stettinius did his part to woo the Senate to the administration's view of the conference decisions. He told a bipartisan Senate committee about the atmosphere at Yalta, where they avoided bickering. It was apparent that Stalin and the Soviet government had decided that the USSR should take its place among the United Nations, and he had frequently made concessions on political, economic, and security matters. Roosevelt had presided, because he was the only actual head of state among the Big Three, and he had taken up the military situation first and foremost.[9]

In the Soviet Union the mood was almost euphoric over the results of the conference, which could not help but encourage members of the Roosevelt administration to feel that their own optimism was warranted. Averell Harriman recounted the Soviet press reaction, which acclaimed Yalta "as [a] further step forward on [the] path of cooperation between the three principal Allies and as evidence of their desire to work together not only to achieve victory over Germany but for the postwar as well." There was special satisfaction "over agreement reached concerning [the] international security organization, postwar control of Germany, settlement of [the] Polish question, and treatment of [the] liberated countries of Europe."[10]

---

[8]See for example, Kennan to Stettinius, DSF 861.911 RR/4-1945; 4-2745; and 5-745. See also DSF 861.404/2-345; 2-845; and 3-945. Kennan was quite accurate in his assessment of the objectives of the state, but he did not fully understand the patriarch's position, which rested on a belief that the church could benefit by cooperation in bringing back to the fold of the "one true faith" the strayed Uniates in eastern Europe and others who might find the "final center" of world Christianity as the rock of their faith. For an exposition of this view of the Russian Orthodox church and its leadership see Edward M. Bennett, "The Russian Orthodox Church and the Soviet State, 1946–1956: A Decade of the New Orthodoxy," *Journal of Church and State* 7:3 (Autumn 1965): 425–39.

[9]Stettinius daily notes, March 16, 1945, Records of Harley A. Notter, Miscellaneous Subject Files, Box No. 29, Lot 60D-224, Stettinius daily notes, December 14, 1944-March 16, 1945.

[10]W. Averell Harriman to Stettinius, March 15, 1945, Post Files, Box 1372 B Moscow, 800-801.2, 1945, 800-USSR. When Soviet perspectives on questions relating to postwar problems altered the view of what should be done about Germany, some Soviet historians attempted to "prove" that the USSR never supported division of Germany or any settlement based on the idea that Germany had to be kept down. This strained interpretation appeared as late as 1985. See Alexei Roshchin, "The Crimean Conference and the Postwar Settlement," in Alexander Yakovlev, ed., *Lessons of History: The Yalta Conference, 1945* (Moscow: Novosti Press Agency Publishing House, 1985), pp. 45–46. However, by 1987, Soviet historians, including some whose work appeared in this volume, began to look more objectively at the evidence of the Yalta and other conferences

While Roosevelt hedged on telling the American people about the voting formula worked out for the United Nations, *Izvestiia* laid it out clearly for its readers.  Harriman judged that the article set forth "dispassionately and clearly the Soviet view . . . stressing the profound practical significance" for the effective functioning of the United Nations. The Soviet writer contended that "true international equality can be achieved only by the assignment to the strong peace loving states of full responsibility for preservation of order in the world."[11]  Harriman found this worrisome; but, in fact, it was exactly the perspective that Winston Churchill, FDR, and Stalin had discussed and essentially agreed upon at one stage of their meetings at Yalta.  That this view of the voting formula was presented only in the USSR related not so much to Soviet misinterpretation as to the squeamishness of the British and Americans about telling it like it was.

*Pravda* editorial writer A. Georgiev insisted that there had been only one great enemy, the Fascists, and the United Nations aimed to prevent the revival of fascism.  Roosevelt and Churchill tried desperately at Yalta to get the Russians to agree that their security rested on a viable United Nations. The editorial contended that "we are confident that [the] Soviet Union, Great Britain, and [the] United States, having achieved splendid results in war against aggressors, will be able to construct future peace on [a] firm basis of cooperation in [a] single international security organization."[12] Unfortunately, this article appeared after Roosevelt's death. He would have taken some solace from it.

Even Harriman, who had become quite skeptical about Soviet behavior, thought that there was some possibility of showing the Russians that they were not completely alone in their view of the peace. Concerning their approach to Finland, he agreed with them and thought that they acted with moderation. He suggested to Stettinius that the State Department should authorize a statement that "would be helpful from the standpoint of our relations with the Soviet Government."  There had been criticism of the Soviets for things they did that America did not like, "and it would seem appropriate for us to take a position publicly which would support them in this case where we think they are right."[13] This was done too seldom, and it was thought that the Russians were right hardly ever. But then the reverse was true as well.

Roosevelt knew that he would be criticized for the Yalta decisions relating to both the Far East and Europe, but he was under heavy pressure

---

and admitted that there was certainly a vengeful mood and a fear of German revival on the part of all three powers represented at Yalta. Author's notes on the Moscow colloquium, October 1987, FDRL.

[11]Harriman to Stettinius, March 12, 1945, DSF 711.00/3-1245.

[12]Unsigned dispatch to Stettinius, April 21, 1945, DSF 711.00/4-2145.

[13]Harriman to Stettinius, March 1, 1945, DSF 860D.00/3-145.

from his military advisers, including theater commander General Douglas MacArthur, to involve Russia at all costs in order to shorten the war and save millions of lives. In August 1943, MacArthur had urged Secretary of the Navy James V. Forrestal to push for Russian involvement, and shortly after Yalta the general had voiced approval of what had been done, concluding "that Russian seizure of Manchuria, Korea, and possibly part of northern China was inevitable, and that to deny Port Arthur to Russia would be impractical."[14]

General Dwight Eisenhower appealed for action by the president to persuade Stalin to launch an offensive to aid the American advance in Germany, and this was noted at both the Malta and Yalta conferences.[15] There has been considerable debate about whether a mistake was made when the Americans did not rush to Berlin and seize it before the Russians could arrive. Some critics have reproved Eisenhower for this "error," and some have condemned FDR. It is far better to blame the Germans. The Russians could have made a dash for Berlin, but they believed that they should be fully prepared for a massive and decisive assault and waited until they had 1,125,000 men ready. Eisenhower was under pressure from the British and from some of his own subordinates to make an assault on Berlin for political advantage; he resisted, because he did not believe that he could succeed with the divisions at his disposal when he was 250 miles from the German capital and the Russians were only 35 miles away. Also, he thought that the whole situation might backfire and cause the Russians to react adversely. This, too, was included in Roosevelt's briefing materials at Yalta, and undoubtedly it influenced his approach to the end of the war in Europe.[16]

That FDR was less than totally enchanted with the agreements emerged in his conversations shortly after his return. Eleanor Roosevelt bombarded him with questions and expressed her shock at the surrender of "little countries," such as Estonia, Latvia, and Lithuania, to Soviet control. FDR, who often snapped at his wife when she touched upon a sore spot, retorted: "How many people in the United States do you think will be willing to go

---

[14]John L. Snell, ed., *The Meaning of Yalta* (Baton Rouge: Louisiana State University Press, 1956), p. 154. Other evidence of Douglas MacArthur's position throughout the war favoring whatever deals were needed to get Russia involved is found on pp. 32–33, 133, and 201–2. The "rime" of Yalta to which MacArthur referred in 1955 concerning the Far East did not seem to him so criminal on February 13, 1945; see pp. 153–54.

[15]Ibid., pp. 26–31.

[16]Stephen E. Ambrose, *Eisenhower and Berlin, 1945* (New York: W. W. Norton, 1967), pp. 88–89. Ambrose makes a cogent argument for the wisdom of Eisenhower's decision to halt and regroup on the Elbe River and points out that the Russians had been preparing for their assault for a long time, while the American and British forces were worn out from a long campaign, were badly in need of reinforcements and rest, and had outrun their fuel supply. Eisenhower stated that taking Berlin would offer no advantage if the Germans held out in southern Germany, and he was convinced that the high cost of capturing the capital would be a waste when the Russians would be virtually there anyway.

to war to free Estonia, Latvia, and Lithuania?" She said that she supposed
there would not be many.[17] Adolf Berle, who had long suspected that not
much good would come of dealing with the Russians, also stopped in to see
the president. "Yalta," he shot at FDR in some measure of derision.
Roosevelt threw his hands in the air and said, "I didn't say it was good,
Adolf. I said it was the best I could do."[18] He really believed that it was the
best he could do, and perhaps it was.

## II

While Stalin gave lip service to the concept of security through the United
Nations, he set about providing his own insurance by restoring an alliance
system on the Soviet borders. In early March the Russians concluded a pact
with Yugoslavia and Bulgaria; the Americans, and to a lesser extent the
British, objected on grounds that collective security was intended to
eliminate the necessity for this sort of balance-of-power structure. V. M.
Molotov claimed not to understand their opposition.

Nor were the Soviets only building an alliance system, they also
seemed to be less enamored of the UN idea and flaunted their
disenchantment, announcing that Molotov would not attend the San
Francisco Conference. When the British ambassador, Clark Kerr, warned
Andrei Vyshinski that this was unwise, the Russian told him to mind his
own business. Ambassador Harriman reinforced the "gloomy mood" that
Soviet action regarding the United Nations engendered in the United States
when he called attention to a Soviet press article. This article made clear that
the Russians preferred a defensive alliance system against a German revival
to collective security guaranteed through the United Nations.[19]

When President Roosevelt read Harriman's dispatch, he was alarmed.
He protested to Stalin, suggesting that Molotov attend at least part of the
conference, since all of the other foreign ministers would be present. He
implied that the absence of the Russians would make it appear that they
considered this gathering to be of less importance than did the other
participants.[20] Stalin said that he was sorry, but it was necessary for
Molotov to be in Moscow for a meeting of the Supreme Soviet. He
concluded with a warning that the Russians' actions would not be determined
by anyone's opinions but their own.[21]

---

[17]Bishop, *FDR's Last Year*, p. 468. For a somewhat different version of the
conversation see Joseph P. Lash, *Eleanor and Franklin* (New York: W. W. Norton, 1971),
p. 718.
    [18]Bishop, *FDR's Last Year*, p. 468.
    [19]Records of Harley A. Notter, Section 8, Various Developments Abroad, Soviet
Union, Week of March 18 to April 7, 1945, p. 32.
    [20]FDR to Stalin, March 25, 1945, USSR Ministry of Foreign Affairs,
*Correspondence*, p. 197.
    [21]Stalin to FDR, March 27, 1945, ibid., pp. 199–200.

While the Russians were apparently rebuilding the east European alliance system, a menacing defection appeared possible in the Western camp.  Charles de Gaulle added to British and American woes when he protested against Anglo-American policy on Indochina and asked the U.S. ambassador to France, Jefferson Caffery, "Do you want us to become, for example, one of the federated states under the Russian aegis? When Germany falls they will be upon us. . . . We do not want to become Communist; we do not want to fall into the Russian orbit, but we hope you do not push us into it."[22]  In other words, if Britain and the United States opposed the restoration of French rule in Indochina and other French objectives, they might find France siding with the USSR.

Stettinius recorded other disturbing moves by the Russians. They rejected a request for consultation on a tripartite commission for Romania. Then, they terminated their treaty of friendship and neutrality with Turkey "as a forerunner to a request for modification of the Montreux Convention." Stettinius thought that this was the first step in bringing "Turkey into the Soviet Cordon Sanitaire of Soviet-influenced buffer states."[23]

President Roosevelt spent the last few weeks of his life dealing with the post-Yalta problems, and Poland was at the center of these.  Both Churchill and Roosevelt wrote Stalin to protest deviations from the Yalta accords on Poland.  On March 23, Molotov rejected their interpretations of the agreements.  He contended that the Lublin Poles had to be consulted about any reorganization of their government and that any requests by England or the United States to send observers to Poland had to be processed by them. Although at Yalta it had seemed apparent that the Russians were willing to include Stanislaw Mikolajczyk in any reorganized government, Molotov now refused to consider this.[24]  Churchill asked the president to join him in protesting Molotov's recalcitrance.  The prime minister could not avoid presenting any Polish settlement to Parliament, and public opinion would be hostile if it were unsatisfactory.[25] Roosevelt knew that he faced approximately the same difficulty with Congress.

FDR sent a strongly worded message to Stalin about Poland, with a copy to Churchill.  He told Stalin that the eyes of the world were upon them because of the hopes raised at Yalta.  In reference to the Polish question, he was

frankly puzzled as to why this should be and must tell you that I do not fully understand in many respects the apparent indifferent attitude of

[22]Stettinius Diary, December 1, 1944, to July 3, 1945, Section 7, Various Developments Abroad—Soviet Union, pp. 44–46, Week of March 11–17, 1945, Records of Harley A. Notter, Miscellaneous Subject Files, Box 29, Lot 60D-224.
[23]Records of Harley A. Notter, Section 8, Various Developments Abroad, Soviet Union, pp. 31–41, Week of March 18 to April 7, 1945, pp. 31–32.
[24]Kimball, ed., *Churchill and Roosevelt*, 3:585.
[25]Churchill to FDR, March 27, 1945, ibid., 3:587–89.

your Government. Having understood each other so well at Yalta I am convinced that the three of us can and will clear away any obstacles which have developed since then. I intend, therefore, in this message to lay before you with complete frankness the problem as I see it.[26]

He was disappointed in the Soviet attitude toward Poland *and* Romania. The problem rested on the Soviet interpretation of what had been decided in the Crimean meetings. Roosevelt agreed that the Lublin government should be the base, but it had to be expanded to include other Poles. Any solution resulting in a thinly disguised continuance of the current Warsaw government "would be unacceptable and would cause the people of the United States to regard the Yalta agreement as having failed." He challenged the right of Stalin's Poles to pick and choose who could participate in the formation of the government. The task of creating a new one should be in the hands of the commission on Poland, and there should be mutual veto power of the members, including the Poles.[27]

The president implied that the Soviets' willingness to accept his interpretation and agree to a fair and speedy settlement might determine whether they would continue their much-desired cooperation for the remainder of the war and the following peace. Roosevelt put it in terms that Stalin could hardly fail to understand:

You are, I am sure, aware that genuine popular support in the United States is required to carry out any Government policy foreign or domestic. The American people make up their own mind and no Governmental action can change it. I mention this fact because the last sentence of your message about Mr. Molotov's attendance at San Francisco made me wonder whether you give full weight to this factor.[28]

Stalin acknowledged that the Polish question had reached an impasse, but he disagreed with Roosevelt's reasons. He claimed that the Soviet view of the Yalta agreements was correct and that the Russians had done nothing to violate the Crimean accords. According to Stalin, the American and British representatives were the ones who had challenged the agreements. He contended that the agreed-upon composition included five Lublin Poles "and three from London, not more." The American and British ambassadors wanted the commission to be able to invite unlimited numbers from both Poland and London. Stalin objected that "clearly the Soviet Government could not agree . . . because, according to the Crimea decision, invitations should be sent not by individual members of the Commission, but by the Commission as a whole, as a body." Stalin stated that the Soviet

---

[26]Draft message, Roosevelt to Stalin, March 29, 1945, ibid., 3:596.
[27]Ibid., 3:595–96.
[28]Ibid., 3:597.

government assumed that the invited Poles would be leaders who had accepted the Crimean accords, which would exclude most of the London Poles if Stalin's interpretation were accepted. Included in his desiderata was a statement that no one should be invited who "in practice" did not accept the concept of establishing friendly relations with the USSR. He told Roosevelt that if his points were accepted, "the Polish question can be settled in a short time."[29]

It is unlikely that FDR expected to win on the Polish question; it is probable that he anticipated that Stalin would give way to the form of free elections and self-determination and then create a friendly Poland more quietly. Some observers have contended that subsequent American-Soviet differences resulted from semantic arguments concerning the meaning of democracy. Stalin was determined to have his democrats in control, or Poland would suffer occupation until he had his way. If the Americans and the British wanted the London Poles to be included, it would be on Stalin's terms or not at all; they could either accept his view and go on from there or reject it and expect further trouble all along the line. The Americans chose to continue to argue their case.

Another problem that disturbed the Allied relationship at this juncture was the operation conducted in Bern, Switzerland, by Allen Dulles for the Office of Strategic Services (OSS). Dulles met with various Germans in an attempt to arrange a surrender and possible overthrow of the Hitler regime. Obergruppenführer Karl Wolff had contacted the OSS and met with Dulles, who in turn had reported his activities to his superiors and had received instructions on what he could accept or offer.[30] This exchange was known as Operation Crossword to the British and called Sunrise by the Americans. It was launched in February, and Field Marshal Sir Harold Alexander, the supreme Allied commander in Italy, insisted that the Soviets be informed, and so they were, although not immediately. Part of Dulles's concern was that the Germans might refuse to negotiate if the Russians were involved, and possibly the German fear of the Russians could be exploited if there was no Soviet presence. FDR was not informed at first about what was going on, but he approved continuing the contacts without Soviet participation after he was briefed, lest the Germans be scared off by Soviet inclusion. He did not want to lose the chance to end the fierce resistance in Italy, and he considered that theater of war to be an American operation.[31] Roosevelt did not understand the depth of Russian suspicions about their allies. The Russians approved continuing the talks, but they wanted to be represented.

---

[29]Stalin to FDR, April 7, 1945, USSR Ministry of Foreign Affairs, *Correspondence*, pp. 211–13.

[30]Leonard Mosley, *Dulles: A Biography of Eleanor, Allen and John Foster Dulles and Their Family Network* (New York: Dial Press, 1978), pp. 178–80. See also Kimball, ed., *Churchill and Roosevelt*, 3:586–87.

[31]Mosley, *Dulles*, pp. 178–84; Kimball, ed., *Churchill and Roosevelt*, 3:586.

When they were told that they could be included only in the final surrender negotiations at Allied Headquarters in Italy, Molotov insisted that contact be discontinued and charged the Allies with bad faith.[32]

## *III*

On April 3, Ambassador Harriman recounted a series of incidents that he believed indicated growing Soviet disregard for various agreements reached at Yalta. Unless something were done, he predicted that "the Soviet Government will become convinced . . . they can force us to accept any of their decisions on all matters and it will be increasingly difficult to stop their aggressive policy. We [will] get some temporary repercussions but if we stand firm, I am satisfied it is the only way we can hope to come to a reasonable basis of give and take with these people."[33] Even with a stiffer attitude, he feared that the Russians would continue their effort for all-out defeat of Germany, which no doubt meant taking as much territory as possible, and nothing the United States could do would affect what they might do in the Far East. He wanted the U.S. government to adopt strong measures concerning recovery of American aircraft, crewmen, and base rights in Romania, which would force the Russians to "pay more attention to our requests in other matters of a more fundamental nature such as those that may arise at the San Francisco Conference. If we delay adoption of this policy I am convinced that we will have greater difficulties as time goes on."[34]

Allen Dulles's discussions in Bern continued to be a problem, which FDR tried to alter by a direct denial to Stalin of anything underhanded. Ambassador John G. Winant wrote from London that the Japanese had been used by the Germans to tell the Russians about the surrender discussions at Bern, an obvious attempt to sow discord in the Allied ranks. He believed that Soviet suspicions had been allayed by Roosevelt's explanation to Stalin and that this message "was responsible for the breaking of the Russian-Japanese agreement and the resignation of the Japanese Cabinet. I may be wrong but I believe you have completely wiped out Russian distrust."[35]

Winant may have believed that the Russians were becoming more trustful, but the Department of State did not. General John E. Hull received

---

[32]Kimball, ed., *Churchill and Roosevelt*, 3:586.

[33]Harriman to FDR, April 4, 1945, Map Room Papers, Presidential Trips 000.9 (17–18) January 11-April 13 (Except Yalta) Warm Springs Trip March 29-April 12, 1945 Folder, Box 23, FDRL.

[34]Ibid.

[35]Winant to FDR, April 4, 1945, ibid. For the complete file of the exchanges between the president and Stalin on the Bern negotiations see memorandum by WDL (Leahy), June 5, 1947, with seven letters exchanged between Roosevelt and Stalin, March 24–April 11, 1945, Map Room Papers, Sextant Conferences, Box 28, Documents Concerning the Transfer of Presidential Papers, to the Department of State, February 4, 1946, FDRL.

a memorandum on April 3 reporting the department's conclusions that had been passed on to the army people: "There is considerable confusion and lack of proper estimate of the Russian aims and the underlying reason for their actions." According to the department briefers, there were two groups in Moscow: "The liberals, which include Stalin, who are trying to work along with the rest of the world and the Isolationists, who believe in grabbing everything that is necessary for a self-contained Russia and dispensing with outside dealings." Despite differences over relations with the West, most Russians were devoted to doing "only what will help Russia. They will use any means to force others to accept their interpretation of an agreement." The State Department crew told the army that Stalin had granted big concessions at Yalta, but afterward "the Isolationists set about delimiting the interpretation of the Yalta agreement." They forced Stalin to get tough, because toughness had worked before, and "in this they were helped by British actions." The British had adopted a tough stance on the Balkans and eastern Europe, apparently to enhance their influence, and the Russians were bound to react forcefully.[36]

According to this memorandum, Stalin and his advisers had come to mistrust the Americans because FDR had refused the postwar loan for Russian rehabilitation, and because the Soviets did not believe FDR's explanation that Congress had to approve the loan. The Soviets suspected the motives of the Americans in reducing the flow of supplies to them as the end of the war with Germany was in sight. Previously, the Americans had been willing to give freely to the Soviet Union despite its rudeness. The change in their approach must therefore have been the result of an American belief that the alliance was a marriage of convenience and that, with the demise of Germany, the cause of the marriage had been removed. Accordingly, the Russians were paying close attention to loose talk in London about a coming war with the Soviet Union, and they apparently thought that the Americans were in collusion with the British.[37]

Thus, the isolationists in Russia were convinced that Soviet entry into the Pacific war was their last hole card and that once they played it the United States would be in control. Therefore, they were rushing to get everything that they could possibly want immediately. They also suspected the Americans because "the Russians view every other nation according to what they would do under similar circumstances." The rapid Allied advance in western Germany was "suspected of being the result of a deal with the Germans to concentrate their defenses against the Russians." American demands for observers and an increased American presence in eastern Europe,

---

[36]Memorandum, John E. Hull from John S. Wise, Lt. Col., GSC, Liaison Section, OPD, April 3, 1945, U.S. Joint Chiefs of Staff Files, Subject File (TS) "Russia," Secretary of War (Stimson), Record Group 218, National Archives and Federal Records Center, Suitland, Maryland.

[37]Ibid.

especially in Poland, reinforced Russian suspicions. Citing Harriman's appeal to Roosevelt for a tougher stance when dealing with the Soviet Union, the Department of State contended that, if Harriman's advice were taken, they would back down. The department briefers were pleased with Roosevelt's response to Stalin: "The President has given every indication not to give way to the Soviets at this time and to stick to our position and insist upon a reasonable interpretation of the Yalta agreement."[38]

One State Department officer insisted that the United States should prepare for the worst. It was time for the president to "call a special meeting of the Secretaries of War, Navy and State, at which the Joint Chiefs of Staff would be present, for the purpose of coming to a final and definitive decision as to the course of action to be followed hereafter."[39] The briefers contended that such a meeting might result in a decision to tell the Russians that their part of the war was drawing to a conclusion and that any further supplies they desired would be given only on a cash-and-carry basis. This was to be done after informing the Soviet leaders that the United States did not need their assistance in the Japanese war. The State Department team concluded that as the "conservatives" were playing games to grab as much as they could while they held the trump card of entering the Pacific war, they could be brought into line by letting them know that the United States no longer needed them. When the Department of the Army commented at the beginning of this memorandum on the confusion that existed, it was correct. The source of the confusion was the assessment by the State Department, which blamed the British for Soviet suspicions because of Britain's "get tough policy." The State Department then hoped for a similar policy to emanate from a meeting of the secretaries of war, navy, and state with the Joint Chiefs of Staff present.

President Roosevelt was not ready to go as far as some in the State Department and the military wanted in confronting the Russians, but he was certainly angry and let Stalin know it. He flatly told the Soviet dictator that he resented Stalin's implications about the Bern discussions. Stalin answered with a less inflammatory message, and FDR was ready to work for solutions again.[40] The day before his death he wrote to Churchill, suggesting that they tone down their differences with the Russians: "I would minimize the general Soviet problem as much as possible because these problems . . . seem to arise every day and most of them straighten out as in the case of the Bern meeting." Nevertheless, this did not mean acquiescence

---

[38]Ibid.

[39]Ibid.

[40]For the exchange of messages between FDR and Stalin for the period March 4 through April 13, 1945, see USSR Ministry of Foreign Affairs, *Correspondence*, pp. 194–214.

in Soviet policies: "We must be firm, however, and our course thus far is correct."[41]

On that same day, Roosevelt expressed a similar sentiment in his last communication with Stalin, which was received in Moscow the day after the president's death. He thanked the Soviet leader for the "frank" explanation of his view on the Bern incident, "which it now appears has faded into the past without having accomplished any useful purpose." Then he appealed for continued good relations: "In any event, there must not be mutual distrust, and minor misunderstandings of this character should not arise in the future. I feel sure that when our armies make contact in Germany and join in a fully coordinated offensive the Nazi armies will disintegrate."[42] This is where matters stood when, on April 12, 1945, President Roosevelt suffered a cerebral hemorrhage at 1:15 P.M. and died at 3:35 P.M.

It is fitting that FDR's last speech, which he had intended to deliver on Jefferson Day, April 13, struck several notes that capsulized his feelings about war and peace. He referred to the need to work for a peace that would end the rivalries that could lead the world to its final destruction. He clearly rested his hope for this sort of world in the United Nations, which he planned for and prayed would be a success.[43] That undelivered address illustrated one last time the buoyancy and striving for an improved world that kept him going through thirteen of the most critical years in American and world history.

---

[41]Kimball, ed., *Churchill and Roosevelt*, 3:630.

[42]FDR to Stalin, April 11, 1945, USSR Ministry of Foreign Affairs, *Correspondence*, p. 290.

[43]Commager, "F.D.R. Speaks," side 12. The speech was read on this recording by Franklin D. Roosevelt, Jr.

# Epilogue

AMERICAN-SOVIET RELATIONS during World War II needed more trust than was available for a genuinely close alliance. The Russians were Communists; furthermore, their history and culture made genuinely friendly relations unlikely, indeed, virtually impossible. Yet historic forces made it necessary for Franklin Roosevelt and Joseph Stalin each to attempt to win the other to an active and fruitful coalition in the name of national interest. They really had no choice, for the alternative was destruction.

President Roosevelt perceived Russia and its leader as the key not only to a successful war but also to a lasting peace. It was not simply an American victory he was after; he sought peace for the preservation of civilization. He went so far as to state that the world could not survive another conflict like World War II. FDR was not thinking of atomic warfare; that was yet to come. He thought of the tremendous waste of manpower and resources that could so exhaust the world as to reduce it to the barbarism of the medieval era.

Beginning with the Moscow and Tehran conferences of 1943, and moving on through Dumbarton Oaks in 1944 and Yalta in 1945, the president's focus gradually shifted to the future. When the world conflict commenced he said that it was necessary to change from Dr. New Deal to Dr. Win the War; by 1944 he had begun to plan for Dr. Win the Peace. Here he faced the quandary of satisfying American foreign policy principles on the one hand and confronting the realities of Soviet fears of capitalist encirclement and accretion of power on the other. As a pragmatist he was bound to try various ways to reconcile these antipodal positions. In the end he focused his efforts on an international collective security organization. As plans for the United Nations developed at the Dumbarton Oaks Conference in late 1944, the Russians fought over the number of seats they would have and stubbornly insisted on veto power in the Security Council.

How serious a matter this was for the Russians emerged in a series of interviews that Maxim Litvinov granted to Richard C. Hottelet of CBS

Radio in 1946. Since Stalin would no longer listen to his former commissar of foreign affairs, and Litvinov knew that he was on his way to an ignominious retirement, he could afford to be very blunt. He stated that the alliance of the war era was gone irretrievably; Soviet Russia had abandoned the hope of getting along with the West in favor of a return to tsarist imperial ambitions intended to promote national security by extending Russian influence throughout the Balkans and eastern Europe. In reference to the United Nations, the voting formula had been important because the Russians knew that they would be outvoted in the organization and feared this prospect, justifiably, Litvinov believed.[1]

It is easy to simply charge that Stalin planned for world domination beginning with eastern Europe and the Balkans and possibly extending into the Far East, but this is not the likely scenario. Given the American and British focus on the United Nations, it is far more likely that, mixed with the desire to have no enemy governments on the borders of Russia, Stalin desperately wanted satellite votes in the new organization, which the Soviets perceived as another League of Nations. Stalin visualized a threat to both security and the Soviet system, and he clearly implied this when he told Churchill at Yalta (and reiterated this perspective thereafter) that he and his colleagues could not forget that they had been outvoted and kicked out of the League of Nations by British and French action bordering on an anti-Soviet crusade in December 1939.

FDR thought that Stalin knew that he meant Russia no harm. All he had to do was show some sensitivity to American public opinion and to the principles set forth in the Atlantic Charter, and then they could get on with the business of making peace. Stalin consistently misread the extent to which American public opinion influenced Roosevelt and other officials in Washington when they visualized what kind of Russian policy they might be able to develop and maintain. Litvinov explained this very fundamental reality of U.S. foreign policy to Stalin over and over again, with no visible effect. Stalin would not listen to Litvinov's attempts to persuade him that some attention had to be paid and some concessions had to be granted to American public opinion if there were to be genuine cooperation with the United States.

Although Franklin Roosevelt did foresee the need for Soviet assistance during and after the war, he also made mistakes in his approach to the Soviet Union and Joseph Stalin. There were numerous reasons for Roosevelt's vacillations in his dealings with the Russians, but too often they resulted from indecision and from misreading the need for diplomacy in approaching a power whose leadership operated consistently in the realm of realpolitik. Probably the most accurate criticism that can be leveled against

---

[1]Richard C. Hottelet, "Interviews with Maxim Litvinov," *Washington Post*, January 21–25, 1952.

the president concerns his procrastination in making definitive agreements with the Russians about the limits of their influence in the postwar era. FDR hoped that Soviet policy would change, although there was little prospect for this and little evidence that Stalin ever altered his foreign policy except to serve personal and national ambitions in an extremely calculating fashion.

Adam Ulam was probably correct in his assessment of Stalin at Yalta in that the Soviet dictator took a vacation from his role as paranoid and tyrant, but Ulam was equally accurate in his judgment that after Yalta, Stalin's paranoia returned. The Soviet leader suspected all capitalists and, in fact, mistrusted nearly everyone. He once told the Yugoslav Communist, Milovan Djilas: "Perhaps you think that just because we are allies of the English that we have forgotten who they are and who Churchill is." He accused the British of being sneaky and said that they had tricked Russia in World War I. He characterized Winston Churchill as a man who would dip into a person's pocket for a single kopek. Roosevelt, he said, was not like that. "He dips his hand only for bigger coins."[2] This was not an insult; Stalin admired those who were after the biggest coins. He did not have much faith in the prospects for fair treatment by his allies in the postwar world. He also told Djilas that neither the British nor the Americans would be satisfied to see the Red flag over so large an area as Soviet Russia.[3]

George Kennan has characterized Stalin's view of the world as something deeply rooted in the Russian psyche rather than a peculiar manifestation of Communist behavior. Kennan has noted that "at the bottom of the Kremlin's neurotic view of world affairs is [the] traditional and instinctive Russian sense of insecurity." This fear was more the response of the leaders than of the populace and was based on the conviction that "their rule was relatively archaic in form, fragile and artificial in its psychological foundation, [and] unable to stand comparison or contact with [the] political systems of western countries." In Kennan's view, Stalin fit the mold of the traditional tsars.[4]

Was there a chance for Roosevelt's approach to Stalin and American-Soviet relations to prevail? Possibly FDR could have weaned Stalin away from the extreme paranoia that characterized him so often during his rule of Russia. This appeared to be the case at the beginning at Yalta; however, it is doubtful that Stalin would have changed all that much. When he heard of

---

[2]Djilas, *Conversations with Stalin*, p. 73. This work is replete with illustrations of Stalin's paranoia and mistrust of nearly everyone who worked with him, especially of those who were not under his direct control. However, Djilas also gives numerous examples of Stalin's inclination to admire grudgingly persons whose power was great or some, like Djilas, who had no real power at all.

[3]Ibid., p. 74.

[4]Kennan to secretary of state, February 22, 1946, Record Group 107, Joint Chiefs of Staff Files, Office of the Secretary of War (Patterson), Subject File RPP/Russia, Safe File, National Archives and Federal Records Center, Suitland, Maryland.

Roosevelt's death, he illustrated how deep-seated were his paranoid responses to unforeseen and unwelcomed events. He ordered Ambassador Andrei Gromyko to demand to see FDR's body and would not accept the explanation that the casket would not be opened because the hemorrhage had disfigured the president's face. Gromyko tried to get Eleanor Roosevelt to reverse her decision and was less than polite about it. When Stalin ordered his officials to do something, they did it. Gromyko was less concerned about upsetting the Roosevelt family than he was about what his boss would think. Stalin suspected that the president had been killed by his enemies. When he received Averell Harriman shortly after FDR's death, Stalin expressed his condolences with apparent sincerity and then questioned the ambassador closely about the cause of death.[5] Stalin told Elliott Roosevelt in late 1946, "They poisoned your father, of course. Just as they have tried repeatedly to poison me." Elliott asked who "they" might be. " 'The Churchill gang!' he roared."[6]

Another problem in the Soviet-American relationship was the fundamental difference in how Russians and Americans viewed the world. B. H. Sumner once tried to compare Russian and American development by applying the Turner thesis to Russian expansion into Siberia.[7] Theoretically, the open frontiers in both countries attracted adventurous souls who adapted to their environment and became more democratic and individualistic than their countrymen in the more settled regions. They were also more suspicious of the power of the central government, which did not understand their needs, and were less willing to accept involvement in international struggles.

This analysis is too simplistic. American isolationism rested on the vastness and insularity of the North American continent once it came preeminently under the control of a single nation. Protected by two ocean frontiers, America developed by taming the land rather than by fending off powerful and aggressive neighbors. Russia has had to struggle for its existence against constant invasions from east and west because it has no defensible borders. Modernization and adaptation to external influences on the society have consumed much energy since Peter the Great's time and have conditioned the populace to look to a strong leader for protection. Reaction against foreign ideas has produced periods of extreme xenophobia, and America's failure to understand this has been a part of its problem in trying to deal with the Soviet Union. Americans, too, have experienced periods of xenophobia and paranoia, but they have largely escaped the more

[5]Morgan, *FDR*, p. 766.

[6]Elliott Roosevelt, "Why Stalin 'Never Forgave' Eleanor Roosevelt."

[7]B. H. Sumner, *A Short History of Russia* (New York: Harvest/HBJ Book, 1949), pp. 1–11ff. See especially the quote from Frederick Jackson Turner on p. 9.

extreme side effects of the latter phenomenon.[8] They have not been surrounded by aggressive powers constantly reinforcing their fear of foreign attacks; their enemies have been more imagined than real, which has enabled them to feel less threatened than the Russians.

Both Russians and Americans, however, have had bouts with inferiority complexes when forced to face older and more sophisticated nations that have been unwilling to recognize size and bumptiousness as a substitute for maturity in foreign policy development and implementation. Alexis de Tocqueville recognized the potential for the development of powerful national appetites in the two colossal nations when he wrote about them in the 1830s. He cautioned the older and more developed societies to beware of the latent messianism in the Russian and American psyches.

Roosevelt and, to a lesser extent, Churchill relied too much on reordering the world according to Western ideals. The Tehran, Dumbarton Oaks, and Yalta conferences should be viewed as a whole when fathoming Roosevelt's postwar goals. He wanted an international structure built on cooperation of the major powers to ensure the peace. These hopes ran against Stalin's territorial ambitions and fears of a resurgent capitalist encirclement as well as his traditional Russian xenophobia. A structure founded on democratic ideals could not appeal to Stalin; this made failure of communication inevitable. Churchill was at least more attuned to traditional calculations of national self-interest, and his dealings with Stalin illustrated this basic difference between his view of the world and Roosevelt's. However, Churchill, like FDR, vacillated and changed his approach to the postwar world as circumstances and whim dictated. For example, when his allies and some of his own people looked askance at his plan to attack the "soft underbelly" of Europe to cut off Soviet expansion from the south, he claimed that he did not approve of the idea, which he insisted had originated with Anthony Eden.

FDR mixed idealism and realism in his approach to Soviet-American relations, but under pressure from Secretary of State Cordell Hull and others he relied too much on the efficacy of idealism in his postwar planning at the expense of a realistic assessment of the available alternatives. Often the

---

[8]James Chace and Caleb Carr, in their book *America Invulnerable: The Quest for Absolute Security from 1812 to Star Wars* (New York: Summit Books, 1988), concluded that the United States was never isolationist except concerning European entanglements and then only when the national leaders did not feel immediately threatened. They have reflected a consensus that it is possible to attain absolute security, and they have used military pressure to do so. The authors emphasize American moralism and fear of foreign influences. If this is true, then Americans are even more like the Russians than they are different from them. This thesis is intriguing and has some merit, but it is somewhat exaggerated. The authors are quite accurate, however, when they warn that a major failing of U.S. policymakers has been to leave commitments and power out of balance while leaning toward an overweening universalism (pp. 318–21). For a thought-provoking exposition on American paranoia see Richard Hofstadter, *The Paranoid Style in American Politics: And Other Essays* (Chicago: University of Chicago Press, 1979).

president read Soviet intentions clearly and then acted as though he did not need to consider those objectives in making policy. The president's optimism helped him to overcome many difficulties, but it also clouded his vision in dealing with the Russians. He would have been far better off accepting the advice of those who urged him to bind the Russians to decisions on boundaries in 1942, which could have been held up as commitments at Yalta. Russell Buhite has charged that Roosevelt should not have gone to Yalta; instead, he should have left the making of peace to those more practiced in such matters.[9]  One would question whether Edward R. Stettinius, Jr., could have done a better job of facing Molotov and Eden than FDR did in dealing with Stalin and Churchill.  Given Roosevelt's determination to establish the United Nations, there was no chance that he would turn this task over to others.

Franklin Roosevelt's error was not in pursuing the United Nations Organization; there were good reasons for him to do this, including the need to persuade Americans that they could no longer be isolationist.  His error was in believing that the United Nations could be used to settle disputes among the Great Powers.  For reasons partly related to his Russian policy, however, he did secure the other primary objectives he sought: The Axis powers were defeated, a chance for democracy was preserved, and he got far more than the twenty-five years of peace he once said he hoped to ensure. Whatever his errors, he deserves kudos for both his effort and his results: He succeeded in his search for victory.

---

[9]Russell Buhite, *Decisions at Yalta* (Wilmington, DE: Scholarly Resources, 1986), pp. 132–33.

# Bibliography

## Archives and Manuscript Collections

Houghton Library, Harvard College Library, Cambridge, Massachusetts
  Joseph Clark Grew Papers
Library of Congress, Washington, DC
  Cordell Hull Papers
  Laurence A. Steinhardt Papers
National Archives, Washington, DC
  U.S. Department of State Files (DSF). Record Group 59
  ——. Records of Harley A. Notter, 1939–1945
  ——. Records of the Office of European Affairs, Policy Planning
    Staff
National Archives and Federal Records Center, Suitland, Maryland
  Office of the Secretary of War. Record Group 107
  U.S. Department of State, Foreign Service Post Files. Record Group
    84
  U.S. Joint Chiefs of Staff Files. Record Group 218
Public Record Office, London, England
  Cabinet Minutes (CAB)
Franklin D. Roosevelt Library, Hyde Park, New York
  Harry L. Hopkins Papers
  Henry Morgenthau, Jr., Papers
  Franklin D. Roosevelt Papers
    Map Room Papers
    Official File (OF)
    President's Personal File (PPF)
    President's Secretary's File (PSF)
    Press Conferences

# Government Publications

U.S. Department of State. *Foreign Relations of the United States: Diplomatic Papers. Conferences at Cairo and Teheran, 1943.* Washington, DC: Government Printing Office, 1961.

———.———. *Conferences at Malta and Yalta, 1945.* Washington, 1955.

———.———. *Conferences at Washington, 1941–42, and Casablanca 1943.* Washington, 1968.

———.———. *Conferences at Washington and Quebec, 1943.* Washington, 1970.

———.———. *The Soviet Union, 1933–1939.* Washington, 1952.

———. *Papers Relating to the Foreign Relations of the United States: Diplomatic Papers.* Vol. 3, *British Commonwealth and Europe, 1944.* Washington, 1965.

———.———. Vol. 3, *British Commonwealth, Eastern Europe, Far East, 1943.* Washington, 1963.

———.———. Vol. 3, *Europe, 1942.* Washington, 1961.

———.———. Vol. 2, *Europe, 1943.* Washington, 1964.

———.———. Vol. 4, *Europe, 1944.* Washington, 1966.

———.———. Vol. 1, *General, 1943.* Washington, 1963.

———.———. Vol. 1, *General, 1944.* Washington, 1966.

———.———. Vol. 1, *General, British Commonwealth, Far East, 1942.* Washington, 1960.

———.———. Vol. 1, *General, Soviet Union, 1941.* Washington, 1958.

———. *Nazi-Soviet Relations, 1939–1941: Documents from the Archives of the German Foreign Office.* Edited by Raymond J. Sontag and James S. Beddie. Washington, 1948.

Union of Soviet Socialist Republics, Ministry of Foreign Affairs. *Correspondence between the Chairman of the Council of Ministers of the U.S.S.R. and the Presidents of the U.S.A. and the Prime Ministers of Great Britain during the Great Patriotic War of 1941–1945.* 2 vols. New York: E. P. Dutton, 1958.

———.———. *Stalin's Correspondence with Roosevelt and Truman.* New York: Capricorn Books, 1965.

# Published Documents

Degras, Jane, ed. *Soviet Documents on Foreign Policy.* Vol. 3. London: Oxford University Press, 1953.

Kimball, Warren F., ed. *Churchill and Roosevelt: The Complete Correspondence.* Vol. 3, *Alliance Declining, February 1944–April 1945.* Princeton: Princeton University Press, 1984.

Loewenheim, Francis L.; Langley, Harold D.; and Jonas, Manfred, eds. *Roosevelt and Churchill: Their Secret Wartime Correspondence.* New York: Saturday Review Press/E. P. Dutton, 1975.

Roosevelt, Elliott, ed. *The Roosevelt Letters: Being the Personal Correspondence of Franklin Delano Roosevelt.* Vol. 3. London: George G. Harrap, 1952.

Roosevelt, Franklin D. *Roosevelt's Foreign Policy: Franklin D. Roosevelt's Unedited Speeches and Messages.* New York: Harper & Brothers, 1942.

―――. *Roosevelt's Foreign Policy: Franklin D. Roosevelt's Unedited Speeches and Messages.* New York: Wilfred Funk, 1941.

## Interviews

Feis, Herbert. National Archives, Washington, DC. Spring 1958.

Perkins, Frances. University of Illinois, Urbana, Illinois. Spring 1958.

Roosevelt, Eleanor. Hyde Park, New York. Summer 1959.

## Books

Ambrose, Stephen E. *Eisenhower and Berlin, 1945.* New York: W. W. Norton, 1967.

Barnes, Harry Elmer, ed. *Perpetual War for Perpetual Peace.* Caldwell, ID: Caxton Printers, 1953.

Bennett, Edward M. *Franklin D. Roosevelt and the Search for Security: American-Soviet Relations, 1933–1939.* Wilmington, DE: Scholarly Resources, 1985.

―――. *Recognition of Russia: An American Foreign Policy Dilemma.* Waltham, MA: Blaisdell, 1970.

Berezhkov, Valentin. *History in the Making.* Trans. Dudley Hagen and Barry Jones. Moscow: Progress Publishers, 1983.

Bialer, Seweryn, ed. *Stalin and His Generals: Soviet Military Memoirs of World War II.* New York: Pegasus Books, 1969.

Bishop, Jim. *FDR's Last Year: April 1944–April 1945.* New York: William Morrow, 1974.

Bohlen, Charles E. *Witness to History, 1929–1969.* New York: W. W. Norton, 1973.

Brinkley, David. *Washington Goes to War.* New York: Alfred A. Knopf, 1988.

Brune, Lester H., ed. *Chronological History of United States Foreign Relations, 1776 to January 20, 1981.* Vol. 2. New York: Garland, 1985.

Buhite, Russell. *Decisions at Yalta*. Wilmington, DE: Scholarly Resources, 1986.

Bullitt, Orville H., ed. *For the President: Personal and Secret*. Boston: Houghton Mifflin, 1972.

Burns, James MacGregor. *Roosevelt: Soldier of Freedom*. New York: Harcourt, Brace, Jovanovich, 1970.

Chace, James, and Carr, Caleb. *America Invulnerable: The Quest for Absolute Security from 1812 to Star Wars*. New York: Summit Books, 1988.

Churchill, Winston S. *The Second World War*. Vol. 3, *The Grand Alliance*. Boston: Houghton Mifflin, 1950.

Clemens, Diane Shaver. *Yalta*. New York: Oxford University Press, 1970.

Dallek, Robert. *Franklin D. Roosevelt and American Foreign Policy, 1932–1945*. New York: Oxford University Press, 1981.

Davis, Lynn Etheridge. *The Cold War Begins: Soviet-American Conflict over East Europe*. Princeton: Princeton University Press, 1974.

De Santis, Hugh. *The Diplomacy of Silence: The American Foreign Service, the Soviet Union, and the Cold War, 1933–1947*. Chicago: University of Chicago Press, 1980.

Djilas, Milovan. *Conversations with Stalin*. New York: Harcourt, Brace, 1962.

Florinsky, Michael T. *Russia: A History and an Interpretation in Two Volumes*. Vol. 2. New York: Macmillan, 1958.

Gardner, Lloyd C. *Architects of Illusion: Men and Ideas in American Foreign Policy, 1941–1949*. Chicago: Quadrangle Books, 1970.

Graebner, Norman A. *Ideas and Diplomacy*. New York: Oxford University Press, 1964.

Harriman, W. Averell, and Abel, Elie. *Special Envoy to Churchill and Stalin, 1941–1946*. New York: Random House, 1975.

Hofstadter, Richard. *The Paranoid Style in American Politics: And Other Essays*. Chicago: University of Chicago Press, 1979.

Hull, Cordell. *The Memoirs of Cordell Hull*. Vol. 2. New York: Macmillan, 1948.

Kravchenko, Victor. *I Chose Freedom*. New York: Garden City Publishing, 1946.

Larrabee, Eric. *Commander in Chief: Franklin Delano Roosevelt, His Lieutenants and Their War*. New York: Harper & Row, 1987.

Lash, Joseph P. *Eleanor and Franklin*. New York: W. W. Norton, 1971.

Leahy, Admiral William D. *I Was There*. New York: Whittlesay House, 1950.

Levering, Ralph B. *American Opinion and the Russian Alliance, 1939–1945*. Chapel Hill: University of North Carolina Press, 1976.

Litvinov, Maxim. *Notes for a Journal.* New York: William Morrow, 1955.

Maddux, Thomas R. *Years of Estrangement: American Relations with the Soviet Union, 1933–1941.* Tallahassee: University Presses of Florida, 1980.

Mastny, Vojtech. *Russia's Road to the Cold War.* New York: Columbia University Press, 1979.

Morgan, Ted. *FDR: A Biography.* New York: Simon & Schuster, 1985.

Mosley, Leonard. *Dulles: A Biography of Eleanor, Allen and John Foster Dulles and Their Family Network.* New York: Dial Press, 1978.

———. *Marshall: Hero for Our Times.* New York: Hearst Books, 1982.

Payne, Howard C. *The Police State of Louis Napoleon Bonaparte, 1851–1860.* Seattle: University of Washington Press, 1966.

Petrov, Vladimir. *"June 22, 1941": Soviet Historians and the German Invasion.* Columbia: University of South Carolina Press, 1968.

Prange, Gordon W., et al. *Target Tokyo.* New York: McGraw-Hill, 1985.

Roosevelt, Elliott. *As He Saw It.* New York: Duell, Sloan, & Pearce, 1946.

Ruddy, T. Michael. *The Cautious Diplomat: Charles E. Bohlen and the Soviet Union, 1929–1969.* Kent, OH: Kent State University Press, 1986.

Sherwood, Robert. *Roosevelt and Hopkins: An Intimate History.* New York: Harper, 1948.

Shtemenko, S. M. *The Soviet General Staff at War, 1941–1945.* 2 vols. Moscow: Progress Publishers, 1986.

Snell, John L., ed. *The Meaning of Yalta.* Baton Rouge: Louisiana State University Press, 1956.

Standley, William H., and Ageton, Arthur A. *Admiral Ambassador to Russia.* Chicago: Henry Regnery, 1955.

Sumner, B. H. *A Short History of Russia.* New York: Harvest/HBF Book, 1949.

Tuttle, Dwight William. *Harry L. Hopkins and Anglo-American-Soviet Relations, 1941–1945.* New York: Garland, 1983.

Ulam, Adam B. *Stalin: The Man and His Era.* New York: Viking Press, 1973.

Welles, Sumner. *The Time for Decision.* New York: Harper & Brothers, 1944.

Wilson, Charles M., Lord Moran. *Churchill: Taken from the Diaries of Lord Moran: The Struggle for Survival, 1940–1945.* Boston: Houghton Mifflin, 1966.

Woodward, Sir Llewellyn. *British Foreign Policy in the Second World War.* Vol. 3. London: Her Majesty's Stationery Office, 1971.

Zawodny, Janusz K. *Death in the Forest: The Story of the Katyn Forest Massacre*. Notre Dame, IN: University of Notre Dame Press, 1962.

## Articles in Journals and Magazines

Bennett, Edward M. "The Diplomatic Significance of the Trans-Polar Flight from the Soviet Union to the USA, of June 1937." *Soviet Journal of Modern and Contemporary History* 3 (1988): 42–46.

——. "The Russian Orthodox Church and the Soviet State, 1946–1956: A Decade of the New Orthodoxy." *Journal of Church and State* 7, no. 3 (Autumn 1965): 425–39.

Fischer, Louis. "Soviet Russia Today." *Nation* 149 (December 30, 1939): 728–32.

Roshchin, Alexei. "The Crimean Conference and the Postwar Settlement." In Yakovlev, Alexander, ed. *Lessons of History: The Yalta Conference, 1945*. Moscow: Novosti Press Agency Publishing House, 1985.

Sheinwald, Alfred. "The Fruits of Research." *Contract Bridge Bulletin* (March 1988).

Stone, W. T. "Washington News Letter." *Foreign Policy Bulletin* 19 (January 17, 1940).

——. "Washington News Letter." *Foreign Policy Bulletin* 19 (March 22, 1940).

——. "Washington News Letter." *Foreign Policy Bulletin* 20 (June 27, 1941).

## Unpublished Materials

Author's notes from the American-Soviet Colloquium, Moscow, USSR, October 1986. Franklin D. Roosevelt Library, Hyde Park, New York, October 1987.

## Newspapers

Hottelet, Richard C. "Interviews with Maxim Litvinov." *Washington Post*, January 21–25, 1952.

Roosevelt, Elliott. "Why Stalin 'Never Forgave' Eleanor Roosevelt." *Parade Magazine*, February 9, 1986.

"The Strengthening of Soviet-American Friendship." *Izvestiia*, November 16, 1943.

# *Recordings*

Commager, Henry Steele, ed. Introduction by Eleanor Roosevelt. "F.D.R.
Speaks: Authorized Edition of Speeches, 1933–1945." Washington,
DC: Washington Records, 1960.

# Index